Tony Harrison

COLLECTED FILM POETRY

Tony Harrison was born in Leeds in 1937. His volumes of poetry include *The Loiners* (winner of the Geoffrey Faber Memorial Prize), *Continuous, v.* (broadcast on Channel 4 in 1987, winning the Royal Television Society Award), *The Gaze of the Gorgon* (winner of the Whitbread Prize for Poetry) and *Laureate's Block*. Recognised as Britain's leading theatre and film poet, Tony Harrison has written extensively for the National Theatre, the New York Metropolitan Opera, the BBC, Channel 4, the RSC, and for unique ancient spaces in Greece, Austria and Japan. His film *Black Daisies for the Bride* won the Prix Italia in 1994; this and his volume of film/poems *The Shadow of Hiroshima and Other Film/Poems* and his feature film *Prometheus* are published by Faber and Faber. His most recent film/poem was *Crossings* (LWT), 2002. His *Collected Poems* are published by Penguin simultaneously with this volume.

To Eddie
with much love,
Bas x
24-5-23

D1513061

TONY HARRISON

Collected Film Poetry

Arctic Paradise

The Big H

Loving Memory

The Blasphemers' Banquet

The Gaze of the Gorgon

Black Daisies for the Bride

A Maybe Day in Kazakhstan

The Shadow of Hiroshima

Prometheus

Metamorpheus

Crossings

with introductions by
Tony Harrison and Peter Symes

faber and faber

This collection first published in 2007
by Faber and Faber Limited
3 Queen Square, London WC1N 3AU

Typeset by Country Setting, Kingsdown, Kent CT14 8ES
Printed in England by Mackays of Chatham plc, Chatham, Kent

This collection © Tony Harrison, 2007
'Flicks and this Fleeting Life' © Tony Harrison, 2007
'It's All Poetry to Me' © Peter Symes, 2007

Copyright and first publication details for individual plays
may be found following each part-title page

The right of Tony Harrison to be identified as author
of this work has been asserted in accordance with Section 77
of the Copyright, Designs and Patents Act 1988

A CIP record for this book is available from the British Library

ISBN 978-0-571-23409-7

2 4 6 8 10 9 7 5 3 1

Contents

Flicks and This Fleeting Life

TONY HARRISON

I was an early and avid film devotee. My street in Beeston, Leeds, was within walking distance of a number of cinemas: the Pavilion in Dewsbury Road, where I went to Saturday-morning showings of serials and cartoons, Laurel and Hardy, Abbot and Costello, the Three Stooges, the Marx Brothers, Tarzan with Johnny Weissmuller, costume flicks with Errol Flynn. There was the Crescent, also in Dewsbury Road, and the Rex at the end of the same road, near Middleton. On the Beeston Hill side there was the Malvern, near to where my dad was born and to his dad's former pub, The Harrisons. Further on, a slightly longer walk or a two-stop tram ride took me to the Beeston Picture House. I remember my mother taking me to *Bambi* and *Snow White and the Seven Dwarfs* at the Malvern and later going with my father to see gangster films, especially James Cagney. I'll never forget *White Heat* and Cagney's 'Top o' the world, Ma!' as he goes down in a hail of gunfire on the top of a globe-shaped gasometer. I saw it with my dad when I was twelve. I have written one of my *School of Eloquence* sonnets, 'Continuous', about this experience:

> James Cagney was the one up both our streets.
> His was the only art we ever shared.
> A gangster film and choc ice were the treats
> that showed about as much love as he dared.
>
> He'd be my own age now in '49!
> The hand that glinted with the ring he wore,
> *his* father's, tipped the cold bar into mine
> just as the organist dropped through the floor.

He's on the platform lowered out of sight
to organ music, this time on looped tape,
into a furnace with a blinding light
where only his father's ring will keep its shape.

I wear it now to Cagneys on my own
and sense my father's hands cupped round my treat –

they feel as though they've been chilled to the bone
from holding my ice cream all through *White Heat*.

Flicks were classified as U films and A films. U films you could go alone to as a kid, but you had to be accompanied by an adult to go into an A. Sometimes by myself and sometimes with my friends I would wait outside the Pavilion and accost people to take us into the A film. 'Will yer tek us in, mister (or missus)?' I saw as many flicks as I could.

Calling it 't'flicks' associated the filmic process with flick books, which had successive drawings on each following page that when flicked by the thumb made a continuous movement. I often drew and made my own. I drew them on the corners of school exercise books and Latin grammars, and it made me grasp early that combination of stillness and momentum that is the heart of film creation: so many 'frames per second'. It was a cheap movie version of Pollock's Toy Theatre. But I made cut-out theatrical figures too, which I coloured and arranged on the biggest dinner plate from the set my parents had been given as their main wedding present, a great oval one which I still serve my Christmas goose on.

So I made 'flicks' and theatre, not in a Pollock's proscenium but 'in the round' or more accurately 'in the oval', more like the ancient spaces in Greece or the Roman amphitheatre on the Danube that I was much later to do some of my pieces for. After I'd seen ice shows in Blackpool, where we went for our holidays, I made figures that I blew gently on so that they skated across the surface of the same plate. That I did these more or less simultaneously gave me, I think, a simple but early understanding of the difference between cinema and theatre. The kind of theatre I saw most often was late music hall, or 'variety', and panto, and though it was in proscenium theatres like the Empire, the fourth wall was broken down by the direct address of the comics I saw there: Norman Evans, Frank Randle, Old Mother Riley, Albert Modley, Robb Wilton, and even Laurel and Hardy live on stage.

When I first saw a play in a proscenium theatre like the old Theatre Royal in Leeds, with actors only addressing each other and pouring drinks and smoking cigarettes, I felt bored and excluded. But I could enter into the realism of cinema because it was not a live exchange. The actors didn't know I was there. I grew up loving both cinema and theatre, but because I've felt so conscious of how different they really are, I have always hated any video recording of my theatrical works, and when I have deliberately embraced the ancient ephemerality of the one performance of a theatre piece, as with *The Trackers of Oxyrhynchus* in the stadium of Delphi or *The Kaisers of Carnuntum* in the Roman amphitheatre of Petronell-Carnuntum, I have forbidden any filming of it.

A tram ride into town took me to the big cinemas: the Odeon, and the Majestic, where the blockbuster Hollywood films were shown. There was also a small cinema, the News Theatre, now the Bondi Beach Bar, next to the City Station and the Queen's Hotel in City Square. It was there just after the Second World War ended that I saw the newsreel footage of the Nazi concentration camps. I don't remember who took me – I think maybe my grandfather, the retired Hunslet signalman who lived with us – but there was something overwhelming in seeing such terrible images on a large screen, much bigger than life size. I think my reaction was almost on the scale of those early viewers of the Lumière Brothers' film of the train arriving in a station in 1895. It wasn't that I tried to escape from the heaped corpses moving towards me, but I felt that jumbling cascade of bulldozed emaciated Belsen bodies were being dumped on to the Art Deco carpet of the cinema and into my consciousness for ever. It almost blighted my life, it had such a powerful effect on me, and made me draw a line between what I knew in my heart was 'pretend', the films that entertained me and made me laugh, and what was news: real dead bodies bulldozed into pits at Bergen Belsen. I have never forgotten that introduction to the filming of real life or, in this case, real and terrifying death. Nor how jarring the voice-over narrations were! What narrator could find the right tone for such terror? This newsreel changed my attitude to life and film for ever.

When poetry became my chief obsession it didn't diminish my interest either in theatre or film, and I saw all the great classics at the Leeds University Film Society showings from Eisenstein to the GPO Film Unit and *Nightmail* with the famous verse sequence by W. H. Auden and music by Benjamin Britten. At the other side of City Square was another small cinema that showed new foreign films as they came out – Bergman, Antonioni, Visconti, etc. – something it's hard enough to find now even in London. I didn't know how I could ever commit to both poetry and film and never imagined I'd find a way eventually.

As I believed that some of the greatest poetry was in the greatest drama I also wanted to write poetic plays, though Eliot and Fry were to dry up the taste for them, and I only began to clear a space for myself as a poet in the theatre by translating, from the languages I'd learned, plays from that two-thousand-year-old tradition, starting with the great Greek tragedians, of drama by poets. My first translation was a version of the *Lysistrata* of Aristophanes I did in Zaria, Northern Nigeria, in March 1964 for a group of students, in which I incorporated local village drummers and dancers. It was called *Aikin Mata* (Hausa for *Woman's Work*) and was written in collaboration with my old friend, the Irish poet James Simmons. We had collaborated at Leeds University on writing and performing revues with, among others, Barry Cryer and Wole Soyinka. We also directed *Aikin Mata*, and it began with a montage from newsreels and documentaries projected onto the back wall of the theatre – suggesting, by visiting US audio-visual specialist Paul Robinson's editing, instead of innocent Hausa horsemen honouring the Emir of Zaria, more aggressive cavalry charges and battle preparation. Magajiya, the Lysistrata of the original, flung a large water pot at the back wall to put an end to the warlike images. That was my first brief glimpse into the practicalities of the editing process and how you could make a shot mean many different things by changing what it was juxtaposed with, and how something seemingly quite innocent could be made sinister by editing in a terrified reaction. There is something also in the process of translation, in this case of an ancient Greek play into a modern Nigerian setting, that trains the mind in searching for equivalents, attempting to stay open to all local impressions but having to remain within the confines of an original drama. A combination of fixed form and fleeting content.

My hesitations about the creative co-existence of poetry and film were deepened when my first book of poems *The Loiners* won the Geoffrey Faber Memorial Prize in 1972 and because of that was given some minutes on a TV arts programme. I read some poems on camera and someone went out and shot some images to go with the reading that were so clumsily and clunkily cut into the text that I had to switch the programme off. It was as if the 'director' had only read the nouns in the poems and decided that we wouldn't understand them without a show-and-tell picture. Over thirty years later that kind of clumsy illustration can still be seen accompanying poetry. It is everything a film/poem shouldn't be. That experience made me wary of entrusting poems not specifically written for it to TV until Richard Eyre directed my reading of my long poem *v.* in 1987 for Channel 4, with a great sensitivity to the poetic text.

Sadly, after my *Lysistrata* in Northern Nigeria it was ten years before I did another work for the stage, *The Misanthrope* of Molière for the National Theatre at the Old Vic in 1973. One of the results of this venture's success in London, Washington DC and on Broadway was that I was asked to work on more than one film, though producers soon lost interest when I innocently enquired what metre they imagined the text would be in! But there was one director who saw the play and thought he wanted the kind of verse he'd heard on the Old Vic stage. George Cukor, who had recently directed Alec McCowen with Maggie Smith in the film *Travels with My Aunt* (1973), came to see him playing Alceste and felt that he wanted some of those 'couplays' as he always called my rhyming couplets, for his new film, *The Blue Bird*.

So the first film I ever worked on was *The Blue Bird*, based on the play by the Belgian poet and dramatist, Maurice Maeterlinck (1862–1949), who won the Nobel Prize in 1911. Although I have been frequently mocked for this sentimental skeleton in my closet, I have some fond memories of being involved in it. Despite the fact that it became one of Hollywood's greatest disasters, I learned a great deal on the project, that I didn't realise I would draw on when I finally started to make film/poems. *The Blue Bird* had its very first production in Moscow directed by Stanislavsky in 1908. I saw a production at the Moscow Art Theatre in 1967 when I had been invited over to read my poetry at Moscow University, and the programme I'd kept and later pasted into my *Blue Bird* notebook still credited the director as Konstantin Stanislavsky.

It was translated into English by Alexander Teixera de Mattos and produced at the Haymarket Theatre in London by Herbert Trench in 1909. In a souvenir programme for the production I found in a junk shop Herbert Trench called *The Blue Bird* 'a transcendental pantomime'. Although I was thrilled by scenic transformation and metamorphoses in panto as a kid I wasn't so keen on them straining for transcendence and I wasn't, I fear, naturally suited to the material of *The Blue Bird*. There had been a film version in 1940, intended as 20th Century Fox's rival children's fantasy to MGM's *The Wizard of Oz*. It was denounced as 'hideous kitsch' and was a great flop even with Shirley Temple as the little girl Mytyl. But Hollywood likes to repeat its mistakes.

My brief was to write lyrics for the songs that the Russian composer Andrei Petrov was going to write for the film. The Music Arranger was Irwin Kostal, who had done the same job on Leonard Bernstein's *West Side Story*. The composer and arranger fell out very early and I found myself working in separate rooms with them both, trying to mediate. It didn't make for an atmosphere of détente, and the shuttling back and forth didn't help my creativity much. Even when I was away I would get a letter from Kostal warning if he sent a telegram or phoned me saying 'All is well with Kostal and Petrov' it meant the opposite! Their squabbles over credits were deeply boring. Kostal was quoted in *Newsweek as* saying: 'This is a ship of fools. I've got a fight with Andrei Petrov every day. It's a matter of national pride. He wants me completely off the picture one moment and the next we're great buddies. The problem is he wants to write American jazz, and I want Volga boatmen music. But it will all work out.' But it never did! Our interpreter Sasha was doing a doctoral thesis with the title 'Creative and Sociopsychological Interaction during the Shooting of the First Soviet-American Co-Production, *The Blue Bird*'. The interaction he witnessed and sometimes had to find wounding words for in both English and Russian was often turbulent!

Petrov had the premiere of his opera *Peter the Great* at the Kirov while I was there in June 1975. I was invited. Old women tutted at the length of my hair. Young men tried to buy my denims. I think Petrov felt he was too grand for Hollywood. And I thought that I just wasn't right for Hollywood, miscast as a musical lyricist for such potentially mawkish themes. I often felt in jaundiced mood when I came face to face with great art as in my trips to the Hermitage when I wasn't required on set. I came across an old notebook marked 'Leningrad 1975' with a note about going to see Rembrandt's *Descent from the Cross* (1645). I jotted down details of the hyena-like dog's head with green eyes glaring through a clump of thistles, the pincers pulling out the nail that held Christ's left hand to the cross. I wrote 'How much more human than the fucking *Blue Bird*! . . . I find myself trapped in a film where the categories of approval are "charm" and "prettiness".' Charm and prettiness! Not my most outstanding qualities as a poet! And certainly not the qualities a poet would need to give a voice to the Rembrandt or the terrifying corpses dumped on to the carpet of the News Theatre in City Square.

Although *The Blue Bird* ended up in a book called *The Hollywood Hall of Shame: the Most Expensive Flops in Movie History* (1984) it had given me the opportunity to get to know a legendary director, and to involve myself every day on the set, getting used to how things were done both behind and in front of the camera. Behind the camera was the great British cinematographer Freddie Young, of *Lawrence of Arabia* and *Dr Zhivago*. The second camera was operated by Jonas Gritsus, who had been director of photography on Kozintsev's *Hamlet* and *King Lear*. I watched them at work and stored what I could for the distant day when I might have need of it. And with them behind the camera was the Hollywood veteran George

Cukor, renowned as a great director of women, though when anybody said that he retorted what about Clark Gable, Cary Grant, James Stewart, Spencer Tracy . . .? Because he was directing another band of renowned women, all the press on *The Blue Bird* listed his previous 'temperamental women' credentials. Cukor had directed Garbo, Joan Crawford, Katharine Hepburn, Judy Garland, Judy Holliday, Marilyn Monroe, Vivien Leigh, Ingrid Bergman, Sophia Loren, etc. In front of the camera in Leningrad were Elizabeth Taylor, Ava Gardner, Jane Fonda, Cicely Tyson. There was also a young Russian actress, Margarita Terekhova, playing the role of Milk, who one day asked me if I would like to go with her to see a film, in which she had the starring role, that had just been made and released grudgingly and in a limited way in the Soviet Union in 1975. ('Not a single poster, not a single advertisement', noted the director in his diary entry for 8 April 1975.) The film was *Mirror*, directed by Andrei Tarkovsky, which I thought was brilliant and a very welcome relief from the film I was writing my lyrics and couplets for. According to the Russian critic Maya Turovskaya, '*Mirror* is the most documentary, and the most poetic' of Tarkovsky's films. The stark documentary and the poetic were interdependent. The film moved from colour to black and white, from lyrical fields to newsreels of the Spanish Civil War and more extended footage of the Red Army crossing Lake Sivash during the Soviet advance of 1943. Tarkovsky explains in his *Sculpting in Time*, which I bought and read when it came out in 1986, what drew him to the sequence:

The film affected you with a piercing, aching poignancy, because in the shots were simply people. People dragging themselves, knee deep in wet mud, through an endless swamp that stretched out beyond the horizon, beneath a whitish, flat sky. Hardly anyone survived. The boundless perspective of these recorded moments created an effect close to catharsis.

It was not simply the power of the images captured by an army cameraman who was killed the day it was filmed. Over the sequence was the voice of the director's father, the poet Arseniy Tarkovsky, reciting a poem called 'Life, Life', which was, the son wrote later, 'the consummation of the episode' because it 'gave voice to its ultimate meaning'.

> On earth there is no death.
> All are immortal. All is immortal. No need
> To be afraid of death at seventeen
> Nor yet at seventy. Reality and light
> Exist, but neither death nor darkness.
> All of us are on the seashore now,
> And I am one of those who haul the nets
> When a shoal of immortality comes in . . .
> I only need my immortality
> For my blood to go on flowing from age to age.
> I would readily pay with my life
> For a safe place with constant warmth
> Were it not that life's flying needle
> Leads me on through the world like a thread.
>   Arseniy Tarkovsky
>   *translated by Kitty Hunter-Blair*

Although I knew little Russian and though I got some whispered translations from my companion, there were no English subtitles as the cinema was in Leningrad, but I could hear the strong metre and the rhymes of the poem, and the combination went deep into my heart. A clue perhaps to dealing with those terrible images I saw at the News Theatre in Leeds thirty years before. As that other Russian poet Joseph Brodsky wrote: 'At certain periods of history it is only poetry that it capable of dealing with

reality by condensing it into something graspable, some-
thing that otherwise couldn't be contained in the mind.'
Was the poem the fittest narration for terrifying newsreel
screen images? *Mirror* first compelled me to ask that
question.

There was another poem of director Tarkovsky's father
over an extended shot in black and white of Margarita
Terekhova walking down a very long corridor in the print-
ing works where the mother she was playing worked. It
made you both watch and listen to the poem. It also
stayed deep in my memory and was still there when Peter
Symes and I were filming *Black Daisies for the Bride*
(1993) in High Royds hospital in Menston, Yorkshire,
and found a similar but more sloping corridor for our
brides to walk down singing. I think also the idea of a
snowstorm made out of wedding confetti was also some-
how influenced by that Russian film I saw in a welcome
break from *The Blue Bird*.

So that, though involved in the kitsch of *The Blue Bird*,
I had had my eyes opened to a modern cinema which was
unashamedly poetic, which had poems read by the poet
himself, which made the images you saw, even from news-
reel reality, mean a great deal more. One depended on the
other. It sowed seeds I was only partially aware of then,
though I longed more for the world of *Mirror* than that of
The Blue Bird.

The other seeds were sown in a more jocular but, in
retrospect, equally significant way. In 1974–75 I was in
Leningrad four times, in the Lenfilm studio in the winter
and on location in the park of Pavlovsk in June 1975, do-
ing some of my writing in a room overlooking the battle-
ship *Aurora*, which fired the first shot in the October
Revolution, moored on the river Neva. I was rather im-
pressed that the Lenfilm studio was where one of my great
heroes, Eisenstein, had made *Battleship Potemkin* in 1925.
The British actor Richard Pearson, who played Bread,

made a speech on his arrival at the studios saying how honoured he felt that he was to be working in the studio where Eisenstein had made his great film fifty years ago. The Russian cameraman, Jonas Gritsus, smiled and said, 'You won't feel half so honoured when you realise we're using the same equipment!'

When I had to be away from *The Blue Bird* with the National Theatre and *The Misanthrope in* the United States I would receive cables from George Cukor in Leningrad, the teasing tone of them scarcely concealing their desperation. The first when I was in Washington staying at the infamous Watergate Hotel and working in the Kennedy Center:

TONY OH MY POET TONY WHERE ARE THEM COMIC COUPLETS WITH THE TOUCH OF ASPERITY FOR LIGHT AFTER SHE HAS CREATED FIRE WATER AND A CHARMING BUT BRIEF VERSE AS THEY ALL ARE OFF TO CATCH THE BLUEBIRD STOP MY TONGUE IS HANGING OUT STOP COULD YOU FIND IT IN YOUR HEART TO WIRE THEM STOP SHAKESPEARE AND MILTON ALWAYS SENT THEIR SONNETS BY WIRE SO WHY CAN'T TONY HARRISON?

YOUR DESPERATE ADMIRER GEORGE

Then a few weeks later, when we opened on Broadway at the St James's Theatre, I got another cable at the stage door:

DEAR TONY I KNOW YOU WILL TAKE NEW YORK BY STORM BUT DON'T ABANDON YOUR POOR FRIEND IN RUSSIA STOP HOW ABOUT A COUPLE OF COUPLETS KID.

LOVING REGARDS GEORGE

Although I was used to writing and rewriting in rehearsals from work with the director John Dexter on the National Theatre *Misanthrope* I hadn't yet liberated myself from the practice of having to retire to a room on my own to write. It was some years later when I started to direct my own plays that I developed the ability simply to change a text verbally and have the stage management write it down, so the idea of wiring poetry by Western Union was not then what I felt I could take to naturally, but with George Cukor's gentle goading I began to wean myself off being only able to create after long hours of brooding. This developed in me and stood me in great stead when I began to make film/poems, or write political squibs for the newspapers or write from a battle in Bosnia and send the poem via satellite to the *Guardian* in London. But the gently mocking cables of George Cukor somehow began the process, though I wasn't aware of it then.

When I'd cabled my couplets I would get a teasing courteous picture postcard of Lenin from George: 'Grateful thanks to my favourite Long Distance poet!' Then another sentence begging me to make another trip to Leningrad though the added caution of 'only if a working harmony is established between Petrov and Kostal' hinted that the strained relations between composer and arranger were little better. Then he concluded: 'The white nights will be upon us, what an opportunity for Britain's greatest poet (Newcastle Division). Huge thanks, Anthony, and affectionate regards, George.'

He also sent me contact strips from photographs in the studio or on location taken by Henry Wynberg, the used car salesman who was Elizabeth Taylor's beau between her first and second marriage to Richard Burton. One of them shows Cukor in his black beret gesturing to someone. That someone had been me when we were discussing some of my couplets on location in Pavlovsk. He had inscribed the one of himself as 'a character'. This was joined to two of me listening to Cukor. He had captioned them as 'the brooding poet'. I heard of his death on 24 January 1983 on the one o'clock news, and then the

obituary in *The Times* used the same photo as he had sent
to me, the contact print that he was addressing me from.
I wrote the following poem:

LOSING TOUCH

in memoriam George Cukor, died 24 January 1983

I watch a siskin swinging back and forth
on the nut net, enjoying lunchtime sun –
unusual this time of year up north
and listening to the news at five past one.

As people not in constant contact do,
we'd lost touch, but I thought of you, old friend,
and sent a postcard now and then. I knew
the sentence starting with your name would end:
'the Hollywood director, died today.'

You're leaning forward in your black beret
from *The Times* obituary, and I'd add
the background of Pavlovsk near Leningrad
bathed in summer and good shooting light
where it was taken that July, as I'm
the one you're leaning forward to address.
I had a black pen poised about to write
and have one now and think back to that time
and feel you lean towards me out of Nothingness.

I rummage for the contacts you sent then:
the one of you that's leaning from *The Times*
and below it one of me with my black pen
listening to you criticise my rhymes,
and, between a millimetre of black band
that now could be ten billion times as much
and none that show the contact of your hand.
The distance needs adjusting; just a touch!

You were about to tap my knee for emphasis.
It's me who's leaning forward now with this!

I grew very fond of Cukor during our work in Leningrad and my two visits to his house in Hollywood, and I only wish we could have worked on something more congenial to my own talent and more worthy of his. But I learned a little of how to collaborate, happily with him and less so with the warring musical factions. Their quarrels made me aware that it was important to find other artists who were truly open for collaboration and not scrabbling to buff up their own egos or squeeze a more prominent credit. It made me very choosy about composers, and the wariness created by this early film experience made me grateful to discover composers I could collaborate with in theatre and film, such as Harrison Birtwistle, Dominic Muldowney and Richard Blackford.

In my *Blue Bird* notebook there are some 'couplets' that I wrote but were never used where I can see myself trying to match image and word in a way I found myself doing later in the film/poems I had a fuller and more creative involvement in. Some are for a scene where the children of the poor woodcutter, Tyltyl and Mytyl (played by the seven-year-old Patsy Kensit) watch as the rich children skate on the lake, eat, and watch fireworks. The word 'rich' is associated with the hiss of skates on ice, the spray of shaved ice as a skater stops a glide, foaming champagne, the sharpening of knives to cut a roasted joint, the whoosh of sky rockets, the swish of skirts, the drawing of curtains, servants sweeping the crumbs up off the floor of the banquet:

> Six white horses pull a sleigh
> of laughing children who can say
>
> we're rich, rich!
>
> The fireworks cascade, each spark
> that swooshes through the dark
>
> says rich, rich!

Look, the ice skates as they glide
hiss and hiss, self-satisfied

rich rich!

Look at all the childen skating,
what's everybody celebrating?

being rich!

The champagne bubbles effervesce
in surfeits of rich happiness . . .

rich, rich!

The happy boy who only eats
one or two from heaps of sweets

is rich, rich!

The happy girl who'll only taste
her cake and leave the rest to waste

is rich, rich!

The swish of silken crinolines
swirling as the lady spins

says rich, rich!

The knives being sharpened for the meat
for all the well-fed guests to eat

says rich, rich!

The velvet curtains that are drawn
by servants in the chilly dawn

say rich, rich!

The brushes that sweep up the mess
of other children's happiness

says rich, rich . . . !

This was a kind of song/montage that might have used some of the later techniques of my film/poems had it ever got any further than my notebook. I seem to remember it was considered to have tipped a degree too far towards the 'Soviet' half of the co-production! As was a duet I wrote between the Dog (George Cole) and Cat (Cicely Tyson), the one inciting the forest trees into revolution and the other suggesting appeasement:

CAT

I sing to you this day of days
the forest kingdom's Marseillaise.
The time has come, you forest glades,
to use your boughs as barricades.
Be chopped no more to logs and sticks,
you servile trees, turn Bolsheviks.
The end's in sight to saw and axe
the tyranny of lumberjacks.
O sycamore, O elm, O beech
Liberty's within your reach.

DOG

Don't listen to those servile lies
there's always room for compromise.
O little shrubs and trees think twice
compromise can be rather nice.
I beg you all to reassess
Man's power and your powerlessness.
You humble trees were never meant
to question the Establishment.
You vegetables learn your place
to live and serve the human race.

etc. etc.

Admittedly uninspired, but it helped to teach me to write quickly when needed and also to bin lines almost immediately. It was good training for my later film/poems, when I was trying to articulate things closer to my heart, or a greater burden on my spirit, but with something of the same pressures to produce the poetry.

I went over to Hollywood to see Cukor after the film had been almost universally savaged except by a loyal Cukor fan on the *Los Angeles Times*. The reactions depressed him, but he showed it only fleetingly. It fared so badly it was never released in the UK, so I went to see it at a cinema in LA, and was horrified. I couldn't tell George Cukor that the critics were wrong and I tried to make him feel better by saying that I felt that I had let him down. It seemed to me he was thinking that *The Blue Bird* that had turned into a turkey had finished him in Hollywood. It finished me before I got started, though I'd always known it wasn't the place for me and didn't care. Seeing Tarkovsky's *Mirror* in the middle of the making of *The Blue Bird* stamped my poetic film priorities for the rest of my career. I felt sorry for George, but he wasn't so depressed that he couldn't go on making fun of me, of both what he called my 'humble origins' and my much-mocked 'elevated status' as a translator of 'highbrow' classics, with a hit on Broadway. 'I thought,' he said, 'that someone of your humble origins might like to be picked up in a green Rolls-Royce.' And that's what he sent and I rode in it down Sunset Boulevard. I'd given him some of my books of poems and theatre texts and he said that he'd put me in his library with other authors who had been his friends and had inscribed books to him. He wasn't sure, he mocked, quite where I belonged and pointed out my tomes wedged between Thomas Mann and Irving Berlin. Katharine Hepburn, who lived next door, dropped in for tea. He showed me the place in the garden where Laurence Olivier and Vivien Leigh had a blazing row.

When I was next in Hollywood I took my son Max with me. I had been asked to meet with John Williams, the film composer most famous for *Jaws* and *Star Wars*, to discuss the possibility of working together on a musical based on Bernard Shaw's early novel, *Cashel Byron's Profession*. Max, though still very young, had also been inspired by the great cinematographer Freddie Young when I'd taken him with me to Leningrad on one of my *Blue Bird* trips. He had by this time an 8mm cine camera and was filming in George Cukor's garden, where I was talking with George and another person, who told Max not to intrude. Cukor threw a fit and berated his other guest for discouraging the boy. Then he went through the motions of setting up the scene for Max and calling 'action!' Max wasn't discouraged. We also went to the studios to watch John Williams conduct the recording of his soundtrack to John Frankenheimer's film *Black Sunday*. John Williams and I came to a mutual decision that we weren't really suited to each other and my Hollywood career ended for ever.

These were seminal experiences also for Max. It was my son Max who was to teach me many of the technicalities of film and deepen my understanding of the process. From an early age he had a brilliant grasp of the medium. I remember him coming with me to Cinecitta, the great film studios in Rome, where Franco Zeffirelli was shooting *La Traviata*, with my then wife, Teresa Stratas, singing the role of Violetta. Zeffirelli gave Max a giant wheel of Dolcelatte cheese as a reward for spotting that in the sets for *Traviata* at Cinecitta you would see the camera and crew reflected in the highly polished and gilded antique furniture. We watched films together and he would provide a fascinating commentary on how the shots were set up. He came with me when we were filming *The Blasphemers' Banquet* in Bradford and in London. Before his cruel illness he became a camera assistant and worked in that capacity on Peter Greenaway's *The Cook, The Thief, His Wife and Her Lover*. My son taught me a great deal about film, passed on as he learned it with passionate commitment himself.

Certain seeds had been sown in these early experiences which meant that the tentative first verse commentary I made for *Arctic Paradise* in 1981 was not a venture into totally unknown territory, though it was my first experience of the cutting room, which by degrees became the place I did more of my work than in a secluded room or study. For this film, produced by Andree Molyneux, I used the metres of Robert Service, the Scots-born Yukon Balladeer. This story for a *World About Us* slot was of a young man, Roger Mendelsohn, who'd left his job in the city to go and live as a trapper with his wife and family in the Yukon. The first thing that struck me in trying to write verse for already cut film was that I often needed a longer hold on the beginning or end of shots. Even later I've found cameramen, even those who've worked with me on more than one film, using their free eye to raise an eyebrow at the length of time elapsing before being asked to cut. In a second shoot in the new Yukon gold rush, Andree Molyneux brought back longer shots and it helped the verse to develop a story in a different, more concentrated way than in coinciding with a continuous quickly intercut sequence. Later, working with my great collaborator, Peter Symes, we developed an understanding of the length of holds on close-ups and the pace and momentum of tracking and crane shots. Peter Symes goes into the details of these discoveries in his generous introduction to this volume.

Arctic Paradise was a tentative beginning but it led to another work for television produced by Andree Molyneux, *The Big H* (1984), not strictly a film/poem of the kind Peter Symes and I pioneered, but again another step on the way to understanding the processes that made verse work or not on the screen. It was also the beginning of a screen collaboration with the composer Dominic Muldowney, who later worked with me on *The Blasphemers' Banquet* (1989) and *Black Daisies for the Bride* (1993) as well as the ambitious theatre piece for the National Theatre, *Square Rounds* (1992). *The Big H* (1984) was important too in that poet and composer collaborated from the beginning, even before the text was finished. All stages towards the fluid collaborations of the later film/poems.

What I really needed, I thought, was an involvment in the entire process, so that I could join up all my fragmentary film experiences. And this is exactly what began to happen when I started to work with Peter Symes, first on *Loving Memory* (1987), then *The Blasphemers' Banquet*, *Gaze of the Gorgon*, and *Black Daisies for the Bride*, a collaboration with a brilliant and patient colleague with whom l shared locations and cutting room in an increasingly creative partnership. We began from scratch with no ideas of models and slowly evolved a way of working that became increasingly organic, open and fluid.

In enterprises as collaborative as theatre or film I like to work with the same people, and go from one project to another, taking the discoveries made from project to project. In theatre it was the twenty-year relationship with the great designer Jocelyn Herbert, who also designed my feature film, *Prometheus*, which grew out of both my verse for the theatre and my TV film/poems. With films it has meant rich, fruitful collaborations on eight films with the director Peter Symes, on five films with the cameraman Alistair Cameron, with the Bristol editor Peter Simpson, and the composer Richard Blackford, who has worked on *A Maybe Day in Kazakhstan* (1994), *The Shadow of Hiroshima* (1995), *Prometheus* (1998), *Metamorpheus* (2000), and *Crossings* (2003) as well as plays like *The Kaisers of Carnuntum* (1995), *The Labourers of Herakles* (1995), *The Prince's Play* (1996), and who will be working on my new play *Fram* for the National Theatre early in 2008.

The irony is that now I have found a brilliant team to work with, no one seems to want me to make any more films. The ranks of producers swell up with the stupid, the timorous and the mercenary. Few people, except those that were a part of it, understand how these film/poems were made. Neither film people nor the sad poetry world. This volume, *Collected Film Poetry*, could well have been called *Complete Film Poetry*, as I don't think it's likely that I'll ever get funding for another film/poem, though I am fuller of ideas than ever. There is much more for me to discover in the film/poem.

The most apparently prosaic can be poetic. The camera's eye can make the most familiar or unregarded object or person worthy of new attention and regard. It was a feeling of this kind that I had when I wrote one of my 'couplays' solicited by a Cukor cable for Elizabeth Taylor in her role as Light in the 'transcendental pantomime' of Maeterlinck:

> I am the Light that helps men see
> the radiance in reality

Sadly this 'couplay' is still in the film, but I had taken the idea from the main theme of the original play. Even Maeterlinck was saying that the trail of the transcendent leads back to the illuminated, transformed ordinariness of home. When the two children in *The Blue Bird*, Tyltyl and Mytyl, return from their adventures in the Land of Memory, the Palace of Night, the Forest, the Palace of Happiness, the Kingdom of the Future, they have in Act VI, Scene ii, 'The Awakening': Maeterlinck's stage directions read: 'The same setting as in Act I, but the objects, the walls and the atmosphere all appear incomparably and magically fresher, happy, more smiling.' Tyltyl looks at his turtle dove in its cage: 'Hello, why he's blue . . . But it's my turtle dove! . . . But he's much bluer than when I went away! Why that's the blue bird we were looking for! . . . We went so far and he was here all the time!'

It is here and now all the time, not in any hereafter. It is the nature of the combined prosodies of film and poetry to keep on making this simple discovery. It is not in the hereafter, it is here and now all the time in both its ghastly agony and its glories.

When I did my *Lysistrata* of Aristophanes in the predominantly Muslim Northern Nigeria in 1964 I put an epigraph in the programme and the published text from a translation of a sentence in the Koran about the Greeks: 'They care for this fleeting life but of the life to come they are heedless.' Which also describes my own feelings about this life and the hereafter and I went back to the phrase when searching for something to be sung by a life-affirming voice against the ugliness of fundamentalist rant that we filmed in the controversial film Peter Symes and I made defending Salman Rushdie and blasphemy in *The Blasphemers' Banquet*:

Oh, I love this fleeting life!

The recognition of the fleeting nature of this life is certainly the most fruitful condition for the loving of it. The flickering momentum of the flicks is a condition for the framing and focus of the camera lens, and the metrical beat of poetry makes the mind both aware of the inbuilt transience of temporal motion and also relishingly sensible of the sensual sounds of combined vowels and consonants carried by that unstoppable beat. Metrical ictus and screen scansion reflect what is fleeting and can keep up alongside savouring the detail each passes through. 'Prosody,' wrote Joseph Brodsky, 'is simply a repository of time within language.' Committing to metre is to emphasise the time that ticks away as our lives get shorter. It opens itself without panic to the time that is counting down to our ends. Again, as Joseph Brodsky has written in the same wonderful essay on Akhmatova, 'prosody absorbs death'. It was no accident, I think, that I began to realise these connections in a really organic way when Peter Symes and I made our first four films of the *Loving Memory* sequence. *Loving Memory* revealed this structure to me more clearly than ever before, partly because it involved so many graveyards and cemeteries. What I dramatised in the films was the struggle between memory that resists time and oblivion that lets time have its way. The scansions of the screen and the prosodies of poetry co-exist to create a third kind of mutually illuminating momentum that is the film/poem whose potential range and depth has not been fully explored. These texts only partially represent my own various attempts at the form. They will always require the films they are an organic part of to be fully understood.

Newcastle-upon-Tyne, 2006

It's All Poetry to Me

PETER SYMES

Ladies and gentlemen, you have seen that the little
show we have presented for you this season has been
under a great deal of criticism. You have seen that
certain citizens, some of them quite eminent, have seen
fit to call our performance 'filthy', 'obscene', 'offensive',
and that may well be their opinion, but I come to
you, ladies and gentlemen, and ask you to be my final
judges. I am, like you, a simple man, born of simple
folk, a man of the industrial north of England. My
pleasures are simply my packet of Woodbines, my
glass of Guinness. The simple joys of the seasons.
Simple people of our kind understand the facts of
life in a way that many of our critics don't. You will
know that my little bits of fun are founded upon the
facts of life and because you understand life and the
realities of life, I ask you to be my judges.[1]

These words are not Tony Harrison's, though (Woodbines
aside) they certainly resonate with his experience. Who
can forget the *Daily Mail* headline when *v.* was broadcast:
'Four-Letter TV Poem Fury'; or the campaign by the
Archbishop of Canterbury to stop transmission of *The
Blasphemers' Banquet*? Rather they belong to one of
Harrison's early heroes, the music-hall comedian Frank
Randle, wearily justifying himself to his audience when,
towards the end of his life, he had yet again been targeted
by the moral guardians of the time. He belonged to a
peculiarly public art, an art that entertained and excited,
which talked directly to its audience in words they could
understand. Tony Harrison is old enough to have been

able to see many of the great acts of the music hall, and he adored them. It was an art which, like his, frequently offended, and it is no surprise to find it sitting alongside another great art that the poet frequently cites as a central influence on his own: classical Greek theatre.

It is not fanciful to compare the two, though modern audiences have only recently been reintroduced, by the poet himself, to Greek theatre's true humanity: its insistence on the bawdy alongside the tragic, its practice of always accompanying a tragedy with a satyr play. When he staged his own production of *The Trackers of Oxyrhynchus* and we were presented with the wonderful sight of priapic satyrs, their great penises waving about as they did their life-affirming clog dance, the worlds of Greece and Blackpool merged. Here was Randle, resurrected, come to tell us something serious, demanding our attention, but entertaining us with spectacle and theatre in a truly exciting way. Here was no proscenium arch and tidy drawing room, but a sand-strewn arena ready for the rites of a performance; and when at the end of the play the back doors of the National Theatre stage opened and invited us to view the homeless on the South Bank, it spoke directly to us all, sitting in this time and space: it demanded that we take notice.

The primacy of language, set in a stylised frame, underpins ancient Greek theatre. Language was an elemental force, as it was for Randle. His own delight in words, albeit pretty colourful ones, lay at the heart of his comedy. It transported audiences already familiar with the ritual of his stage business. Harrison is attracted to tragedy and comedy, but would deny that there is a polarity, seeing both merely as parts of a whole, essential to our understanding of the world. Underlying it all is the centrality of the spoken word, and the ritual. It is not surprising he was eventually attracted to film and television.

All his life he has been passionately concerned with the business of making language public, using the page and the stage to do this before he turned his attention to the small screen. And he has done this by resolutely not rejecting his working-class roots or his Yorkshire dialect. His is a public poetry, for public display, and it is a poetry that sits comfortably upon the foundations mentioned above. While President of the Classical Association, in 1988, he delivered an address that contains an illuminating insight into this, and into his own assessment of the importance of the poet. Harrison was discussing the Muses, and more particularly his own, commenting that he regarded poetry as being unclassifiable, and impossible to place under the care of any specific Muse from the nine of Greek mythology: 'It's all poetry to me, whether it is for the printed page, or for reading aloud, or for the theatre, or the opera house, or concert hall or even for television.' However, if there were to be one Muse, then it would probably have to be Melpomene, the Muse of Tragedy. He went on to outline why.

> Robert Jay Lifton, the American professor of psychology, who has charted the effect of the Nazi concentration camps and the nuclear holocaust on our imaginations, and the deeply numbing effect of what must be the most petrifying Medusa-like gaze of all on our sense of futurity, has called for artists to discover a 'theatre that can imagine the end of the world and go beyond that . . . [a theatre] that can believe in tomorrow', what he later has to call 'a theatre of faith'. It sounds to me like a call for the rebirth of tragedy. And this theatre he calls for, this tragedy, has to believe in the primacy of the word. I think my obsessive concern with Greek drama isn't about antique reproduction, but part of a search for a new theatricality and also a way of expressing dissatisfaction with the current theatre where I work as a poet.[2]

This restless 'search for a new theatricality' has meant that we have a poet who is now at home in print, in the theatre and within the confines of the film frame, and this new collection of Harrison's film/poems is a celebration of the long journey he has taken into that world which John Boorman so memorably described as 'converting money into light'. Film is a magical medium. Twenty-four static images flash before your eyes every second, giving the illusion of movement, and we immediately enter a make-believe world. One second follows the next, and the process of juxtaposition is extended to scenes and amplified with sound, yet at its base lies this formal mechanism of stillness. What better vehicle for a poet to use? Are not the still words, combined into lines, undergoing a similar process, not for the eyes but for the ears? What more exciting process, then, but to combine the two?

It seems now the most natural thing in the world that Harrison should have gravitated to television, that relentless eye in the corner of our sitting-room that looks at everything and often at nothing, and used it to extend his experiment with theatre and with poetry. Can the use of verse in this context help us to look at the future? Can it also allow us to look at our past and our present with unblinking eyes? And can we adapt this modern music hall, this increasingly mindless televisual frame, to something serious? With typical commitment Harrison has embraced this challenge, and my aim here is to chart his journey, from an initial commission from the BBC in 1981 through to his own directorial work for Channel 4 and ITV.

*

Since 1936, when Auden took those first tentative poetic steps into the world of 'moving' pictures with his famous collaboration on the GPO documentary film *Night Mail*, there have been a number of poets brave enough to sup with the devil, daring to combine their poetic skills with the skills of a film maker. John Betjeman was perhaps the most assiduous early practitioner, and there have been others, but it was not until Tony Harrison turned his attention to the form that we saw the beginnings of a real development and the creation of a body of work that actually moved the process onto a different plane. Here at last was work that was beginning to create its own agenda, and in which one can discern a development both in form and in content. It was work that took great risks, and which challenged much orthodoxy. It brought poetry into the homes of millions of people, and made it immediate. It was work that attempted to face up to the changing society we live in. In this collection you can see laid out the results of over a quarter of a century of work in this medium.

Characteristically, it all started in a wine bar in London when he met up with the BBC producer Andree Molyneux in May 1979. Molyneux was already at work on a film about the Scots-born Canadian poet Robert Service, which endeared her to Tony, and out of this meeting grew a collaboration on another film, called *Arctic Paradise*. This film was about a young family living in the wilds of the Yukon in North America, and Tony decided to use a metre Service himself had employed to comment on sequences in the film around the documentary material. This decision to use a particular metre, and to involve himself closely with the editing process, laid the foundations for what would become an established way of working. Between them they began to experiment with the use of verse and visual image, discovering during the edit some of the problems that would later be tackled in the documentaries where verse alone became the engine driving the story forward. It led to a second collaboration, this time not on a documentary but on a kind of nativity play for television called *The Big H*, which focused more on the massacre organised by Herod (the big H of the title) than on the birth of Jesus. This time the poet was involved from the outset, and although the end result was a studio production, Tony was able to immerse himself in the whole process, from development through testing out different ideas up to the final recording. It is an original and challenging take on the old story, with its witty and caustic use of H to ram home the message: Herod, horror, Hunslet, and a wonderful group of recalcitrant Leeds youngsters who insist on dropping their 'h's' as a typical Harrisonian marker about the value and pride in your locality. These two works proved to be a valuable launch pad for what came later, from the initial experience of the cutting room to the collaboration with the composer Dominic Muldowney, who went on to work with Tony and myself on *The Blasphemers' Banquet* and *Black Daisies for the Bride*. Before that could happen, however, came four films which were to prove a vitally important learning experience for us all; four films that were to be the start for me of a creative collaboration, stretching as it now does over more than two decades, that has been one of the most satisfying and exciting in my career.

It was in September 1986 when I approached Tony with the suggestion that he work on a documentary series about cemeteries to be called *Loving Memory*. He was about to record his published poem *v.* for Channel 4, a poem also set in a cemetery, this time in Leeds, and dealing with the vandalism of his parents' graves: perhaps this predisposed him to our project. Aside from writing the verse sections in *Arctic Paradise* he had never been involved closely with a documentary production, and *v.* was a record of poetry that was already in existence. What he was to propose was something very different. At our meeting he laid down some conditions: he would do it, provided *all* the commentary was in verse, and provided we approached the commission as a true collaboration. He was no longer interested in producing verses for sequences or for sections that already existed. I was sitting in a rather dingy Soho restaurant with Michael Hutchinson, the Assistant Producer, and Gordon Dickerson, Tony's agent, and I took a very healthy swig from the wine glass before nervously assenting. We were entering virgin territory, territory that my superiors certainly considered dangerous. It was a leap into the dark.

From the outset we started to experiment with a new way of working. Those of you who have been privileged to peek inside the famous Harrison notebooks (most destined for the Brotherton Library at the University of Leeds) will have had an insight into his working methods. Mounds of research are reduced to cuttings, pictures, scribbled lines, as page after page of ideas fill up the blue notebooks with their red bindings. This is an ongoing process that starts long before filming and continues up to, and sometimes beyond, the final post-production.

Then, with notebook under arm, poet and team proceed to the locations. Filming is affected by and affects the ideas. More ideas go into the books. Then the whole effort relocates to the cutting room. Here two rooms are always booked, one for the poet and one for his comrade-in-arms, the film/video editor, and the exhilarating job of the rhythmical juxtaposition of image and sound begins. Gradually we developed our own techniques for the edit: a quick review of the images in the morning; writing and editing, followed by constant trials with the verse using rough recordings; rewriting and rejection of visual or verbal ideas; and as much of a complete viewing as was possible before staggering home each evening. This constant reviewing of the programme each day may sound indulgent to some, tedious to others, but it proved to be invaluable. It allowed the editor to get an overall feel for the whole pulse of the film as it developed, and it allowed Tony to keep the complete work in focus while he struggled with individual quatrains during the day. It was also made palatable by the poet's civilising insistence on champagne and nibbles at around six o'clock; our cutting room with its small fridge and bowl of fruit and exotic nuts attracting much envious comment.

As our confidence increased, so this creative process began to diverge quite radically from the one a documentary film maker would normally employ. The conventional process of making a documentary film involves research and pre-production planning that might include a detailed shooting script, or, in the case of an observational documentary, long acquaintance with the subject. There is usually a clear idea of the structure of the film. Filming having been completed, the edit then follows this line, albeit with some flexibility. In the case of the film/poems the approach was different. There was always lengthy research, but this would be to add to the poet's already extensive reference, and would be concerned with imagery and ideas. This would suggest locations. There would then be a limited initial recce, but this would be more along the lines of searching for a central idea (for instance, the disused churches in *The Blasphemers' Banquet*), and poet and director would arrive on the location with the aim of collecting imagery, often without a clear idea of where that imagery might appear in the finished product. Frequently new images would be discovered, and would change the direction of the piece, allowing us to respond quickly to new discoveries. It was eerie how this process sometimes worked: a disused church is named after a Persian poet; we decide on using the poet as a central idea; then we find him quoted on a gravestone in a cemetery we had entered merely to obtain a better shot of Bradford; that quote then becomes one of the centrepieces of the whole film.

This approach also offered the film editor enormous latitude which, in the cases of Peter Simpson, who edited most of these films, and Liz Thoyts, who bravely led the way with the first *Loving Memory*, they embraced wholeheartedly. In these films the role of the editor is central. They are faced with a mass of material to play with, and need to attempt numerous versions of sequences. Often this throws up new ideas, and we quickly developed a schedule that allowed us to return to locations, sometimes taking with us a sequence that we could expand with a new and more constructed scene. One such is in the auction rooms in *The Blasphemers' Banquet*, where the original auction scene was embellished at a second visit with our own objects 'for sale'. Supporting all this work, therefore, is the crucial artistry of the editor, and that artistry was given great creative freedom. In 1986, however, when our collaboration began, all this lay in the future.

When he started work on *Loving Memory*, Tony had not been present at some of the filming for the series, but he joined us early enough to allow us to throw everything up into the air and begin again. The original idea for a documentary series focusing on various cemeteries became a meditation upon death, memory, and the apparent futility of commemoration in the twentieth century. We were able to plan a beginning that would involve a typical village churchyard, of the sort familiar to Thomas Gray, so that the metre of the famous *Elegy* could then provide the poet with a verse form that he could use throughout. With this in mind, for our first film, *The Muffled Bells*, we chose Breamore in Hampshire, where there was a church still linked to the estate, and where the village population was still involved in all its affairs. Having decided on the metre, Tony could then sit down and think about what needed to be said, and he started work on the film that eventually ran second in the strand: *Mimmo Perrella non è Piu*.

The choice of metre, and its linkage to the subject of the film, has become a trademark. So, *Arctic Paradise* uses Robert Service. *The Blasphemers' Banquet* uses the famous quatrain of Fitzgerald's translation of the *Rubaiyat* of Omar Khayyam, thus placing that 'Voltaire of the East' centre stage in a piece about blasphemy. Heine's octosyllabic couplets appear throughout *The Gaze of the Gorgon*, a film that uses the strange story of the displacement of a statue of that famous German poet as the skeleton for an extended essay about war and the twentieth century. And *Loving Memory* uses Gray. This technique offers the poet immense freedom. Once a metre is embedded in the poet's brain, it makes it possible for him to say anything.

Having decided upon his metre for *Loving Memory*, Tony was then able to approach both filming and editing. *Mimmo Perrella non è Piu* is a film about the strange burial customs that exist in Naples. The structure of the piece was proving difficult. There was the obvious progression of a funeral process, but there did not seem to be a central idea or story that could propel us through the film, and there were a lot of disparate elements that needed uniting. Luckily, although much of the filming had been done, we were able to return to Naples with Tony, and it proved to be an important visit.

Arriving at the impressive gates to Poggioreale cemetery, he came across a poster. Upon it, in bold black type, was the announcement that Mimmo Perrella *non è piu* – literally, 'is no more'. Anyone who visits Italy will be familiar with these 'death' notices, which usually announce the date of the funeral and other important family details. Their headlines are seldom quite so brutal, but they are usually plastered everywhere. So Mimmo was chosen as our central character, never appearing, but nevertheless ever-present, a ghost at our feast. The things that happen to other people become the events that will happen to Mimmo in some ill-defined future. The verse commentary, while offering plenty of factual insights, becomes a crucial structural device.

What is more, our poet-presenter was able to produce three quatrains very quickly, and he recorded them as a 'piece-to-camera' in the cemetery. Writing to order during a busy filming schedule is difficult enough in prose – it's something we expect of journalists in the front line, but not of poets. Harrison's metrical technique allows him to do this. So we have an introduction that manages to suggest the narrative line of the film, with its story of Mimmo's journey, while also managing to touch on the often complex exploration of such issues as purgatory and the transitional progress of the soul after death – in convincing verse, and to camera. It's as if Harrison is saying: well, why not in verse, and why not from the front line? With its ringing repetitions, it is an introduction that lingers longer in the memory than most things seen on the small screen, and it serves as an example of the location technique I mentioned above:

> *Mimmo Perrella non è piu*
> Mimmo Perrella is no more.

> *Mimmo Perrella non è piu.*
> Mimmo Perrella is no more.
> This gate his body will be carried through
> he walked past into work not days before.

> *Mimmo Perrella non è piu.*
> Let's follow Mimmo Perrella's fate,
> or, rather, not one single fate but two,
> that of the body brought in through this gate

> and put under marble in a dark, dry hole
> where Vesuvius's soil makes it like leather,
> and that other fate, meanwhile, of Mimmo's soul
> exposed to an uncertain, otherworldly weather.

We learnt many things very quickly during this first long session in the cutting room. The back-and-forwards between writer and editor became a rhythm in itself. As Andree Molyneux discovered in *Arctic Paradise*, we rapidly found out how complex verbal rhythms could cancel out visual ones, and vice versa, but also how close the editing process was to the poetic work being done next door: both poet and editor struggle with the rhythmical juxtaposition of images. We revelled in repetition, something verse and image excel in. We were excited by the possibility offered by the verse of intense and very visual imagery on the sound track that we could juxtapose with gentler or less insistent pictures on the screen. But perhaps the most significant discovery during the filming of this first series was that relating to the subjective. When Tony began to describe what he imagined people were thinking, and it worked, we realised we were on to something. This was something Auden himself noted in 1936 in a reported lecture on film and poetry that was included in his *Plays and Other Dramatic Writings*. He was recorded as saying that 'Poetry can also be used to express the thoughts of characters, in rather the same way as Eugene O'Neill introduces "the interior voice" in *Strange Interlude*.'[3]

The Neapolitan film is centred on a bizarre custom, apparently peculiar to this region, which involves the exhumation of a corpse about two years after burial, and its re-interment in a wall vault. Family members are present at this gruesome ritual, and it provides a moment in the film that was both difficult to record and potentially difficult to screen.

Poetry alters this scene in a number of ways. As we saw earlier, Harrison is a firm believer in verse's ability to look at life unblinkingly, and there is no doubt it operates here in a very interesting way. It also allows the writer the privilege of becoming personal; of moving from a documentary record into a world justifiably imagined without in any way undermining the documentary reality. When the moment comes to face the corpse, he places the words into the mind of the man's widow, and then slips back almost unnoticed into the third person:

Was this the Vincenzo who I slept beside?
Vincenzo Cicatiello non è piu.

xlii

Now, now I know you've really died.
Till now I only half-believed it true.

Being seen in such revolting tatters
wouldn't suit him. He was much too proud!
Although he's dead, she still believes it matters
that they make him feel he looks right in his shroud.

I cannot imagine getting away with this in prose, yet here
it added a depth and compassion to the film that was
intensely moving. It also does something else. For a reason
I am not sure I can explain, I think it *allows* us to watch
without turning us into voyeurs, as much of current tele-
vision is succeeding in doing. Is there a key here for that
'theatre that can imagine the end of the world and go
beyond that . . .'?

As our methods developed, and we began to realise the
exciting possibilities, we discussed ways of filming that
would also assist the process. What shots worked better
than others? Should we stay wide or go for closer shots
whose power might interrupt the flow? Would tracks allow
us to have longer developing shots, which would in their
turn not interrupt the verse metre with visual cuts? And
what of sound? Could we use sound more inventively here,
perhaps even interweaving into the verse the prose words of
people filmed under more usual documentary conditions?

By the time we were working on the third film,
Cheating the Void, the possibilities offered by this tech-
nique were plain. In a film that became a tour both of the
great European cemeteries and of the European century,
we exhumed bodies; reanimated dead singers; interwove
for the first time a prose comment made by an interviewee
into a quatrain; turned the verse into the first person;
used a line from a Jim Morrison song as a conclusion to
a quatrain; and supported the verse with a much more
inventive sound track than existed in the other films. I
have a postcard, sent to the cutting room accompanying

another provisional script, during one of Tony's very infrequent absences. I think it illustrates the system admirably, while also pointing to the process of discovery that continues to this day:

> Herewith a very rough first stab. I can't take it further, till you've taken the next step with it. I think I can then take off from there. I've underlined in red the Jim Morrison bit I'd like edited in [*this was the line 'No one here gets out alive!' from The Doors' 'Five to One'*] and I'd like to experiment a little more with that idea on the spoken bits so that it's like a duet/interview still in metre. It could work very well. I'm going to try some of that with Mr Kemp [*the stonemason we had already filmed at Kensal Green cemetery*] and maybe the girl in Kensal Green, but just go ahead with what there is for now. All this in haste. I look forward to prog. 4 and the Blackpool bits. If we can make the intercutting of speech work properly it gives me a way in to something more densely peppered with speaking faces, etc . . .

Cheating the Void was a testing ground for a number of ideas. Of the four films in the series, it was the one in which we experimented most, and with which we had most fun, in spite of its dark contents. It contains some of the concerns central to Harrison's work: oblivion and memory being linked to darkness and to light, for instance; almost a Promethean echo, the thread of flame running from Hamburg in this series to the oil flares of the Gulf in *The Gaze of the Gorgon* and on to *Prometheus*.

> Oblivion is darkness, Memory light.
> They're locked in eternal struggle. Which
> of these two forces really shows its might
> when death's doors are thrown open by a switch?

And magically, we bring the dead back to life as we see the Lumière brothers' famous factory crowd pouring out of their workplace, rushing home to assignations and appointments now lost in the dust of history: death no longer absolute, as one contemporary critic famously asserted.

The series was transmitted on BBC2 during the summer of 1987 and was a surprise hit, attracting a great deal of attention.

*

It was two years before Tony and I worked together again, and then a chance meeting at the Bristol Old Vic and the actions of Ayatollah Khomeini launched us on *The Blasphemers' Banquet*. This time the documentary was driven by anger, and became a polemical essay about fundamentalists and their fellow-travellers who were intent on attacking free speech. It was a brave toast from a poet to a writer of prose, the novelist Salman Rushdie, at that time just starting his Iranian-imposed exile from normal society.

The Blasphemers' Banquet remains my favourite of Tony's films, and one that is unjustifiably neglected, perhaps because it plays with political and religious fire in a way the Establishment found unsettling. The controversy surrounding its birth was such that it nearly did not receive a broadcast, having no less an authority ranged against it than the Archbishop of Canterbury. It was made with a passion born of intense anger in the ridiculously short space of about eight weeks, on a tight budget, and under very difficult circumstances, yet its invention and daring still startle people.

I have written elsewhere about this collaboration,[4] and the way its core was transformed by the poet's ability to respond to events as they happened, but it is worth reiterating here the *practical* aspects of the operation because a work like this has a truly organic growth, as I outlined at the start of this piece. At the outset there is often only an idea, or at best a fairly sketchy outline, with possibly one or two central scenes. There is usually no verse, but there may be several inimitable Harrison notebooks. There may also be a starting point unrelated to the work, and at this time Tony had for months been toying with the idea of an opera about fundamentalism, to be called 'Heads in the Sand'. The Iranian authorities had started condemning people to be buried up to their necks in the ground, and then stoned to death, and Tony wanted to use this graphic image as the centrepiece of a theatrical work. The project remained under that label until transmission, but the idea of singing heads buried in the sand disappeared, sadly, at the outset. They were replaced by the idea of a banquet, itself the direct result of location research.

A trip to Bradford was the first move once the film had been commissioned, and in April 1989 we arrived at the site of the now infamous book-burning, and immediately found ourselves surrounded by relevant imagery: once-powerful churches reduced to being auction houses or carpet salerooms; a chapel now acting as the Omar Khayyam Tandoori Restaurant; the only new religious building a mosque with a golden dome: rich and ironic possibilities for a man who disdains all this talk of the eternal.

So we started with an initial idea – in this case blasphemy, its importance in our culture, and its place in a specific town in England – and worked from that foundation using extensive reading, enormous amounts of research (much of which was discarded), and the location. Tony's technical skill allows him to remain very flexible, which means he can take full advantage of events as they unfold, discarding verses on the one hand and quickly adapting them on the other as necessary. Gradually, starting from small beginnings, a whole range of ideas and references are brought into play, and the initial simple idea becomes enriched from the multitude of resources stored in the notebooks.

Where does this ability to collect and connect originate? He suggests that it might come from his youth, and his insatiable but undisciplined reading, fuelled by the now famous Thomas Campey, bookseller. Campey's market stall in Leeds (immortalised in the poet's *Ex Libris* stickers and the poem 'Thomas Campey and the Copernican System') offered the young poet an extremely eclectic selection. Tony would devour each set of purchases, taking from them just those ideas that excited him. It became a way of reading, and thus of interpretation, that wide but random selection acting as a catalyst for his imagination. Is it this that underlies the now well-established way he works with film, where an initial idea or event is amplified and embroidered with a variety and artistry that is both personal and very unusual? An artistry that allows him to make the serendipitous connections and elisions that occur while out on location or in the cutting room?

Once we had discovered a church masquerading as a restaurant, *The Blasphemers' Banquet* was designed around a meal. The meal offered opportunities to extol life-enhancing things, particularly alcohol, and it enabled the poet to include the conceit of the various blasphemers who would not be able to accept their invitations to join in this celebration.

A very vague structural frame now existed for the film, but the nature of the main part of it remained open, and continued to change even during the edit. To take one example: the piece-to-camera in the Bradford square where Tony miracles *The Satanic Verses* back into his hand while sitting in the very space where it was burnt was designed as a sequence that would open the film. We thought we knew where we were going when events changed everything, and we had to rethink the whole thing. Once again, it was the Ayatollah who intervened.

We were filming our two absent French blasphemers, Molière and Voltaire, in Paris, when the footage of Khomeini's funeral flickered onto the screens across the world. We sat and watched it in our hotel room, and realised we had a new beginning, and a beginning that underlined much more forcibly the true nature of fundamentalism. The film took on a darker and more aggressive feel. If the fundamentalists could attack us, why could not we, the inheritors of the European rational tradition, attack in our turn? We did so simply by repeating the footage, enhanced here and there either by an occasional trick like slow-motion or enlargement, or by a dazzling score composed by Dominic Muldowney. The poet is nowhere to be heard. Instead he chooses to let the images do the work, and only towards the very end do his words emerge, not as a quatrain, but as a heart-breaking refrain given to the soprano Teresa Stratas, singing of her love for this fleeting life. The refrain, an English translation of a phrase from the Koran, is a Harrisonian inversion. In its original context the phrase is used to warn against attachment to the world. Here it has been appropriated and turned into a hymn of praise for everything fleeting and lovely in this life:

> Oh, I love this fleeting life.

That is an example of the poet leaving well alone, and using the image to telling effect. At the same time, we had started to experiment with techniques that would work better with the verse commentary, and were particularly careful to use longer static and moving shots. One way of achieving a good moving shot in films is to lay a track down, something resembling a railway line, on which you then place a set of wheels for your camera. This we did on several locations, most notably in a little back alley in Bradford. One particular shot starts on an obscene scrawl painted on a boarded-up door. It travels from it across a wall, over an Urdu notice, along a fence, ending finally on the dome of an unfinished mosque. In the finished film it covers four quatrains, and allows an unstoppable momentum to build up in the verse that then continues into the wonderful meditation on transience that lies at the heart of the piece. None of the quatrains that were later to accompany this shot had been written when we filmed it, but nevertheless the ghost of the metre, hummed by the poet as he stood next to the cameraman, Mike Fox, determined the pace at which it was filmed. We had begun to trust each other – on the one hand I would film sometimes disconnected and strange shots with a newfound confidence that they would be connected in the end, and on the other Tony had started to discover what the armoury of film techniques could offer him.

The final sequence in which this shot occurs starts with a picture of two beautiful young girls before cutting to a close shot of the graffiti: 'Scarface bummed his dad . . .' It is graffiti typical of any wall in any city.

> Beautiful sisters in their white and green
> innocent of what these crude words mean
> but maybe they will soon discover beauty
> is inescapably bound up with the obscene.

The tracking shot starts at the beginning of the next verse, with a wider framing of the preceding shot of the graffiti. The movement starts by hugging the ground, moving over some rubbish that lay beneath a sign in Urdu which said 'Leave No Litter', and along the fence, before soaring up towards the mosque, allowing us then to cut to the hill above the city and visually swoop back down again to the next location, the auction rooms of David Bishop. The whole sequence, extending through the stanzas following that quoted above, is covered by two shots, the first the track mentioned above, and the second a pan and zoom from the cemetery above the town. The verse soars along-side them, driving us forward to the sudden juddering halt of the auctioneer's hammer, and the 'going – going – gone of everything'. It is a perfect transition from Frank Randle to Greek tragedy, and then, mischievously, back to Randle when Tony uses the shot of the Queen's face on a biscuit tin, an item in the auction sale, to suggest the possibility of a quick execution by guillotine of both her and other 'high and mighty' people.

Finally, I want to draw attention to the climax of the film, which consists of a bravura montage attacking funda-mentalism everywhere, followed by a long single 360-degree take as Harrison speaks out of the television set directly to Rushdie, hiding as he then was in a secret loca-tion under police protection. The single take allowed the poet a sustained personal statement, amounting to eleven quatrains that he had to memorise, and which were delivered without any filmic intervention. The montage that precedes it was handed over to the film editor, Peter Simpson, and the composer, Dominic Muldowney, who bet-ween them and over a period of several days put together a sequence of great power. The poet remained mute.

Little has been said about the sound track, but with this film we were able to add a third room to our usual two, and in this the composer worked on a Synclavier 9600, a very exciting new piece of equipment at that time, on which he created a unique sound track using a huge range of modified recorded sounds. In exactly the same process used for the words, the sound track was worked on, modi-fied, tested, altered, tested again and so on until everyone was satisfied. In this way the editor and composer were able to refine this particular sequence, in exactly the same way that we were refining the other sequences to suit Tony's words and ideas.

All our films have sound tracks that are the subject of a great deal of care, so it might be worth spending a little

1

time analysing the one that was created for this film. There is an increasing tendency to neglect this side of the art, something that Tony and I feel very strongly about. Working with Andrew Wilson, the Synclavier's operator, the composer assembled a battery of sound effects, some recorded on location, like the demonstration shouts; some, like the helicopter noise, from library discs; and some specially recorded. They also assembled musical samples: tabla [Indian drum]; cabassas [shakers]; Setar [an Islamic version of the sitar]; and a lot of synthesiser bass samples. Many of these were modified; for instance, the bass synthesizer sounds were looped to mimic the helicopter, while other sounds were built up from different samples.

Once all this was in place, it was possible to start work on the sequences that were coming out of the cutting room. We will take one example, the sequence from the Place de la République with its little fairground helicopter, through to the huge London demonstration, surveyed by the real watching helicopters of the police. Here Tony stops, and the sound track takes over. Let Andrew Wilson explain what he did:

We wanted to go into it from the sequence in the Paris fairground, linking from one helicopter to the other. We started with a helicopter approach-and-pass sound but modified it by editing in at the point where the helicopter reached its Doppler shift. The Synclavier gave a waveform display of the whole sample, which was magnified to find the individual rotor passes. Twelve passes were edited out and looped, and that gave us a musical regularity.

Wilson then measured how long the twelve rotor passes were, and calculated how many there were in a minute. This gave a figure of 127.12 beats per minute, and the machine was set accordingly. 'This meant that we could record our musical sounds and keep a musical feel which would match the rhythm of the helicopter.'

A cabassa was added which mimicked the helicopter sound, and Muldowney added his treated shouts which were dropped in as punctuation effects. Then other sounds were included, like the tabla, to help the flow or increase the tension. Distortion was also introduced by simply increasing the volume of a particular sample. Every version was saved, so that they could return to an earlier one if a later one seemed less successful, and the whole tested against pictures in the cutting room, although the composer also had the images to work against in his room. This is just one example, and one short sequence, but it gives an idea of the complexity that underlies this film.

I have dwelt on *The Blasphemers' Banquet* at some length because it illustrates so clearly the ability of this writer to use his adopted medium. To know when to speak, of course, but equally important when to remain silent. The film is a polemic, and wonderful poetry, but it also deserves to be remembered for another reason. In an age of ratings and managerial paranoia, this must seem extraordinary, but *The Blasphemers' Banquet* was screened on 31 July 1989, on BBC1, at prime time directly after the *Nine o'Clock News*. It was a Monday evening. This was the same slot normally occupied by *Panorama*, which always took a summer break, and the audience for the film was nearly four million. Every major broadsheet carried editorials about it on the day of transmission, and every paper in the country reviewed it the day after. It created a storm before it was shown, and had an equally great response afterwards, not just from critics but also from the viewers.

*

The Gaze of the Gorgon was Tony Harrison's next television work, and it was transmitted on BBC2 on 3 October 1992, as part of a season of programmes under the label of *War and Peace*. It was a single work that had originally been planned as a trilogy. Part One in Corfu concerned the German Kaiser, the excavation of a Gorgon's head, and the start of what was to become a very bloody century. Part Two would have moved to Florida, to the town of Arcadia, which Tony had discovered had once possessed in the 1930s the only rattlesnake-canning factory in the world. At the same time as these beautiful if deadly snakes were being destroyed as a gimmick for tourists, at a nearby airport tests on the first flying bomb were taking place. The second film was intended to cover, from this very particular perspective, the middle years of the century, though containing its hint of the later development of Cruise missiles. Part Three was planned to feature Frankfurt and was designed to bring us up to date. We truncated all three into one film.

Omitting the rattlesnakes was painful, but with the help of Heinrich Heine, whose statue stands in Frankfurt, and once stood in Corfu, Tony was able to include the different parts into a single film that is a very powerful overview of the twentieth century. It illustrates very clearly the earlier remark about poetry's ability to look unflinchingly at the unbearable. And it took our techniques into several new areas, most notably the use of the Schumann song, '*Was will die einsame Träne?*', which is woven through the film, both sung in German, played in various arrangements by our composer, Martin Kiszko, and finally rewritten by Tony and sung in English at the conclusion:

> The closing century's shadow
> has darkened all our years
> and still the Gorgon's filling
> my empty sockets with tears.

'*Was will die einsame Träne?*' was written by Heine and set to music by Schumann. When the Empress Elizabeth of Austria built a palace on Corfu, she commissioned a statue of Heine, and he was sculpted clutching the text of this poem in his left hand. Strangely, for a member of the Establishment, the Empress had taken a fancy to this dissident Jewish poet, but when the German Kaiser arrived to take possession of her summer retreat after her assassination in 1898, Heine was the first person he evicted. The statue, shipped back to Germany, occupied an ignoble position in a coffee house before being moved again when the Nazis started to deface it. It stands now in a little park in Toulon, virtually unknown and unrecognised, having survived the war hidden in a crate. Heine becomes the guide for the film, and his octosyllabic form is used as a metrical template.

Once established in Corfu, the Kaiser decided to play at archaeology, and it was during his time there before the start of the First World War that a large head of a Gorgon was unearthed, part of an early Greek temple. The film/poem takes this creature, whose gaze turns men to stone, as a metaphor for what was being unleashed upon our century. The Gorgon's shadow is with us still, even in the frozen eyes of the drug addicts in the Frankfurt Square.

The Gaze of the Gorgon is a difficult work, but it manages to do something I touched on at the beginning of this introduction, and is even more relevant now than it was when it was created. A letter we received from a viewer clearly illuminates this, because it underlines the value and the power of the poetry to speak to us about the unspeakable:

> I don't know if it is the theme which is so strong and hits right at the heart and guts, or the power of the imagery, which I can't seem to forget, and which jumps out in my mind so vividly. I don't think I have seen anything on fascism that touched and excited me

so and at the same time gave me hope. Usually films
on the subject leave me depressed, while the *Gaze* left
me with a sense of understanding, of facing up to that
overpowering threat of fascism; fascism particularly as
it is manifested all around us, yes, in the architecture
and in things we take for granted and which intimidate
and brainwash us – which often paralyse me and
make me shrink. Perhaps this is because you can sense
the intelligent individual standing so calmly but also
so clearly and surely on the other front, making their
statement and passing it on to those of us who allow
themselves to be intimidated and overpowered by
what we see and what we often feel is beyond our
strength to stop or reverse.

The statue of a warlike Achilles raised on Corfu by the
Kaiser was one such fascistic emblem dwelt on in the film.
In the early days of research, before we knew we would
concentrate solely on the Greek island, we had been look-
ing at statues of Achilles in this country. I have another
cherished postcard from Tony, which arrived while we
were amassing this research. It shows a photo of Achilles
in Hyde Park with a large CND poster covering his
infamous fig leaf. On the back Tony has written: 'We should
collect the different signs covering the cock of Achilles.
I have one "No War in the Gulf". Can researcher acquire
as many as possible?' Tony has many more, including one
with its concealing banner reading 'No Blood for Oil', and
another glorious picture with a Frank Randle connection.
Randle, looking like one of the satyrs out of *Trackers*, is
posed with a large stick below the same Achilles that
dominates the Duke of Wellington memorial in Hyde
Park. This time the fig leaf is there for all to see, and it
looks as if Randle is trying to flip it off with his stick.
   We duly acquired as many cocks as we could lay our
hands on, but in the end the only one that illuminated the

film is the one on the Kaiser's statue, another example of the Harrisonian research method. As if to appease us, however, this cock did have a covering of sorts, something picked up by the eagle-eyed poet on our first visit to the island:

> this bellicose, Berlin-gazing totem
> has hornets nesting in his scrotum.

*

The Harrison style was pushed furthest in his portrait of Alzheimer's Disease sufferers, *Black Daisies for the Bride.* Completed and transmitted in 1993, the verse in this film, unlike his other films made with me, was given to performers to sing.[5] I suppose it is not strictly speaking a film/poem, since the poet is not driving the action directly, but it took all the lessons learned earlier and applied them in an exciting way, and it proved to be a trailblazer for later work, notably by the poet Simon Armitage and director Brian Hill in documentaries such as *Drinking for England* and *Feltham Sings.*

Here again, the techniques developed elsewhere come into play. The intense research (including extensive work with all the families concerned), followed by a documentary filming period of two weeks during which time the world of Whernside Ward at High Royds Hospital, Menston, West Yorkshire, was recorded. This was followed by an initial post-production period for documentary editing and writing. At this stage, the composer Dominic Muldowney became involved, and after the rough edit, music recordings, casting and rehearsals occupied our time. The 'drama' shoot was next, taking place over another eight days, consisting mainly of the 'wedding dress scenes' that were shot to playback, the songs having been recorded. I also have in my files an extensive list of additional documentary material that we had decided was required. We then returned to the cutting rooms to edit, and to write 'commentary', which was also sung, Tony now having decided he could do this using the metrical vehicle of 'In the Bleak Midwinter'. Further recordings, using school-children from Menston, followed (echoes of the children in *The Big H*) and the whole was then completed with sound mixes, film printing and on-line editing.

Since this was 1993, we were still shooting on film. After we had completed the film edit, the material was transferred to tape, and an extensive 'on-line' edit took place. For instance, it was here that the bouquets on the ward were mixed into the bouquets in the old black-and-white pictures, and then placed behind the wired glass of the locked door. A similar extended post-production edit took place for *The Gaze of the Gorgon*.

This time something very different was being attempted. For the first time, we were going to interweave perform-ance with documentary, and we were going to do it in an ethically difficult arena. Yet it seemed the only way to offer an insight into the world of the sufferers, placing them centre stage, without the intervention of professionals in white coats, while at the same time allowing us to give the viewer a hint of their past lives. If anything, it harks back to our experiences with our first edit, on *Mimmo Perrella*, with its startling use of the subjective voice in the first person, and it was something we only decided on after considerable research and consultation with both relatives and carers. It left us open to criticism: it appeared pre-sumptive to put words into the mouths of the women who were now so ill. One song was especially singled out, given to the 'young' Kathleen Dickenson, which ends:

With Alzheimer's shredding all remembered time,
the blizzard's blowing, but Godammit I'm . . .
g . . . gl . . . gla . . . glad . . . I'm still Kath and alive!
                      I'm still Kath and alive!
                      I'm still Kath and alive!

How could we presume to know? we were asked. To which I can only say, if you had met Kathleen yourself and worked with her as we did, you would embrace and want to celebrate that wonderful spark of life that still flickered in her eyes, something resoundingly underlined by her lovely unscripted dance later in the film.

Tony had decided to use the music heard on the ward, or discovered in the past lives of the patients, as his template, and so the first editing period found him struggling with words that had to fit into models as diverse as 'Oh, You Beautiful Doll' and Puccini's *Madame Butterfly*. The achievement of putting colloquial words into the operatic framework of Puccini was particularly exciting, and was then carried forward by Dominic Muldowney using musical fragments of the opera as a frame. More than most, this work is unclassifiable. Tony's failure to fit into a neat pigeonhole is illustrated by the fact that *Daisies* received two awards, one for the best documentary and the other for the best drama.

After the success of *Black Daisies for the Bride* in 1993, Harrison moved over to Channel 4, where he made *A Maybe Day in Kazakhstan* and *The Shadow of Hiroshima*, and where he was to develop and make his feature film, *Prometheus*. Working with the producer Andrew Holmes, *A Maybe Day* was co-directed with Mark Kidel, but *Hiroshima* Tony directed himself. Both films contain developments upon the earlier work: the use of synchronous contributions from bystanders that are woven into the verse; the use of music and sound as integral to the whole, some of it emanating from the documentary, the sound even being recorded by the poet or, in the case of *The Shadow of Hiroshima*, by the composer, Richard Blackford, taken on location to act as the sound recordist; the playful and clever transformation, in the verse, of documentary material discovered on location. Hard to forget the witty use of a Trotsky lookalike doll with revolving eyes to make fun of the Soviet ideal of permanent revolution in *Kazakhstan*:

> There, in strange surgical disguise,
> Dr Trotsky rolls his eyes
> drinking his prescribed solution,
> only his eyes in revolution
> and that by no means permanent
> once Dr Trotsky's battery's spent.

The Shadow of Hiroshima in one way brings us back full circle to *Loving Memory*. When it was transmitted on 6 August 1987, the episode *Cheating the Void*, which starts in Père Lachaise cemetery in Paris and passes from nineteenth- to twentieth-century Europe, culminating in the firestorms of the bombed city of Hamburg, left the question of total annihilation open, though it was very much at the forefront of Tony's thoughts.

Cheating the Void started with the Lumière brothers' famous film of factory workers leaving their workplace – shadows on the screen:

> These people are all dead, and yet they walk.
> The first in fact to move on celluloid.
> Though they are silent and won't ever talk
> their very movements seemed to cheat the void.

The Shadow of Hiroshima (transmitted on Channel 4 on 6 August 1995, the fiftieth anniversary) also starts with a shadow, though this time not one on film, but the burnt outline of a man whose body has been photographed, not by celluloid, but by stone. He is one of many thousands killed by the atomic bomb dropped on Hiroshima, but in his case all that was left was the outline of a body etched onto the pavement. Harrison gives him a voice, and a lover, in a film/poem of great emotional intensity. Like Heine and Mimmo Perrella before him, Shadow San becomes our guide, and his story and longing for an ordinary life is interwoven into the build-up for the annual ceremony of releasing the 'doves' that takes place beneath the famous Peace Dome in the city. The doves are in fact pigeons, and they form the other major strand in the film, as we follow them and their keepers from their cages to the park and then, for the lucky ones not savaged by the Hiroshima hawks, home again. I love the fact that in an age when the presenter on television is everything, and when looks are more important than intelligence, we have a poet who has given us three 'presenters', two invisible, and all three dead. I recommend it to producers: their fees are a lot cheaper than those currently being demanded.

The other presence in the film is that of the A-bomb Peace Dome, the famous Hiroshima landmark that is the only remnant from the old city. Tony had originally planned to do a work that featured this exclusively, a kind of 'One Hundred Views' like the famous views of Mount Fuji by the painter Hokusai, and while that idea changed, nevertheless the building is an unsettling presence throughout the film, caught in the back of shots; reflected in the water; seen through the windows of the NHK, the Japanese Television company. For this film the poet became the director, and his composer Richard Blackford became the sound recordist, capturing effects which he later uses in his music to telling effect (as in the wonderful baseball sequence). As Blackford himself has said elsewhere, he becomes here the 'sound designer', and the sound tracks of all these films are worthy of a separate study.[6]

This film contains one of the clearest examples I know of the power and potential of poetry when it is linked with subjects of this kind. In a moving sequence quite near the start of the film, we meet Hara San, a survivor who ritually paints the A-Bomb Dome that is the centerpiece of the Hiroshima memorial each year, perhaps as a way of coming to terms with the horror of his past. We see him as he begins painting the famous skeletal shape. The visual scene is set very simply, the camera transferring its gaze fairly quickly from the painter to the Dome and then onto the slowly moving water below it, with its indistinct reflection. The shots of the water are very long, and we are to some extent mesmerised by the look, texture and motion of the water. But every time I watch this scene, the water is transformed, because overlaid upon it are images of a very different nature, and these we cannot turn away from or ignore. Words stronger than pictures, but in a perfect marriage:

His schoolmates' shrieks from blackened lips
haunt Hara San each time he dips
his brush in water from the stream
to give relief to those who scream,
all his dying schoolmates, those
whose skin slid off their flesh like clothes.
Like clothes, three sizes oversize,
their flayed skin loosens from their thighs.
Burns and blisters, bloated blebs
burst as the Motoyasu ebbs,
the tidal Motoyasu trails
black flaps of flesh like chiffon veils.
Like kimonos with their belts untied
black sloughed-off skin floats on the tide.

*

When Auden started work on his first effort in this field over half a century ago, he little realised how much further his successor would develop it. Auden's thoughts about verse and film, which he made public in a lecture to the North London Film Society, remain intriguingly prophetic, and his conclusion is still relevant today.[7] Having outlined what he saw as the advantages and disadvantages of verse and film (he wrongly thought that accepted metrical forms would not work, a conclusion he came to because of the technical constraints at that time), Auden ended by pointing out that the most difficult element in the equation was finding the right kind of support, both financial and artistic, to enable this process to develop. As I have tried to show here, that development may often take place over an extended period of time, and require a great deal of faith. It may well be that poets need either to learn the business themselves, or develop their skills in conjunction with a compatible film maker. What is certain is that if it is to work this form is something that must be allowed a life of its own, with the space to grow. Poet and film maker must be given the room to develop and experiment.

The two final film/poems in this collection (and I am omitting *Prometheus* which is not part of Harrison's documentary canon) are *Metamorpheus* and *Crossings*. The first is a playful experiment with new technology, made for BBC2 in 2000, while the second brings this film/poem journey to its logical conclusion in that it was the poet's own homage to Auden and to *Night Mail*. It was shown on ITV in *The South Bank Show* in 2002.

Metamorpheus was in one sense an attempt to see if the advantages of the new technology could be harnessed to this old art. Using myself as the sound recordist and general gopher, and with Alistair Cameron (Tony's cameraman on *A Maybe Day*, *Hiroshima* and *Prometheus*) gamely struggling with a simple little DV camera, we set off into the wilds of Bulgaria accompanied by the poet and Oliver Taplin, Professor of Greek at Magdalen College, Oxford. The idea was that the financial savings afforded us by using this simple equipment would allow us to reconnoitre and shoot over the period of a month in Bulgaria and Greece, working in a way not possible had we used a conventional crew. The film is about the myth of Orpheus and explores the idea that, like all Greek myths, it is not set in some mythical landscape but in the real world, with recognisable landmarks in Bulgaria and Greece that are connected to it. It takes up the story after Orpheus has lost Eurydice for the second time, and looks at the later part of the story, his death and dismemberment. Oliver plays the role of the Professor in the film, gamely taking the bardic gibes on his chin, while Tony takes the role of the virtually absent Orpheus . . . until his severed head disturbs the Professor's meditations on the Orphic myth. Richard Blackford again provided the music, giving a voice to the severed head. This was a copy of Tony's made by a most unpleasant process which involved us virtually stifling the poet with latex. The film takes us on the journey Orpheus' severed head was said to have taken, from the source of the Maritsa River above Sofia all the way down to the Mediterranean, and across the sea to Lesbos.

Another and more important journey was taken a few years later, when Tony Harrison decided to use the final closure of the famous mail train service from London to Scotland to offer his own tribute to Auden and to *Night Mail*. In *The South Bank Show*, the original film is analysed first, in a documentary about its creation, and is followed by an excellent short documentary in which Harrison explains very clearly the technique he has developed for creating these works. The third and final part is *Crossings*, a film/poem that is both an elegy and a state-of-the-nation protest.

'I always call my things "film/poems" which is an honest description because I think they involve giving the documentary style an organisation, a structure, that it doesn't have naturally. Even things that are called documentary like *Night Mail* are very contrived,' he states in the middle film, and goes on to explain how he never writes a poem and sends a crew out to illustrate it, but depends instead on a sort of 'creative chaos' where he collects with his team a 'ragbag collection' that is a 'creative serendipity'. He illustrates this by then telling us how, at the beginning of *Crossings*, which takes place at the huge London sorting office with its automatic sorting machine, he was watching the process and discovered that the letters go through something they call 'the salmon leap', and where also there is a large red button labelled 'culler' to literally cull letters. This discovery is used in the film in a typical act of connection to link us both to culled Foot and Mouth cattle in the fields the train passes through, and also to the salmon rivers of its final destination in Scotland.

Crossings, co-directed by Tony with David Thomas, and with Richard Blackford again working his magic on the sound track, takes the 'Lady in Red' on her journey north, and links it to imagined characters for whom letters will be important: the homeless boy on the streets of London; the farmer bankrupted by the Foot and Mouth crisis; the old pensioner putting his money on the dogs; the woman waiting terrified for her HIV test to arrive. Whereas Auden had offered only a very tangential hint at character, here the poet broadens the story out and brings it up to the present as the train speeds north on what will be one of its last journeys before being axed.

The opening, in the sorting office, which takes its metre and rhythm from the original, is a tour de force, spinning us into the journey with the assistance of other voices, including lines from sorting office workers, preparing us for the appearance of other people speaking lines that sit alongside the poet's own. All the usual hallmarks of the process are here: the clever use of technique to isolate the colour red; the dramatic use of sound; the experimentation with different voices; the connections obviously discovered as research and filming progressed; the delight in and confident use of editing. Moments like the one where we leave the broken farmer sitting at the railway crossing –

> I'll lay awake anxious ,till t'letterbox flap
> bangs afore dawn like the spring of a trap

– and we cut to the traps of a greyhound stadium opening with the dogs bursting out onto the concourse in a startling and noisy change of pace.

*

The scripts assembled in this collection, ranging from work done over a twenty-five year period, deserve to be preserved. However, reading them is a poor substitute for *seeing* and *hearing* them. Sadly, even in the age of the DVD, getting hold of these films is not easy, but at the very least being able to study them on the printed page will give a sense of the diversity and range of the work. As you read them, never forget that this is work that is designed to be *seen* and *heard*. It has been specially constructed with pictures in mind. It is specially commissioned work, written and re-written with much trial and error both at the filming and the editing stages, created with often painstaking experiment. Almost as much as survives upon these pages lies on the cutting-room floor, and none of it existed before it was hammered out in front of editing machines or on location.

It has been written only so that it could exist alongside those other elements that go to make up a film – the pictures, obviously, but also the other sounds, ranging from synchronous prose to sung music. It is not for nothing that Harrison has chosen to call his works film/poems, and his willingness to work in this way may seem to many writers to be brave, but to me seems quite natural. He has embraced every new idea and piece of technology, but harnessed it to the oldest art. The classical education; the extraordinary breadth of reference encouraged by Thomas Campey, bookseller; Frank Randle's passion, directness and mordant wit: all these and more have gone into an alchemical mix which has given us this film-poet of outstanding versatility and power. 'It's all poetry to me.'

Bristol, September 2006

NOTES

1 Nuttall, J., *King Twist: a Portrait of Frank Randle* (Routledge, 1978).

2 *Proceedings of the Classical Association*, Vol. LXXXV (1988), page 16.

3 W. H. Auden and Christopher Isherwood, *Plays and Other Dramatic Writings 1928–1938*, ed. Edward Mendelson (Faber and Faber, 1989), page 512.

4 *Bloodaxe Critical Anthologies 1: Tony Harrison*, ed. Neil Astley (Bloodaxe Books, 1991), pages 384–94.

5 *A Maybe Day in Kazakhstan* was conceived for Melina Mercouri, the famous Greek actor and Minister of Culture, but she died before she could perform for the film. *Crossings* (2002) also uses actors and actors' voices.

6 In Part Two of *The South Bank Show* celebrating *Night Mail* (which included *Crossings*), transmitted on ITV on 10 March 2002, both Blackford and Harrison offer insights into their creative process.

7 W. H. Auden and Christopher Isherwood, *Plays and Other Dramatic Writings 1928–1938*, Appendix V, 'Two Reported Lectures: Poetry and Film', ed. Edward Mendelson (Faber and Faber, 1989).

ARCTIC PARADISE
(1981)

Tony Harrison's verse commentary
in Robert Service style for the BBC film
Arctic Paradise is for two voices,
a man's (here represented in roman type)
and a woman's (*in italic type*),
intended to be old-timers of
the Yukon Gold Rush days.

Arctic Paradise was first transmitted in
the *World About Us* slot in October 1981.

Off the beaten track in the cold outback's not what a
    feller thinks
as the perfect place for the human race but more for bear
    or lynx.
The place to be unfenced and free is a place most men
    would shun
but the snowy waste is to the taste of Roger Mendelsohn.

*

A normal day gets under way for a family of four.
The table's spread, hot coffee, bread, but just outside the
    door
is Yukon snow and frost as low as seventy degrees
and the outside air once let in there would make hot
    coffee freeze
and what's between this family scene and the bitter
    Yukon weather
are the walls and doors and wooden floors they learnt to
    build together.

*

*Come June, July, a clear blue sky and the sun up there all
    day.*
*For this paradise, that winter ice was a paltry price to
    pay.*

*

No greens, no fruit, just what I shoot and ice-hole
    fish-lines bring
and one moose can make a year of steak to see us
    through till Spring.

3

All they require, for food and fire, the family never lacks
and never will while they've got skill with net, rifle, trap
    and axe.

*

The white-fisted land opens her hand and is generous
    when she thaws
provided all, both big and small, do all their daily chores.

Spring, Summer, Fall, three seasons all get ready for the
    fourth
with dry wood in store you're ready for a Winter in the
    North.

All they require, for food and fire, the family never lacks
and never will while they've got skill with net, rifle, trap
    and axe.

*

No greens, no fruit, just what he shoots and ice-hole
    fish-lines bring
and one moose can make a year of steak to see us
    through till Spring.

*

The Yukon river's a bounteous giver but you have to
    coax her first.
If you ask her right, the Yukon might not let you starve
    or thirst.

*

Toronto he, California she, though both kids are Yukon
    born
but the dream they'd be completely free is the reason
    they were drawn,

4

and only here, a last frontier, where the climate is
  extreme
and laws are those you self-impose, can you fulfil that
  dream.

*

*The dog-sled team's part of the dream and we had to
  learn to breed
the malamutes, those half-wild brutes, and they're more
  mouths to feed.*

*

*The dogs we've bred to pull the sled we keep on a strong
  chain
if it weren't strong it wouldn't be long before they're
  wild again.*

*

This space we share with wolf and bear is their own
  stamping ground.
There are dogs. There's game. We hunt. We tame. But
  the wild is all around.

*

They're always there, the fox and bear, and when a
  fellow thinks
he's on his own, he's not alone, he's watched by wolf and
  lynx.

*

*Trapping pays when the fashion craze is fur cuffs and fur
  collars
and a tailored fox in an opera box is what wins us our
  dollars.
He sends his haul to Montreal and they send back big
  cheques*

5

and sable wraps from these iron traps get draped round
  scented necks.

The Hudson Bay'll buy all I supply while the rag trade
  preens and prinks.
Paris and Rome maintain our home as long as they wear
  lynx.
From this beast's death-throes to Paris clothes is but a
  stage or two.
What I kill and pack in the cold outback will find its
  way to you.

*

A woman's more than a man's mere squaw when the
  dream is living free.
What you may regard as man's work, hard, she does as
  much as he.

*

It's not he fishes, she washes dishes, we both mend the
  skidoo
and if I'm away he can't 'role-play', he does all I would
  do.

*

Distinctions blur between him and her, the work
  assigned to each.
Both trap with dogs, both cut the logs, both man and
  woman teach.

*

To visit friends a man contends with Winter at its worst.
Though company's nice, with Yukon ice, you think
  about it first.
When the folk next door are twenty miles or more, it's
  only once or twice

you make it through on the old skidoo across the snow
and ice.

*

Come June, July, a clear blue sky and the sun up there all
day
it's then you know, despite the snow, there's no other
place you'd stay.
For this paradise, the winter ice is a paltry price to
pay.

*

Diners bite by candlelight into my salmon grilled
in some chef's pan in Saskatchewan, and feel their
taste-buds thrilled
and such who dine, on fish of mine, with sips of chilled
Chablis
they're the sort, I guess, support my dream of living free.

*

*Nature flees the scars and screes where the yellow metal's
found.*
*She can't refill the ravaged hill, or restock the gouged-out
ground.*
The last frontier will disappear if men flock at this rate.
Now even more seek out the ore than in the Rush of '98.

As they dredge and spray the land away and make the
hills collapse
game disappears for years and years and there's nothing
in the traps.

What it was then was us grizzled men who worked our
claims alone.
Now that same scene's packed with machines that chew
up every stone.

Not one lone man with sluice and pan but companies
    who've planned
to dredge each speck of dross and dreck and devastate
    the land.

*Big companies hose down the screes with high-powered
    water-jet
and what they spill we fear may kill the salmon that we
    net.
Great dredgers chew the trees that grew, the green of
    their terrain,
where dredgers graze no wild-life stays and won't come
    back again.
The dinosaur that grubs for ore leaves the land one
    mangled mess.
Where it's staked its claim, its goodbye game, and
    goodbye wilderness.*

*

The scale that weighs what this gold pays is the balance
    of world power,
and politics, globe-wide, will fix the gold price hour by
    hour.
What's in the pan's the fate of man not just the dust and
    ore,
each ounce's worth across the earth depends on peace or
    war.

*

What men have meant by true content seems something
    like these scenes,
who'd give up this hard-worked-for bliss for growling
    mine machines.

If a scale could weigh this sort of day against a mine that
    struck it rich,

8

and I'd to choose which one I'd lose, I tell you I know
  which;

And if you'd poured *your* sweat into trap and net to
  watch your children grow,
in the wild you share with wolf and bear I think you'd
  also know.

But I hear some say 'Gold all the way' but to this lucky
  feller
whose dream means more, the sought-for ore is just a
  stone that's yeller.

When winter's past and the sun at last stays whole weeks
  in the sky
and the Yukon seems a place for dreams, what more
  could mere gold buy?
For a man who's freed from gold-lust greed and from the
  rat-race rut
whose dream's come as true as it could do, here's true
  contentment. But . . .

*

*the doves and hawks, moscow's, new york's, affect the
  way gold swings,
world strain and stress are what assess the cost of
  wedding rings.*

*

Come June, July, a clear blue sky and the sun up there all
  day
for this paradise the winter ice is a paltry price to pay.

*

*We don't even dent the environment, the resources that
  we use*

9

*for fur or food soon get renewed, and it's Nature who
    renews.*

But Nature flees the scars and screes where the yellow
    metal's found.
She can't refill the ravaged hill or restock the gouged-out
    ground.

*

But when I see my name scrawled on the claim, I feel
    something in me's gone.
Something's died in the former pride of Roger Mendelsohn
and the driven stave's romance's grave, the tombstone to
    the dream
of the paradise of snow and ice, the traps, the dog-sled
    team.

THE BIG H
(1984)

'What a strain it is to be evil.'

Bertolt Brecht

'Ours is not the only language and culture
in which h-dropping among the common people
is stigmatised: we are told that the Galilean speakers
of Aramaic in New Testament times were well known
for this tendency, so that Jesus Christ
almost certainly dropped his h's.'

John Honey
Does Accent Matter? The Pygmalion Factor

The **Big H** was first performed on BBC2 Television on 26 December 1984 with the following cast:

Maths Teacher Barrie Rutter
History Teacher June Watson
Geography Teacher James Carter

and from Woodkirk High School, Tingley, Yorkshire:

The Boys	The Girls
Michael Day	Andrea Cholmondeley
Simon Smith	Paula Yeoman
Timothy McArdle	Cheryl Green
Damon Evans	Amanda Waugh
Jason Fountain	Julie Cliffe
Martin West	Joanne Hall
Philip Grimes	Sarah Squire
Neil Hargreaves	Amanda Trowsdale
Dennis Pinchen	Gillian Curtin
Michael Dunn	Lisa Jarvis
Mark Tyson	Andrea Shales
Simon Goodson	Joanne Madarasz
Matthew Haslam	Lara Thompson
Jason Nowell	Louise Close

Musical Director Dominic Muldowney
Saxophones John Harle, Tim Payne, Dave Roach, Glen Martin
Percussion John Harrod, Tony Wagstaff
Organ Mark Hamlyn

Producer Andree Molyneux
Directors Bill Hayes, Jeremy Ancock
Designers Stuart Walker, Raymond Cusick
Make-Up Designer Elaine Smith
Costume Designer Nicholas Rocker
Production Manager Vivien Rosenz
Production Assistants Marissa Cowell, Thelma Helsby
Assistant Floor Manager Dermot Boyd
Film Cameraman Fintan Sheehan
Film Recordist Ron Brown
Film Editor Alistair Mackay
Stills Photography Peter Lane
Graphic Designers Graham McCallum, Peter Wane
Prop Buyers Monica Boggust, Paul Schrader
Technical Co-Ordinator Alan Arbuthnott
Vision Mixer John Barclay
Camera Supervisor Geoff Feld
Video Effects Roger Francis
Videotape Editor Phil Southby
Sound Supervisor Chick Anthony
Lighting Director John Summers

Overture.

Establishing shots of Leeds.
Children on their way to school.

Shots of the Leeds coat-of-arms on some of the
following locations:
1. Leeds Town Hall, front façade beneath the clock.
2. Stone carving above the offices of Metro Leeds.
3. Cockburn High School, Dewsbury Road. Stained glass
coat-of-arms above school entrance.
4. Old Midland Bank in City Square across road from
Queens Hotel.
5. Leeds Civic Hall. Front façade. PRO REGE ET LEGE
carved on the façade in large letters.
6. Leeds Civic Hall. Side entrance above door. The arms
are in blue, red, gold and therefore have a 'medieval'
look appropriate for Herod.
7. City Library, Headrow entrance. Wrought iron
coat-of-arms, gilded.
8. Cross Flatts Park, old entrance gateposts, Dewsbury
Road end. Blackened sandstone.
9. Metropole Hotel, Wellington Street entrance.
The whole effect should establish the rule of Herod in
every nook and cranny of life.

In the activity of Leeds people going to work and their
children to school, we follow twelve Boys who are
making their way to school. In groups of three, making
four groups.

We notice signs indicating the way to places in and
around Leeds beginning with H: HEADINGLEY, HOLBECK,

HUNSLET, HAREHILLS, HORSFORTH, HOLMFIRTH,
HALIFAX, HECKMONDWIKE, HUDDERSFIELD, HULL,
HEBDEN BRIDGE, HEPTONSTALL, HARROGATE, HARE
WOOD, HOO HOLE, HOG HOLES, HANGING HEATON, *etc.*

*The Children and the three Teachers arrive at school.
Boy 12 is seen running, late. Classroom.*

*We hear the voices of Rachel (the leader of the chorus of
Mams) and the eleven Mams calling the names of their
sons over the Teacher giving register call.*

ALL MAMS
(*voice-over*)

He were a lovely lad

> *Each of the Mams fits in the name of her massacred
> son.*

MAM 1

Our Roger!

MAM 2

Our Johnny!

MAM 3

Our Frank!

MAM 4

Our Malcolm!

> *Boys start softly singing 'We Three Kings' and fade
> out under Mams.*

MAM 5

Our David!

MAM 6

Our Jason!

MAM 7

Our Ronnie!

MAM 8

Our Michael!

MAM 9

Our Peter!

MAM 10

Our Tony!

MAM 11

Our Mark!

MAM 12

Our 'arry!

Register still being called.

RACHEL

He were a lovely lad.
And God alone knows why
my baby had to die!

BOY 12

We were bonny babies so say our mams
but we all got murdered in our cots and prams!

I. THE MATHEMATICAL HEROD

On the blank blackness of the blackboard a hand writes
TEST.

*Then we are in a classroom of twenty-eight kids, the
fourteen boys we have already seen and the fourteen
girls some of whose voices we have heard as Rachel and
the eleven Mams. The Teacher is one of the faces we saw
in the playground.*

The kids protest against the word TEST *written on the
blackboard.*

KIDS

Aw, sir, it's Christmas!

TEACHER

No, it isn't, yet!
We're going to have that maths test I promised you I'd set.

INNER VOICE OF HEROD

Make way for ranting Herod, the Anti-Christ Kid King
who cringes every Christmas when the Noels start to ring.
Make room for me King Herod, your inner Mr Hyde
who'd rid himself of Jesus by unleashing genocide,
searching for that Christ Kid through all Leeds cots and
    prams
leaving bloodstained bundles to be blubbed at by their
    mams.

TEACHER

I want to do more work on parallelograms,
and tonight . . .

BOY 2

Aw, Sir!

TEACHER

For homework you'll revise trapeziums.

BOY 3

Sir . . .

GIRL 2

It's Christmas!

GIRL 3

'omework!

BOY 4

Crumbs!

BOY 12

(*raising his hand for attention*)
I 'ave to 'elp mi mam to 'ang the 'olly . . .

TEACHER
(*emphasising the dropped aitches*)
Have to Help your mother Hang the Holly!
Try to find some aitches on your Christmas tree.
Ask Santa to leave some in the toe-end of your stocking.

INNER VOICE
OK, Dr Jekyll, that's enough of being jolly.
Time for sceptre-shaking and shouting something shocking.
Give me room to rant and rage, and leave the rest to me.
Make way for horrid Herod, your inner Mr Hyde
who's been revving up all morning hatching homicide.
The Homicide I'm Hatching is Hardly against Hommes
– it's boy babies under two I'm after with my bombs!

There should have been a Herod with his heavy mob in
    Halifax.

KIDS
A 'erod with 'is 'eavy mob in 'alifax!

TEACHER
(*emphasising aitches*)
There should have been a Herod with his heavy mob in
    Halifax
descending on he-children with head-cracking hatchet
    hacks
and terminating toddlers with his lethal axe-attacks.
There should have been a Herod who kinged it hereabouts.

KIDS
'ereabouts.

TEACHER
Hereabouts.

INNER VOICE
There should have been a Herod who kinged it hereabouts,
clobbering the kids before they grew up lazy louts.

INNER VOICE & TEACHER

Yes.

INNER VOICE

There ought to be Herod now in Hunslet or in Hull . . .

KIDS

In 'unslet or in 'ull!

TEACHER

In Hunslet or in Hull! In Hunslet or in Hull!

INNER VOICE & TEACHER

Yes.

INNER VOICE

There ought to be a Herod now in Hunslet or in Hull
hammering kids' heads in till the morgue slabs are all full!

INNER VOICE & TEACHER

Yes.

INNER VOICE

There ought to be a Herod alive and well and here . . .

BOYS

'ere! 'ere! 'ere! 'ere! 'ere! 'ere!

TEACHER

Here! Here!

INNER VOICE

There ought be a Herod alive and well and Here
in full infanticidal flow in full KILL-ALL KIDS career . . .

TEACHER

Before they grow up squirting aerosols graffitiing our
    garages,
rip open the upholstery in cup-excursion carriages
and end up with some lass like these in monstrous fertile
    marriages.

Before they grow up to squirt aerosols and start to spray
the few words they can spell right or UNITED RULES OK,
then get some fertile female in the family way . . .
Best batter 'em while they're still brats, yes, batter 'em
    before
they come and squirt four-letter words all over your
    front door.
Before they start percussion bands with your street's
    dustbin lids,
Before they bump on purpose into supermarket soupcan
    pyramids,
then, still kids themselves, start producing their own kids!
Wives traipsing for their ciggies still in their curling pins,
starting boozing first with Babychams then graduate to
    gins,
slopping in worn slippers fringed with orange nylon fur
shopping for their *babies* . . .

  VOICES OF RACHEL AND THE II MAMS
   (*interrupting very tenderly*)
      Gold, frankincense and myrrh!
Shopping for their babies, gold, frankincense and myrrh!

    BOYS I–I2
Myrrh myrrh myrrh myrrh myrrh myrrh myrrh
myrrh myrrh myrrh myrrh myrrh myrrh myrrh.

    TEACHER
   (*his anger escalating*)
STOP that myrrhmyrrhing!

I see her in the future a shapeless shambling cow
with kids I'll end up teaching twenty years from now,
when happiness is crappy nappies lurching round the
    laundromat
and a belly bulging big again with one more bawling brat
and in Herod's world of weeping women the last thing
    we need is THAT.

VOICES OF RACHEL & THE 11 MAMS
A word that's wiped the worn-out WELCOME off the
front door mat.

BOY 1
Sir, mi mam says babies are all bonny.

BOY 7
and mi aunty, sir,
says every baby's worth gold, frankincense and myrrh . . .

BOYS 1-12
Myrrh myrrh myrrh myrrh myrrh myrrh
myrrh myrrh myrrh myrrh myrrh myrrh.

TEACHER
(*loud, at explosion point*)
Stop that bloody myrrhmnyrrhing!

*The Teacher of Mathematics is transformed into King
Herod, and launches himself in the 'Rant of Herod'.*

*The Teacher is on the classroom dais. Behind him,
chalked on the blackboard, is the Leeds coat-of-arms
with its prominent PRO REGE ET LEGE.*

*The classroom is now bare of chairs and tables and
desks and is the performance area for the PREL, Herod's
death-squad (played by the twelve Boys) and for Rachel
and the eleven Mams (played by the twelve Girls).*

HEROD/TEACHER
And now I am a Herod in my proper Herod gear
I'll kick off my campaign by clouting this lad's ear!
Let every so-called innocent be designated X
and let this ruler be the axe that swipes off their 'sweet'
necks!

And now I am a Herod, a true-blue HERODES REX
a REX whose every little word's interpreted as LEX,

your first maths assignment is the measuring of necks!
Now calculate the necessary length of noose
if the gibbet in Judaea has a six-foot hypotenuse!

*We now see the twelve Boys transformed into the
PREL, the deadly death-squad of Herod.*

*The PREL with arms raised simultaneously as if in
competitive eagerness to give an answer to Herod's
question, but giving the effect of a long-drilled Sieg
Heil!*

THE PREL
SSSSSSSSSSSSSSSSSSSSSSSSSSSSSSSSSir!

HEROD
(*warming to the subject*)
If a gallows set in Galilee is .95 metres high
and a toddler 30 centimetres takes .31 secs to die
how long a length of rope does Herod's hangman have
to buy?

A pause while the PREL consider the problem.

*The PREL raising their arms simultaneously to
answer the question and again giving the effect of a
drilled Sieg Heil!*

THE PREL
SSSSSSSSSSSSSSSSSSSSSSSSSSSSSSSSSir!

HEROD
Now this is a hard one: how many furlongs, yards and
chains
would a toddler have to toddle before the PREL beat out
his brains?

*The PREL raising arms, again with effect of drilled
Sieg Heil!*

THE PREL
SSSSSSSSSSSSSSSSSSSSSSSSSSSSSSSir!

HEROD
If 4 MPH's the speed at which an infant fled
and the PREL pursued at 60 how soon was that kid dead?

THE PREL
SSSSSSSSSSSSSSSSSSSSSSSSSSSSSSSir!

HEROD
If the PREL pursue their little prey on speedy roller skates
and the innocents are toddling as two-year toddlers do
one's going at forty, the other a mere two,
calculate the seconds before they meet their fates.
Then tot up the tonnage of TNT
to liquidate all toddlers from Tynemouth to Torquay,
then the whole kid population from North to Irish Sea!

The PREL, with arms raised simultaneously again.

THE PREL
SSSSSSSSSSSSSSSSSSSSSSSSSSSSSSSir!

HEROD
*(holding up his jewelled orb which is
a disguised aerosol)*
If I press this little ruby on my shining regal orb
'Herod rules OK,' OK, is what my orb'll daub.

PRELS 1–11
Herod rules OK.

PREL 12
'erod rules OK.

PRELS 1–11
*(turning on PREL 12, shocked at his lapse, his dropped
aitch)*
HEROD, HEROD, HEROD, RULES OK.

24

HEROD

With my ruby-studded orb I'll daub 'Herod rules OK'
or eliminate this horrid kid by aerosolling X
wherever lives a little lad my PREL platoons should slay,
for I am HEROD, the regal REX and legal LEX.

*The PREL now worked up for their 'prowl', begin to
chant.*

THE PREL

REX! LEX REX! LEX!

HEROD
(*over the chant of the PREL*)

Go out and gut the lot, my goodly ghoulish geezers,
wherever I have squirted X might be the home of Jesus.

*The PREL beginning to form up for the 'prowl' of the
PREL.*

THE PREL

PRO REGE ET LEGE.

HEROD
(*over chant of PREL and pointing to
Leeds coat-of-arms with its owls*)

PRO REGE (that's me, folks) ET LEGE (me too).
I'm the King and the Law, the tu-whit and tu-wu!

THE PREL

PRO REGE ET LEGE!

*Then the PREL 'number off' in Latin and proceed on
'the prowl' to massacre the innocents.*

PREL 1

Unus!

PREL 2

Duo!

PREL 3

Tres!

PREL 4

Quattuor!

PREL 5

Quinque!

PREL 6

Sex!

PREL 7

Septem!

PREL 8

Octo!

   Four beats.

PREL 9

Novem!

PREL 10

Decem!

PREL 11

Undecim!

PREL 12

Er . . .

   The PREL all turn towards him.

PREL 1–11

Duodecim!

PREL 12

Duodecim!

   The PREL, beginning 'the prowl' of the PREL.

PRO REGE ET LEGE! P-R-E-L.
PRO REGE ET LEGE! P-R-E-L.

PREL 1
When the PREL is after prey.

PREL 2
When the PREL is on the prowl.

BOY 1
You'll hear foreboding hootings.

BOY 2
From the left and right Leeds owl.

THE PREL
PRO REGE ET LEGE,
THE MEN FROM THE PREL!

BOY 1
What guarantees a nation
will be free from unrest?

BOY 2
It's swift elimination of all boys at the breast.

THE PREL
PRO REGE ET LEGE,
THE MEN FROM THE PREL!

BOY 3
Our corps goes kid-coshing
and zapping the prams.

BOY 4
We've nabbed some still noshing
the milk from their mams.

THE PREL
PRO REGE ET LEGE,
THE MEN FROM THE PREL!

BOYS

To stop rabble-rousers
and rockers of boats

BOY 6

we mow them with Mausers
and slit their wee throats.

THE PREL

PRO REGE ET LEGE,
THE MEN FROM THE PREL!

BOY 11

Hacking slashing
slitting babes' throats

BOY 8

Keeps the blood splashing
our black leather coats.

THE PREL

PRO REGE ET LEGE,
THE MEN FROM THE PREL!

BOY 9

I dropped one off the top floor
of a high-rise hotel.

THE PREL

Bang! Bang! on the door,
the PREL!

BOY 10

One mailed fist to the jaw
can toll a nipper's knell.

THE PREL

Bang! Bang! on the door,
the PREL!

ALL

Pro rege et lege,
the men from the PREL!

BOY 11

One day I killed a score
when the baby hunt went well.

THE PREL

Bang! Bang! on the door,
the PREL!
BANG! BANG! on the door,
the Prel!

*The members of the PREL reappear in the classroom
and number off in Latin as before.*

PREL 1

Unus!

PREL 2

Duo!

PREL 3

Tres!

PREL 4

Quattuor!

PREL 5

Quinque!

PREL 6

Sex!

PREL 7

Septem!

PREL 8

Octo!

PREL 9

Novem!

PREL 10

Decem!

PREL 11

Undecim

PREL 12

Er . . .

   Prel 1–11 turn towards Prel 12.

PREL 1–11

Duodecim!

PREL 12

Duodecim!

HEROD
(*inspecting his men*)
Well, leader of Group 1, step forward and report
how many lives of little ones your platoon's cut short.

PREL 1

All hail, Herodes Rex
we have done to death this day.

BOYS 1–4

CCVIX.

   Herod writes CCVIX *the blackboard.*

HEROD
(*solemnly*)
The title I hereby bestow upon thee
is Grand Child Eliminator – G.C.E.

Well, leader of Group 2, step forward and report
how many lives of little ones your platoon's cut short.

PREL 8

All hail, Herodes Rex
we have done to death this day.

BOYS 5–8

CCCIX.

Herod writes CCCIX *on the blackboard.*

HEROD
(*solemnly*)
The title I hereby bestow upon thee
is Grand Child Eliminator – G.C.E.

Well, leader of Group 3, step forward and report
how many lives of little ones your platoon's cut short.

PREL 12

All 'ail . . .!

Shocked silence at the dropped aitch.

PREL 12
(*thinking Herod hasn't heard his greeting*)
All 'ail . . .!

Deeper shocked silence.

All 'ail, 'erod . . .

HEROD
Take him to the H-block. Let him cool his heels.
Feed him Preparation H and then see how he feels.
H as in block, H as in bomb,
feel the aitches in your lungs where the air comes from.
The proles may drop their aitches but yours must never
slip.
H-defaulters lose their fan-club membership
which includes the toffee-noses but not your tongue-tied
Tyke
who utters 'eck – instead of Heckmondwike . . .
Harrogate!

31

BOYS

Hunslet!

HEROD

Holmfirth!

BOYS

Hull!

HEROD

Huddersfield!

BOYS

Holbeck!

ALL

HHHHHHeckmondwike!

Again Herod points to the ladder built of aitches.

HEROD

The ladder of aspiration, the more you aspire
the more your aspiration will take you higher.
Those who drop their aitches fall and break their necks.
But those with proper aspirations end up REX and LEX!

End to end laid aitches are a ladder to the top,
so never never let me hear your aitches drop.

THE PREL

ALL HAIL HEROD.

HEROD

Now to reward you for your kills
and honour your kid-killing skills . . .

*PREL 1 steps forward to receive his medal. With
pomp and solemnity.*

HEROD

For blasting the Red
still a babe in his bed

and stopping the Trot
stone-dead in his cot,
for niftily netting
the nippers you nab,
and liberally letting
with slash and with stab
of hatchet and sword a
lot of lads' blood
I hereby award a
Star of Herod Class 1.
Pro Rege et Lege!

THE PREL

Pro Rege et Lege!

HEROD

Well done!
Well done.

> *Herod attempts to pluck the top centre star from the
> Leeds coat-of-arms but finds it stuck. It will later be
> the Star of Bethlehem.*

HEROD

PRO REGE ET LEGE!

BOY 1

PRO REGE ET LEGE!

HEROD

Well done! Well done!

> *Herod plucks the left star from the coat-of-arms and
> pins it on the diligent PREL 1. PREL 1 steps back
> and PREL 8 steps forward.*

HEROD
(*with pomp and solemnity*)

For blasting the Red
still a babe in his bed

and stopping the Trot
stone-dead in his cot,
for niftily netting
the nippers you nab,
and liberally letting
with slash and with stab
of hatchet and sword a
lot of lads' blood
I hereby award a
Star of Herod Class 1
Pro Rege et Lege.

THE PREL

Pro Rege et Lege.

HEROD

Well done! Well done!

Herod attempts to pluck the top centre star from the Leeds coatof-arms but finds it stuck. So he plucks the right-hand star from the coat-of-arms and pins it on the diligent PREL 8. PREL 8 steps back into line.

HEROD

PRO REGE ET LEGE!

BOY 8

PRO REGE ET LEGE!

HEROD

Well done! Well done!

Those are the diligent, those who worked well
and now let us turn to the delinquent PREL.
Fetch back the sacked Duodecim
and let's find a punishment suitable for him.

The PREL march away to fetch PREL 12 from the H-Block.

HEROD
(*considering Boy 12*)

What good's a ratter
who catches no rats?
What good's a bratter
who catches no brats?

PREL I

What good's a ratter

THE PREL

who catches no rats?

PREL I

What good's a bratter

THE PREL

who catches no brats?

HEROD
(*to Boy 12*)

For not doing well
as a member of PREL
with all those who fail
you'll weep and you'll wail,
and, tormented, you'll yell and howl like HELL!

Herod, with a teacher's blackboard pointer, points to the left-hand owl on the Leeds coat-of-arms.

HEROD

Howl!

BOY 12

Owl!

HEROD

Howl!

BOY 12

Owl!

35

HEROD

Howl! Howl! Howl!

BOY 12

Owl! Owl! Owl!

HEROD

If you don't get it right,
nobody'll leave
if we have to stop all night
or till Christmas bloody Eve.
Howl!

BOY 12

Owl!

HEROD

Howl!

BOY 12

Owl!

HEROD

H as in Bomb, H as in Block,
We're stopping here tonight till twelve o' bloody clock.
Howl!

BOY 12

Owl!

HEROD

Howl!

BOY 12

Owl!

HEROD

H as in Rachel, lamenting sons I slew
and the next dead son is going to be you.

HEROD

HOWL!

BOY 12

Owl!

This goes on being repeated and repeated as though indeed they were being kept in until twelve on 'Christmas bloody Eve'. We hear Herod with his three howls and the boy following with his owls over the montage of Leeds coat-of-arms in various locations but focused successively on the three owls on each.

RACHEL & 11 MAMS
(sung)

*Heu! quia memores
nostroque levare dolores
Gaudia non possunt
nam dulcia pignora desunt.*

Rachel and the eleven Mams lament their massacred sons. We see also the thirteenth Mam.

RACHEL
(to the Thirteenth Mam)
Your lad did for my lad.

13TH MAM

My lad?

RACHEL & THE 11 MAMS

Your lad!

RACHEL
Your lad did for every little lamb
and you ought to be ashamed to be his mam!
It must be awful to 'ave given birth
to one of the worst monsters ever on the earth.

Mams hum.

13TH MAM
Some poor woman gave 'im birth
and dandled on 'er knee

37

one of the scourges of the earth
and that poor soul were me.

Somebody put 'im to 'er breast
and taught 'im ABC.
In case you 'aven't already guessed
that somebody were me.

RACHEL
She wishes she'd never given birth
to one of the worst monsters ever on the earth.

13TH MAM
Me and 'is dad we chose 'is name
before our lad's nativity
but when I see what 'e became
I wished 'e'd died in me.

MAM 6
The causers of all cruel wars,
this unjust Judaean king
don't seem so scary when their jaws
gnaw on a teething ring.

MAM 9
A mam's 'eart is the soonest broke!
What mother wants to dream 'er
little boy will be the bloke
who A-bombs 'iroshima?

RACHEL
Your lad did for every little lamb.

13TH MAM
And I'm ashamed to be 'is mam.

ALL
(*Sung*)
And God alone knows why
my baby 'ad to die!

We see the Teacher with the class register as we hear the voices of Rachel and the eleven Mams.

MAM 1

You can cross our lads off your list –

MAM 2

It's not like other days they've missed.

MAM 4

It's not the croup or chickenpox.

MAM 5

It's not a bad case of the runs.

MAM 6

The *Rex* did for our sons.

MAM 7

'erod has put 'em in a box.

MAM 8

Mowed down by men with guns.

MAM 9

And they won't come to school no more . . .

MAM 10

And they won't come to school no more.

MAM 11

And they won't come to school no more.

MAM 3

And they won't come to school no more.

We see the pen of the Teacher cross out the names of twelve Boys.

Blackboard. Blackness. Blackout.

Silence.

Then we see another hand write TEST *on the blackboard.*

II. THE HISTORY HEROD

We are in an identical classroom, this time devoted to History, and the decorations and wallcharts are appropriate to the subject. The Teacher of History is a woman. It is her hand that has written TEST *on the blackboard behind her.*

KIDS

Aw, miss, it's Christmas!

BOY I

And 'ist'ry's boring!

TEACHER

(*quite pleasantly, correcting the dropped aitch*)

History, Michael, History's boring. Why's it such a bore?

BOY 8

You've only got to say the word and everyone starts
  snoring.

GIRL I

It's just king after king, war then war then war,

BOY 2

First World, Second World, White Rose and Red.

GIRL 2

It's all boring 'cos it's all about the dead.

BOY 3

Can't we do somebody living for a change instead?

TEACHER

(*being calm and reasonable*)

Well, tell me what else can history be about?

There is a general cacophony of suggestions, including pop-groups, popular individuals, footballers and football teams, etc.

TEACHER

Come on, hands up, please don't shout.

The hands are raised, not as with the PREL
simultaneously like a Sieg Heil, but in a bored, ragged
wave.

INNER VOICE OF HEROD

Please is the first word a king can do without!

Teacher, as though not hearing her inner voice, picks
one hand out of the twenty-four.

GIRL 3

'air! miss!

TEACHER

Aviation, yes, we could give that a try.

INNER VOICE

Actually it's me that's about to bloody fly
into the loudest rage ever heard in any Anno Domini.

GIRL 3

No, *'air*, miss, *'air*, like we 'ave on our 'ead!
Instead of all this boring stuff about the boring dead.

INNER VOICE

The Bethlehem barber Herod employs
cuts off heads as well as hair when he barbers boys.
He's a boring barber with a boring skill
of boring babies' bonces with a Black and Decker drill.

TEACHER
(*finding it harder to keep control*)
What other things in history can we study?

Arms up.

INNER VOICE

Something about babies, beastly, black and bloody!

Teacher points to a Boy.

BOYS
Murder, miss, and weapons, and how the bomb gets bigger.

INNER VOICE
And how my finger itches on my sten-gun trigger!

GIRL 4
Miss, can you tell us, who got it in 'is 'ead
that stuff about the olden days can give some folk a thrill.

TEACHER
Herodotus, an ancient Greek, or so it's sometimes said.

BOY 5
Well, your ancient Greek, what's 'is name, makes me
feel ill.

TEACHER
Herodotus.

GIRLS
'erodotus?

BOY 12
Who the 'ell's 'e?

TEACHER
(wearily resigned and stressing the aitches)
He when He's at Home invented History!
His name's a hard one. He's an ancient Greek.
You've forgotten him already, though I mentioned him
last week.

GIRLS
Last week's ancient 'ist'ry by now though, innit, miss?

TEACHER
Better get your notebooks out and make a note of this.

Teacher begins to write down the name of Herodotus.

very slowly, separating the letters to make it easier to remember.

The class begin to copy it out laboriously, saying it to themselves mechanically as the elements come out.

Teacher writes HE –

BOYS
(*writing*)

'e –!

Teacher turning from the blackboard automatically to correct the permanently dropped aitch.

TEACHER

He –!

Teacher writes HER –

GIRLS
(*writing*)

'er –!

TEACHER
(*correcting*)

Her!

Teacher writes HERO –

CLASS
(*writing*)

'ero –!

TEACHER
(*correcting*)

HERO!

Teacher writes HEROD –

CLASS
(*writing*)

'erod –!

*The Teacher of History is transformed into King
Herod as the Teacher of Maths before her.*

*The Girls have disappeared and the Boys 1–12 have
been transformed into the PREL once more, ready for
the prowl.*

THE PREL
(*chanting*)
HE–HER–HERO–HHHHHHHHHEROD!
HEROD the HE/HER HERO
all HAIL, HEROD, the REX and the LEX.

HEROD/TEACHER OF HISTORY
These days of full equality he comes in either sex!

And now I am a Herod in my proper Herod gear
let's say, historically speaking, that equality is here.

PREL
(*raising their arms to answer
like a drilled Sieg Heil*)
SSSSSSSSSSSSSSSSSSSSSSSSSSSSSSir!

HEROD
In these days of freedom the flogger and flesh-render
can also be a Herod of the feminine gender.
If you think mass-murder is monopolised by men
watch how this King Herod does it, then think again.
HIStory is HERstory, girls, now mark this well
you too might be recruited into Herod's PREL.

PREL BOY 1
Lasses in our legions?

BOY 2
Like bloody 'ell!

HEROD
A lass can be a foremost and famous infant slayer
like that jealous, jilted wife, the babe-murdering Medea . . .

Who was who?

PREL 1–12
(raising their arms to answer like a drilled Sieg Heil)
SSSSSSSSSSSSSSSSSSSSSSSSSSSSSSSir!

PREL BOY 3
Don't be bloody barmy, this Herod is a Her!

HEROD
Tomorrow's Mussolini needn't be a muscleman
– a Jill can kill as jollily as Jack the Genghis Khan.
So, great macho masters, give us girls a year or two
and we'll turn out our Herods horrider than you!

BOY 12
'erod's 'orrider.

Pause.

HEROD
Who's that dropping aitches?
I'll put you in the corridor.

Those who drop their aitches like those types who down
    their tools
never had an H-block in their infant schools.
O yes, great macho masters, just wait a year or two
and we'll turn out our Herods horrider than you.
Tougher than tormentor and tongue-twister Torquemada.

Who was who . . . ?

PREL
*(raising their arms to answer
like a drilled Sieg Heil)*
SSSSSSSSSSSSSSSSSSSSSSSSSSSSSSSir!

HEROD
O all right SIR . . .
tougher than tormentor and tongue-twister Torquemada

like a HErod but a SHErod horrider and harder.
Though I might wear slinky numbers, I still know how
  to slay
and for the massacres I mistress-mind I'm asking equal pay.
If Herods can be feminine I wonder if that means
that Jesuses in future could be Janets, Janes and Jeans.
By my tormentor's twinset and my persecutor's pearls
does that mean our massacre must murder baby girls?

THE PREL

Yes sir! Yes sir! Yes sir!

HEROD

And now before I send you into town on cot attacks
I want to check what each of you have in your 'terror
  packs'.

BOY 1

A-bomb, airgun, axe, ammonia,
aerosols of acid and an anaconda, sir,
arsenic-laced apples and an assegai.

BOY 2

Blackjack, belladonna, bacilli,
blowpipe, boomerang, bicycle chains,
and a blood-stained battleaxe for bludgeoning brains.

BOY 3

Catapult, cutlass, Cruise missile, cosh.
Cannonades of cowclap, caustic squash.

BOY 4

Depth-charger, dagger. DDT.

BOY 5

Enfields and other guns starting with an E.

BOY 6

A flask full of infected farts . . .

46

BOY 7

. . . gooly-grinders, gas –

PREL 12
(*engineered into wrong place*)
'arpoon, 'owitzer.

Shock. Horror.

HEROD
HHHHarpoon and HHHHowitzer and what else!

PREL 12
'arpoon and 'owitzer, MISS!

HEROD
(*mad*)
HHHHHarpoon and HHHHowitzer and . . .?

PREL 12
'arpoon and 'owitzer, SIR?

HEROD
(*threateningly*)
HHHHarpoon and HHHHowitzer and . . .

Silence.

HEROD
Harpoon and Howitzer and H-bomb, OK?

PREL 12
But H-bomb, miss, begins with an A!

Shock. Horror.

HEROD
(*in the solemn voice reserved for rewards
and punishment*)
For saying that H-bomb begins with an A
you'll stay behind and Howl while the PREL go out to
play!

*Herod stands beside the Leeds coat-of-arms with his/
her blackboard pointer about to start the punishment
of PREL 12.*

Herod 1 suddenly appears.

HEROD 1

I also am a Herod in my proper Herod gear.
I thought I'd help you punish him, King Herod, dear!

HEROD 2
(*offended*)

I think I can manage quite well on my own;
but think how many kids I'd kill if I had a clone.

HEROD 1

Your Herodship is great alone, but Herod's twice as
    gruesome
when the solo slayer's cloned and turns up as a twosum!

HEROD 1

UNUS.

HEROD 2

DUO.

The two Herods begin the punishment of Boy 12.

*They begin to point to the owls on the Leeds coat-of-
arms, Herod 2 to the left owl, and Herod 1 to the
right owl and both together to the owl in the centre.*

HEROD 1

Howl!

BOY 12

Owl!

HEROD 2

Howl!

BOY 12

Owl!

HEROD

Howl!

BOY 12

Owl!

During this 'punishment' the PREL have left to go on the prowl. We hear the PREL and the howl/owl together as we see the montage of the Leeds coat-of-arms with the focus on the owls.

As before the howl of the Herods and the 'owl' of Boy 12 bring in the genuine tragic howl of Rachel and the eleven Mams.

The Mams huddle together.

MAM 1

Your lad did for my little Lamb.

MAM 2

And you ought to be ashamed to be 'is mam.

MAM 3

It must be awful to 'ave given birth

MAM 4

to one of the worst monsters ever on the earth.

13TH MAM
(*sung*)

A nice lad and so sweet to me
a dear when 'e were littler,
'ow could I know 'e'd grow up to be
an Adolf bloody 'itler!

MAM 9

She doesn't see Attila –
or that more recent 'un –
or any kind of killer –
when she gazes on 'er son –

MAM 6

All swaddled in warm baby clothes
'is mother's little darling.
Who'd know 'e'd grow mustachios
and end up Joseph Stalin.

RACHEL & 13TH MAM

From boils on bum to H-bomb blast

13TH MAM

I'd shield 'im from disaster

RACHEL

she'd shield 'im from disaster

13TH MAM

but 'ow I groan and stand aghast

RACHEL

but 'ow she groans and stands aghast

13TH MAM

when my boy is the blaster.

RACHEL

when 'er boy is the blaster.

MAM 8

It's not their throats that are sore.

MAM 9

It's not the boils on their backside –

MAM 10

They won't come to school no more –

MAM 1

They've been killed in your Herod's kiddicide.

MAM 11

They won't come to school no more –

THE BIG H

ALL MAMS
(*sung*)

It's 'erod's mam who mourns the most –
who wails at the world's news –
when she reads in t'*Yorkshire Post*
'er lad, 'erod's on the loose.

13TH MAM

A mam loves 'er baby bad or not,
even 'erod was to 'er
still summat special in his cot
and worth gold, frankincense and myrrh.

12 MAMS

Gold, frankincense and myrrh.

General myrrhmyrrhing.

TEACHER
(*tears in her eyes*)

Stop that myrrhmyrrhing.

III. THE GEOGRAPHY HEROD

*Again, an identical classroom, this time devoted to
Geography, and the decorations and wall chart are
appropriate to the subject being taught.*

*The Teacher of Geography is a man. He has a slightly
'religious' air. Pedantic and a bit prim.*

It is his hand we now see write TEST *on the blackboard.*

KIDS

Aw, sir, it's Christmas!

TEACHER
No, it isn't, yet!

Were going to have that test I promised you I'd set.

And, Ronnie, I'm aware it's near the birthday of God's son.
But now it's geography. Ready! Question One!

BOY 1

Aw, sir.

Having another try.

BOY 2

It's Christmas!

TEACHER

The fact that Jesus Christ was born 's
as relevant just now to what were going to do
as that He ended his life on a cross crowned with thorns.

INNER VOICE OF HEROD

And that's the sort of school-cap I'd fit on most of you!
Babies' bonnets should come with thorns or made of briar
their little heads be bound with the rustiest barbed wire.

*The Teacher of Geography is the first of the teachers
to acknowledge the presence of the inner voice of
Herod, which he does with slight facial winces
of a rather prim kind, as if afflicted with twinges
of indigestion.*

BOY 3

Aw, SIR, it's Christmas!

TEACHER
(*insisting*)

The fact our Lord was born's
got nothing whatever to do with our immediate task
namely the questions that I'm going to ask.
So no more about Christmas and
(*As if to the inner voice.*)   no more about thorns.

BOY 12
(*quoting a sweet ad*)
'Thornes gives Leeds the lead in toffees.'

TEACHER
(*looking round the class*)

Alright! Who?

The Teacher searches the faces and lights upon that of Boy 12.

I might have known. How come it's always you?
Well, that earns you ten thousand lines OK?
Write ten thousand times: Christ is born today!
It'll take you until Christmas before you've done.
That might teach you to blaspheme against God's Son.
Right, Geography, Question One.
The river Mississippi, name its source.

BOY 12
(*quoting Yorkshire Relish ad*)

'The sauce that takes the name of Leeds to the ends of the earth.'

TEACHER

Twenty thousand lines!
(*Loud, angry.*)   Is that understood?

Quietens himself.

I don't want any mockery about Our Lord, who gave his blood.

INNER VOICE

Well, I wish he'd gone and given it thirty years before
instead of three decades spent flouting King and Law.

TEACHER
(*to Inner Voice*)

Whatever devil that you are, you won't take over me.
I'm a Christian, a Pacifist. I belong to CND.

INNER VOICE
(*bored and cynical*)

I don't know why you bother. You'd do better with the bomb.

*Teacher with some difficulty getting on with the
lesson.*

TEACHER

Right, where does the Mississippi start flowing from?

*Boy 8, suppressing a giggle, hoping to get Teacher on
to a pet subject and off geography.*

BOY 8

When we pray at dinners, sir,
what's that language that you speak?
It sounds that funny, sir,
I bet it's Ancient Greek.

TEACHER

I know it's just my test you're trying to avoid.

INNER VOICE

Go on, get the whole damn lot of 'em destroyed!

Smugly, but having trouble keeping the Herod down.

TEACHER

But I'll tell you, Walshaw, just so we can proceed
that the language is Latin, that I once learned to read.

KIDS 10/5/6/7

Go on, sir.

ALL KIDS

Go on, sir.

BOY 7

Let's 'ear you 'ave a go.

*Teacher seeing the trap but knowing no way to avoid
it.*

TEACHER

There are some Latin words that all of you should know
and that's the motto of your city which is: *Pro*

Rege et Lege, for King and Law.
How many have never heard those Latin words before?

He finishes writing PRO REGE ET LEGE *on the board. The Kids have begun saying it to themselves as if trying to memorise it.*

TEACHER

PRO!

CLASS

PRO!

TEACHER

REGE!

CLASS

REGE!

TEACHER

ET!

CLASS

ET!

TEACHER

LEGE!

CLASS

LEGE!

TEACHER

PRO!

CLASS

PRO!

TEACHER

REGE!

CLASS

REGE!

TEACHER

ET!

CLASS

ET!

TEACHER

LEGE!

CLASS

LEGE!
PRO REGE ET LEGE!
PRO REGE ET LEGE!
PRO REGE ET LEGE!

THE PREL

HEROD!
HEROD!
HEROD!
HEROD!
HEROD!

All hail, Herod, the Rex and the Lex.

The Teacher cowers in fear behind his desk and resists being taken over by Herod (like Jekyll resisting Hyde), but at the insistence of the chanting by the PREL, flash! He finally becomes Herod.

HEROD 3

How I became a Herod in my proper Herod gear
is something of a mystery, and not at all too clear,
but I might as well let rip and rant, seeing as I'm here!

Liquefy all lousy lads and have their liquids poured
drop by nauseating drop in Norway's deepest fjord.
Which is. Where?

The Prel arms raised to answer like a drilled Sieg Heil.

THE PREL

SSSSSSSSSSSSSSSSSSSSSSSSSSSSSir!

HEROD

Or weathered and eroded and denuded down to bone

and powder the remainder and dissolve it in the Rhône . . .
Which is where . . .?

THE PREL
(arms raised etc.)
SSSSSSSSSSSSSSSSSSSSSSSSSSSSSSSIR!

HEROD
The Rhône's good for drowning but maybe all you need's
to tip your lorry load of toddlers in the River Aire at Leeds.
Far or near, near or far, there's all the water that you'll
    need
whether Lake Tanganyika or the rivers Tyne and Tweed.
Which are where?

THE PREL
(arms raised etc.)
SSSSSSSSSSSSSSSSSSSSSSSSSSSSSSSSir!

HEROD
Every mam's sweet darling, every daddy's little pride
whirled in person-processors and Irrawaddyfied.
Every nipper Mississippified and splurted down a sewer,
the Volga's volume growing as the solid kids get fewer.
Where's the Volga . . .?

THE PREL
(arms raised etc.)
SSSSSSSSSSSSSSSSSSSSSSSSSSSSSSSSir!

HEROD
All the infants that you find two years old and younger
drag 'em up and drop 'em down K2 or Kanchenjunga,
Which is higher? Hands up those who know!

THE PREL
(arms raised etc.)
SSSSSSSSSSSSSSSSSSSSSSSSSSSSSSSSir!

57

HEROD
(*aside*)
I think my little death-squad's all revved up to go!
Drown 'em in any water but the Okhotsk Sea.
(*Pause.*)   Why?
Because there's no damned *rhyme for* it, you go ahead
    and try.
All the hidden babies, each ferreted out lad,
chain 'em all together and chuck 'em in Lake Chad . . .
What's its area . . . ?

THE PREL
(*arms raised etc.*)
SSSSSSSSSSSSSSSSSSSSSSSSSSSSSSir!

Herod 1 appears.

HEROD 1
I also am a Herod in my proper Herod gear –

Herod 2 appears.

HEROD 2
I also am a Herod just as good as these two here.

HEROD 1 & 3
Off we go then, Herod.

HEROD 2
After you then, dear.

HEROD 1
UNUS!

HEROD 2
DUO!

HEROD 3
TRES!

*And all the three Herods launch themselves off onto a
final trio rant.*

HEROD 1
I'll get that rabble-rouser Jesus jelly-babified by jiminy!

HEROD 2
Destroy all babies born between year dot and 2 Anno
Domini.

HEROD 3
Teeny-weenies under two, all tots still at their mothers' tits.

HEROD 1
Cherished chubby little cherubs, choke and chop to little
bits,

HEROD 2
Bazooka all bambinos that are newly born in Bethlehem.

HEROD 3
If you have to murder millions then go ahead and
murder 'em.

HEROD 1
Millions of bloody babes I'll butcher and I'll barbecue,

HEROD 2
Boil the buggers down to bones and bubbly barley sugar
goo.

HEROD 3
You get Herod's kingly go-ahead to gun the kindergartens
down.

HEROD 1
Massacring all manikins from China up to Chapeltown.

HEROD 2
Annihilate each nursery, carnageizing creche and cribs,

HEROD 3
Pour petrol into diapers and benzine over bibs,

HEROD 1
Napalm nippers still in nappies from New York to
  Northumberland.

HEROD 2
Sling the swaddled sucklings into never-ending slumberland.

HEROD 3
Daub their dummies and their teats with diptheria bacteria

HEROD 1
and when the children all get killed . . .

ALL HERODS
KING HEROD WILL BE CHEERIER.

The Prel leave to go on the prowl.

The Massacre of the Innocents takes place to percussion.

The PREL return from the prowl.

HEROD 3
Step forward, 1, and tell me all the once-infested spots
you've made entirely free, for me, of toddlers and tots.

PREL 1
(stepping forward)
Hiroshima, Hanoi, Hamburg . . .

HEROD 1
And how many?

PREL 1
Thousands and thousands!

*Herods write on the board the thousands in roman
numerals: MMMMMMMMM etc.*

HEROD 3
The title I hereby award to thee
is Grand Child Eliminator – G.C.E.

PREL 1 steps back into line.

Step forward, 8, and tell me the once-infested spots
you've made entirely free, for me, of toddlers and tots.

PREL 8

Hong Kong, Hungary, Holland –
Hawaii, Houston and Harlem –
Honduras, Haiti, Hyderabad –
Helsinki and the whole of the Hague –

PREL 5

Heidelberg, Hanover, Hilversum.

PREL 6

Hove, Hastings, Havant.

PREL 5

Harpenden, Hull, Harlow.

PREL 6

The Hebrides, Haddington, Hamilton.

PREL 8

Holyhead, Harlech, Halewood.

PREL 5

Holborn and Hillingdon High Street.

PREL 6

Hemel Hempstead, Hatfield, Harwich.

PREL 7

Haywards Heath, Habberly and Hallow.

PREL 8

Harrogate, Haywood, Headingley,
the whole of Humberside,
Horsforth and Holbeck,
Heckmondwike, Helmsley and Haxby,
and Halifax, Hunslet and Hull.

HEROD

. . . and how many!?

PREL 8

Hundreds and hundreds!

The three Herods write hundreds and hundreds on the board in roman numerals: CCCCCCCCCCCCCC . . .

HEROD 3

The title I hereby award to thee
is Grand Child Eliminator – G.C.E.!

PREL 8 steps back into line.

Herod 3 is about to call PREL 12 forward, but PREL 12 with a resolve we have so far not seen in him steps forward of his own accord much to the shock of all assembled.

PREL 12

Sir!
It's 'orrible, sir! I'm sick of all this 'orror!'

Pause.

The rest of the PREL are shocked.

HEROD 3
(*with the manner of Teacher 3*)
Thirty thousand lines! *And* by first thing tomorrer!
Now, 12, tell me all the once-infested spots
you've made entirely free, for me, of toddlers and tots.

PREL 12

None! It's Christmas, sir, women shouldn't weep
and the lion shouldn't lurk to kill the little sheep.
We've run about killing and we're all that out of breath,
can't we 'ave an 'oliday from all this blood and death?

Pause.

THE BIG H

HEROD 1
(correcting Boy 12's perennially dropped aitch)
It's Holiday!

HEROD 2
Holiday!

3 HERODS
Holiday!

PREL 1
Thank you, sir.

3 HERODS
Holiday!

PREL 2
Thank you, sir.

3 HERODS
Holiday!

PREL 3
Thank you, sir.

3 HERODS
Holiday!

PREL 4
Thank you, sir.

3 HERODS
Holiday!

PREL 5
Thank you, sir.

3 HERODS
Holiday!

PREL 6
Thank you, sir.

3 HERODS

Holiday!

PREL 7

Thank you, sir.

HEROD 1

Hey, who said you could go away?

3 HERODS

Holiday!

PREL 8

Thank you, sir.

3 HERODS

Holiday!

PREL 9

Thank you, sir.

3 HERODS

Holiday!

PREL 10

Thank you, sir.

3 HERODS

Holiday!

PREL 11

Thank you, sir.

HEROD 1

You drop all your aitches so you'll have to stay
behind and howl while the rest break up for holiday!
Howl!

HEROD 2

Howl!

HEROD 3

Howl!

64

Again we go through the montage of the Leeds coat-of-arms in various locations.

The montage comes to rest on the arms of the front façade of Leeds Town Hall clock.

BOY 12

I know that to you kings the owl's a bird of prey
but to me it means wisdom, at least for today!
Owl! owl! owl!
The owls are for wisdom not for pain.

We hear the lamentation of the Mams slowly stop and then their voices take up a new song, but still very far away.

RACHEL & 11 MAMS
(sung under Boy 12's speech)

In terra pax
hominibus bonae voluntatis alleluia! alleluia!

BOY 12

The owls are for wisdom not for pain
and being evil must be such a strain
and I tell you by that flashing star –

The flashing star is the one left in the centre (top) of the Leeds coat-of-arms.

– and I tell you by that flashing star
you're going to follow near and far,
you're no longer Herods, now you are
UNUS! DUO! TRES!

The three Herods become Three Wise Men.

BOY 12

UNUS! DUO! TRES!

Speaking to the tune of the Christmas carol 'We Three Kings'.

The Rex that men of peace are all pro
isn't a 'erod.

HEROD 1

No!

HEROD 2

No!

HEROD 3
No!

BOY 12
(*still speaking to the tune of 'We Three Kings'*)
Where the fleece is the King of Peace is
and that's where we all must go.

1, 2, 3, all stand in a line
let's check you over, you'll do fine
with your crowns on, Wise Men's gowns on,
go follow the Big H sign.

ALL
Ooooo Big H sign in white and blue
H for 'ope depends on you.
From tomorrer H for 'orror's
banned with 'erod's 'ellish crew.

*We see road signs, the H in white and blue for
Hospital, with arrows going forward, left, right,
forward again, until we reach Leeds Maternity
Hospital. Town Hall clock starts striking midnight.
Stills of Boys 1–12 mixing with their baby pictures.*

BOY 1

One!

GIRL 1

Our Roger.

As if counting the dead in some distant past.

66

BOYS 1 & 2

Two!

GIRLS 1 & 2

Our Johnny.

*After the second stroke of twelve we should be aware
that the second lion on the steps of Leeds Town Hall
has left its place near the sign reading* POLICE *and gone
about walking as the Leeds legend insists that it does.*

Town Hall clock: Bong 3!

BOY 3

Three!

GIRL 3

Our Frank.

BOY 4

Four!

GIRL 4

Our Malcolm.

BOY 5

Five!

GIRL 5

Our David.

*Between each bong we should see the Three Wise
Men making their way to the nativity followed by the
class of children, who walk towards the Leeds
Maternity Hospital outside of which is a big H sign
in white and blue.*

BOY 6

Six!

GIRL 6

Our Jason.

> BOY 7

Seven!

> GIRL 7

Our Ronnie.

> BOY 8

Eight!

> GIRL 8

Our Michael.

> BOY 9

Nine!

> GIRL 9

Our Peter.

> BOY 10

Ten!

> GIRL 10

Our Tony.

The road signs we should see are those we saw at the beginning, signs pointing to places round and suburbs of Leeds: HEADINGLEY, HOLBECK, HUNSLET, HAREHILLS, HORSFORTH, HUDDERSFIELD *etc., except that now they are aitchless and read:* EADINGLEY, OLBECK, UNSLET, ARE ILLS, UDDERSFIELD.

> BOY 11

Eleven!

> GIRL 11

Our Mark.

Twelve Mams coming closer: 'Alleluia' etc.

Town Hall clock: Bong 12!

ALL

Twelve!

GIRLS

Our 'arry!

Procession. Girls sing under Boy 12's speech.

BOY 12

The white Town Hall lions came to life
as midnight chimes on Christmas Eve
and they look for the joiner Joe and his wife
and you'll see them walking if you'll only believe . . .
The lions that stirred when the first stroke was struck
they stroll down the 'eadrow to take a look
at the baby of Mary and the joiner Joe
and the cops have problems with the traffic flow
as loads of folk come to Leeds to see
the North's most noted Nativity,
and the lions lay down with the lamb,
and the lions lay down with the lamb!
They lick the 'ands of 'is dad and mam
and the lions, the lions lay down with the lamb,
and they lovingly lick the lad in his pram,
and the lions, the lions lay down with the lamb,
and the lions lay down in Leeds with the lamb,
and the lions lay down with the lamb.
And the roaring lions pipe down to a purr
and there's a midnight feeling over the earth
and a sense of somebody special's birth,
a sense of somebody special who's worth . . .

ALL

GOLD!

FRANKINCENSE!

and MYRRH!

We see the class and the three Teachers singing a carol ('We Three Kings') round a Christmas tree in the Leeds Maternity Ward. We see a sequence of babies in incubators.

ALL

Every babe's worth . . .
GOLD . . . FRANKINCENSE . . . and MYRRH!

Classroom. Boy 12 is alone writing his thirty thousand lines: 'Christ is born today.' The classroom is decorated for Christmas. The blackboard now reads MERRY CHRISTMAS, *made from an M and a C from the Roman numerals of Herod's score of dead innocents.*

BOY 12

And he'll grow up to be a teacher!

The End.

LOVING MEMORY
(1987)

Loving Memory, a series of four film poems written and presented by Tony Harrison, produced and directed by Peter Symes, was first broadcast on BBC2 in July and August 1987.

The Muffled Bells was first broadcast on 30 July 1987.

Cameraman Steve Saunderson
Sound Recordist Trevor Gosling
Dubbing Mixer Alan Dykes
Lighting Electrician Alex Scott
Grips Alan Imeson
Graphics Paul Johnson
Production Assistant Lisbet Heath
Research Florence Minnis
Film Editor Peter Simpson

Mimmo Perrella non è Piu was first broadcast on 23 July 1987.

Photography John Goodyer, Graham Frake
Sound Recordist Roger Long
Dubbing Mixer Alan Dykes
Production Assistant Lisbet Heath
Researcher Tiziana Toglia
Film Editor Liz Thoyts
Director Michael Hutchinson

Cheating the Void was first broadcast on 6 August 1987.

Photography Brian Hall, Steve Saunderson
Sound Recordists Roger Long, Trevor Gosling
Dubbing Mixer Alan Dykes
Lighting Electrician Dusty Miller
Grips Alan Imeson
Production Assistants Lisbet Heath, Catherine Barnes
Assistant Producer Michael Hutchinson
Associate Producer Colin Rose
Film Editor Peter Simpson

Letters in the Rock was first broadcast on 16 July 1987.

Cameramen Steve Saunderson, Paul Morris
Sound Recordists Trevor Gosling, Lyndon Bird
Dubbing Mixer Alan Dykes
Lighting Electrician Alex Scott
Grips Alan Imeson
Graphics Paul Johnson
Research Florence Minnis, Nick Shearman
Production Assistant Lisbet Heath
Assistant Producer Michael Hutchinson
Associate Producer Colin Rose
Film Editor Peter Simpson

NOTE

The anniversary of Hiroshima came at the end of the available transmission dates, and it was decided to place *Cheating the Void* on 6 August. As will be clear from the dates above, the first transmission order was therefore not the one followed here. This is the preferred order, and was adhered to for subsequent transmissions, as it makes more sense both of the historical and poetic arguments.

The Muffled Bells

Int. church: muffles being put on bells.

They're muffling the bells for Stanley Hall.
Stanley Hall the Breamore miller's dead.
Clappers in cowhide cladding peel and call
all those who used his flour in their bread.

Farmer with geese.

He hears the curfew toll for Stanley Hall,
Ed Trim seen fattening his Christmas geese
will be one of four friends who'll bear his pall
when the Breamore miller goes to rest in peace.

Horses ploughing, cows standing in water, etc.

Muffled curfew, flock of geese, the plough,
some things survive from 'how things used to be',
though much is vanishing and threatened now
Breamore's bells are pure Gray's *Elegy.*

'*The Curfew tolls the Knell of parting Day,*
The lowing Herd winds slowly o'er the Lea,
The Plow-man homeward plods his weary Way,
And leaves the World to Darkness, and to me.

Now fades the glimmering Landscape on the Sight,
And all the Air a solemn Stillness holds;
Save where the Beetle wheels his droning Flight,
And drowsy Tinklings lull the distant Folds.

Beneath those rugged Elms, that Yew-Tree's Shade,
Where heaves the Turf in many a mould'ring Heap,
Each in his narrow Cell for ever laid,
The rude Forefathers of the Hamlet sleep.

Far from the Madding Crowd's ignoble Strife,
Their sober Wishes never learn'd to stray;
Along the cool sequester'd Vale of Life
They kept the noiseless Tenor of their Way.

Yet ev'n these Bones from Insult to protect
Some frail Memorial still erected nigh,
With uncouth Rhimes and shapeless Sculpture deck'd,
Implores the passing Tribute of a Sigh.

Their Name, their Years, spelt by th'unlettered Muse,
The Place of Fame and Elegy supply:
And many a holy Text around she strews,
That teach the rustic Moralist to dye.'

A lichened quatrain chiselled in the year
Seventeen fifty when the poet Gray
first wrote the Elegy I'm reading here,
this 'rustic moralist', what does he say?

    Tombstone.

'Come hither mortal, cast an eye
Then go thy way prepared to die.
Twill be thy doom to know thou must
Like me at last be turned to dust.'

Strange how poetry most people think a bore,
poetry that people of our period despise
or if they don't despise it just ignore,
seems to surface fast when someone dies.

    Tombstone.

'I was but young and in my bloom
My morning sun was set at noon
Grieve not for me my glass is full
It is the Lord his will.'

Craftsmen, wheelwright, blacksmith, undertaker,
who also turned a skilled hand to the plough

gathered in harvests grateful to their Maker
are in decline, as Gray's own craft is, now.

Now that the village's last miller's dead
his craft of milling flour has also died.
Flour from Breamore fields went into bread
that's been replaced by pre-sliced *Mother's Pride*.

Breamore village.

The new commuters eye the empty mill,
the sequestered vale's a teeming motorway.
But in spite of creeping yuppies Breamore's still
the sort of churchyard known to Thomas Gray.

Though the curfew's being tolled for the old ways
and the mill and manor are developers' desires,
Breamore's going to stay the way it stays
while it's Sir Westrow Hulse, the present squire's.

VICAR
(*with Sir Westrow and Lady Hulse by church door*)
    '*Morning to you. I gather it was all a great*
    success yesterday, did it go well?'

The squire who owns Stan's mill and all the land
that gives harvests that they've come to thank God for.
He pays the rector who's just shook his hand.
He enters the Saxon church by his own door.

Breamore remembers in its autumn prayers
and memories are in Sir Westrow's head
for those who lie outside in seven layers
the village's long roll-call of the dead.

Norman Dymott, sexton, rings the bell
for families of men who marched away
in World War One and those of them who fell
are marked on the Roll of Honour with a K.

Roll of Honour.

Two congregations: one, in seven layers,
stays silent as the other sings the hymns,
the Vinces and the Walkers and the Wares,
the Witts, the Dymotts and the Trims.

Int. church: congregation stands.

> *'Come ye thankful people come,*
> *Raise the song of harvest-home:*
> *All is safely gathered in,*
> *Ere the winter storms begin,*
> *God, our Maker, doth provide*
> *For our wants to be . . .'*

The choir consists of thirty generations
though most of them are muffled underground.
The minority, this present congregation's
singing for the dead who lie all round.

> *' . . . the song of harvest-home.*
> *All this world is God's own field,*
> *Fruit unto his praise to yield . . .'*

The man who'll dig the grave for Stanley Hall,
thrusting his sexton's spade in with his boot,
is the same who gave the bell's unmuffled call
to Breamore's blessing of its flowers and fruit.

> *'Ripening with a wondrous power*
> *Till the final harvest-hour:*
> *Grant, O Lord of life, that we*
> *Holy grain and pure may be.'*

NORMAN DYMOTT (*sexton*)
> *'The majority of the people that's buried here are*
> *parishioners and you've lived with them, and*
> *been brought up with them and therefore you*
> *know there's a personal touch in them, and it's*

78

*a lovely feeling that you can still walk back into
your old village church and churchyard and find
that your old relatives and workmates are still
there with you.'*

Marking out grave.

> 'The first thing sort of with any funeral, I get a
> phone call from the undertaker and he gives me
> the person concerned, the size of the grave, the
> time of the funeral and from then on we, you
> know, make preparation for digging the grave.'

> 'My father he actually took over from William
> Nicklin that lived in the cottage near the church,
> he got killed in the 1914–18 War and father was
> then pleaded out of the Army and he took over
> from him, and it's just carried on. I helped him
> when I was old enough and when father died
> I took over from father and we're today carrying
> on, with the help of John, my friend here to do
> the donkey work.'

They're measuring the ground for Stanley Hall.
They don't need to know what Stan's statistics are,
they were his neighbours and they know how tall
the man was they stood next to at the bar.

Coffin-making.

John Shering gives hard elm a final shave
to demonstrate another dying trade,
most people these days go into the grave
in a coffin of veneer that's factory-made.

The grooves a carpenter bends coffins by
he calls the *curfs*, a local Hampshire word
that, like what it describes, will also die
and, like the Breamore miller, be interred.

JOHN SHERING (*undertaker*)

'*I've been undertaking for forty years and the family have been undertakers for the last two hundred years. All the Sherings, all that time, have all been carpenters and the village carpenter was the undertaker.*'

'*Coffins aren't like this very often now, this is too hard work for us all. The fresh method is they're made in factories with machines that cut each board, they mitre the corners, they use machines to tack them together, they're a lot lighter. This method is the method that has been used for hundreds of years and when I started we always made coffins just like this. This is elm that was cut down after it was caught with Dutch elm disease. Cut down about a mile away from here, and sawn up, and we've kept this wood for ten years, and it's got good and hard now. Hard to work. We've still got some more board if anybody needs one.*'

NORMAN DYMOTT

'*When you chat about coffins these days they're nearly all veneered to what they were solid oak or elm in the days gone by. To prove how long an oak coffin will last against a veneered one, in the corner of the churchyard there I've exhumed a body that had been there for twenty-five years and that coffin was still absolutely intact and solid and the lid and everything was absolutely solid still. Admitted it was in gravel soil that was you know was draining, good drainage, but goes to prove the difference between a veneer coffin and a solid oak coffin. The veneered coffin I should say you could give it twelve months and*'

the lid's caved in, specially in wet heavy soil,
there's a vast difference in the lasting power and
also the price.'

JOHN SHERING

'And my father and I used to carry a coffin out
at dusk, 'cause most people stayed in their houses
in those days, and we would carry a coffin at
dusk on our shoulders through the town, and
really nobody took a lot of notice of us. I don't
know what would happen now if someone was
seen carrying a coffin through the town at dusk,
but everything seemed normal then.'

'Being an undertaker isn't just dealing with the
coffin and the one who has died. The most
important people we look to are the relatives
because we do everything for them, we
undertake to do everything for them, even if it's
just talking, or even if it's not just talking, but
sitting and maybe holding their hands. I think it's
important that you talk about the person who
has died, just because they've died and maybe
been buried or cremated, they're still people in
people's memories and you should talk about
them.'

John buries people but exhumes the past.
His museum helps the village to recall
with village things and photos he's amassed,
like maybe the miller's tools of Stanley Hall.

Brass plates in museum.

Off solid oak and elm these coffin plates
from the layer before the one where Stan will lie
are all that's left of those who met their fates
in what Norman Dymott calls 'the days gone by'.

CHILDREN (*rehearsing* Annie, *singing*)
    'It's a hard knock life
    Got no folks to speak of so
    It's the hard-knock row we hoe . . .'

JOHN SHERING
    'The museum is used for lots of things. The
    choral society use it for a sort of practice room.
    We rehearse plays in there.'

CHILDREN (*singing*)
    'Don't it feel like the wind is always howling,
    Don't it seem like there's never any light?
    Once a day, don't you wanna throw the towel in?
    It's easier than puttin' up a fight.'

    'No one's there when your dreams at night get
      creepy,
    No one cares if you grow . . . or if you shrink
    No one dries when your eyes get . . .'

JOHN SHERING
    'These funeral cards are collected over the years
    and people hand them in. They were sent out as
    mourning cards, not used now.'

CHILDREN (*singing*)
    '. . . running free in NYC
    Bet she finds her folk
    Like that
    Mom and Dad
    Right off the bat
    Lucky duck, she got away
    But we're gonna have to pay
    Gonna get our faces slapped
    Gonna get our knuckles rapped
    It's a hard knock life
    Yes it is
    It's a hard knock life . . .'

Maybe Stanley Hall made this girl weep –

CHILDREN (*singing*)
  '. . . *yes it is*
  It's a hard knock life . . .'

Maybe Stanley Hall pulled these girls' hair –

CHILDREN (*singing*)
  '. . . *it's a hard knock life –*
  Yes it is!'

Most and not maybe are now six feet deep,
forming the country churchyard's seventh layer.

Tombstone.

Catherine Sarah Taunton, 33,
who passed away in 1859
a century too late for *Gray*'s elegy
but at least still legible enough for mine.

Tombstone.

'*A wife so kind a friend sincere*
A tender mother lieth here
We weep on earth in vain
But in Heaven we hope to meet again.
Here then in hope of endless life
Rest three children and a wife.'

  Damaged stones with names of Snow, Frost, Dew.

Not many tombs survive from Gray's own day,
gravestones afforded only by the few
after their occupants themselves decay,
worn down by Hampshire rain, Snow, Frost and Dew.

Who were also Breamore rectors whose remains
are appropriately close together
but none, though in his element, sustains
the pressure of their eponyms of weather.

TONY LIGHT

'Gravestones were an important aspect of
historical research, but as with memories of the
more recent families in the village, their use is
fairly limited, and we really need to use the
historical documents which survive to build up a
proper picture, a more complete picture of many
of the families, and I've been cataloguing the
documents up at the House here for the past ten
years or so.'

'My, I think it was great-great-grandfather came
to Breamore as coachman to the family at the
house here in about 1860 and they've been
resident in Breamore ever since.'

'Only one gravestone survives from before 1700,
and even for the past two centuries probably no
more than one in six of the villagers ever had
their own memorials erected because of the cost.'

'The very richest and the highest actually laid
claim to a place in the church itself for burial
and the aim was always to get as near to the
door of the church as possible if you couldn't
actually afford to get inside, and as we go further
away from the church itself the number of box
tombs actually becomes very small generally,
and there's a general mixture of dates and types
of tombs and all classes of people, except the
very poorest of course, who aren't actually
commemorated.'

Unmarked grave (mound).

'Until relatively recently most villages were
virtually self-sufficient in the basic crafts and
many of the gravestones actually refer to these

families because of their importance to the village through their trades. They tended to be the most prosperous of the families and could afford the gravestones.'

Tombstones of Hobbs family.

'*One such were the Hobbs, who were the village carpenters and weavers until under ten years ago. The documentary record is often the only one for many of them. Although there were more than sixty members of the family buried in the churchyard, according to the registers we only have surviving gravestones for sixteen, and without the documentary record there would actually be very little detail of many of them.'*

RON HOBBS

'*I remember grandfather very well, he was very good to me as a schoolboy. I remember he bought me my first bicycle, yes.*

'"*In remembrance of Isaac Hobbs", that was my grandfather. He started the first business at Breamore. There was a lot of work done there, before harvest time there were as many as perhaps twenty wheels to be repaired. The farmers used to bring them in before the harvest you see so that they be ready in time to carry in the food produce and so on. He was the wheelwright, but of course after the last war tractors came in and then a lot of the farmers they had their wagons converted to rubber wheels to go behind the tractor, you see, and therefore in my time there wasn't so much wheelwrighting done.'*

TONY LIGHT

'Another craft family within the village were the
Edsalls, who were to become the village
blacksmiths in the eighteenth century. About
1753 one of the Edsall family moved to a forge
near the Marsh and this was the start of the
blacksmith business. The forge today is still
actually being run by a direct descendant of the
family, although the one at the Marsh closed
some years ago and now operates as a
motor-mower repair shop.'

TREVOR KIMBER (*blacksmith*)

'There were four uncles, and I can remember all
of them working at the different shops, the one
at Downton and the one here and the one at
Alderholt, the other uncle he most of the time
worked with Uncle Les in this shop, he didn't
have a blacksmith's shop on his own, he worked
for this one.'

'I'm probably the last one of the family still
doing this type of work. What happens after
that, well . . . I wouldn't be sure.'

NORMAN DYMOTT

'This is a cremation we had here of two brothers
which were blacksmiths, one in our village and
one at Downton.'

Plaque on ground: Lesley Edsall.

'Lesley, the one here, I know very very well, was
a great character in the village and always a
great friend of the publican because he was a
frequent visitor there and his favourite saying
was always when you went in, "Well, are you
going to buy one?" But he was a wonderful

character and many a tale he's told in the pub
used to keep the whole place in roars of
laughter.'

Leslie Edsall drank with Stanley Hall
though those who drank with Les bought all the beers.
Blacksmith and miller at the *Bat and Ball*
drinking to precarious careers.

Houses, one with 'For Sale' sign.

Wheelwright's and blacksmith's workshops both are sold,
each a des. res. and the sequestered vale
as each craftsman's like the miller's curfew's tolled
is less and less sequestered and for sale.

For Stanley Hall they're knotting their black ties,
they're buffing their black shoes to mirror shine.
With him some more of Breamore village dies,
he was the Breamore miller, last in line.

Bearers load coffin onto hearse.

For Stanley Hall they've brought the big black hearse,
buffed like their black shoes to high-gloss shine
to be taken to a grave without a verse.
If the job of miller's dated, so is mine.

NORMAN DYMOTT
'The majority of the people that's buried here are
parishioners and you've lived with them and
been brought up with them and therefore you
know there's a personal touch in them, and it's a
lovely feeling that you can still walk back into
your old village church and churchyard and find
that your old relatives and workmates are still
there with you.'

JOHN SHERING
'I don't know what would happen now if someone

*was seen carrying a coffin through the town at
dusk, but everything seemed normal then.'*

Funeral procession.

VICAR

*'I am the Resurrection and the life, saith the
Lord: he that believeth in me, though he were
dead, yet shall he live: and whosoever liveth and
believeth in me shall never die.'*

*'I know that my Redeemer liveth, and that he
shall stand at the latter day upon the earth: And
though after my skin worms destroy this body,
yet in my flesh shall I see God: whom I shall see
for myself, and mine eyes shall behold, and not
another.'*

*'O remember not the sins and offences of my
youth but according to thy mercy think thou
upon me O Lord for thy goodness' sake.'*

Stanley Hall on photo.

This was the Stanley Hall who made girls cry,
this is Stanley Hall in choirboy's gear
escorting a coffin from the days gone by
of solid elm, not mass-made and veneer.

Mourners and Vicar round grave, coffin lowered.

Mr Trim's at his friend Stanley's head.
He'll be back home in time to feed his geese.
The man he drank his bitter with is dead,
the Breamore miller's gone to rest in peace.

A country churchyard burial in times
when most end up as ashes in cheap urns.
Pity the miller's headstone won't have rhymes,
quatrains as antiquated as his querns.

VICAR
> *'We commend unto thy hands of mercy most*
> *merciful Father the soul of this our brother*
> *Charles Stanley Hall departed and we commit his*
> *body to the ground; earth to earth, ashes to*
> *ashes, dust to dust . . .'*

And white dust gathers on the mill's grindstones.
Next year the miller Stanley will be mute
with forebears layered below already bones
when Breamore blesses Harvest flowers and fruit.

VICAR
> *'. . . ever and ever, Amen.'*

The village's last miller's in his hole
that the village's last sexton's got to fill,
The thudding sods begin their grim drum roll
and new commuters eye the empty mill.

One dying trade inters a now dead trade
and one by one the craftsmen pass away.
Soon the miller's grindstone and the sexton's spade
will be in John's museum for display.

NORMAN DYMOTT
> *'He's just part of the village and that's it. The*
> *village . . . cricket . . . shooting – he was a very*
> *keen shot and a good shot too, old Stan's one of*
> *the real old-timers and very very sadly missed.*
> *Very sorry to think we're here today to do it.'*

Some other local sits in Stanley's pew.
Someone else does his churchwarden's chores
and men from outside Breamore come to 'view'
will find Stan's footprints on the floury floors.

CONGREGATION
> *'. . . raise the song of harvest-home*

All is safely gathered in,
Ere the winter . . .'

There'll be one rusty voice, one Amen less
when all is safely gathered in again
and the folk of Breamore hear their rector bless
grapes freighted in from Italy or Spain.

'. . . come to God's own temple, come;
Raise the song of harvest-home.'

'Oft did the harvest to their sickle yield,
Their furrow oft the stubborn glebe has broke;
How jocund did they drive their team afield!
How bow'd the woods beneath their sturdy stroke!

Let not Ambition mock their useful toil,
Their homely joys, and destiny obscure;
Nor Grandeur hear with a disdainful smile,
The short and simple annals of the poor.

The boast of heraldry, the pomp of pow'r,
And all that beauty, all that wealth e'er gave,
Awaits alike th' inevitable hour.
The paths of glory lead but to the grave.'

CHILDREN (*singing*)
'It's the hard knock life for us
It's the hard knock life for us
Steada treated
We get tricked
Steada kisses
We get kicked
It's the hard-knock life.'

'Got no folks to speak of so
it's the hard-knock row we hoe
Cotton blankets
Steada wool

Empty bellies
Steada full
It's the hard-knock life.'

'Don't it feel like the wind is always howlin',
Don't it seem like there's never any light?
Once a day don't you wanna throw the towel in?
It's easier than putting up a fight.'

'No one's there when your dreams at night get
    creepy
No one cares if you grow or if you shrink
No one dries when your eyes get wet an' weepy . . .
It's a hard knock life.'

Mimmo Perrella non è Piu

Bay of Naples.

Vesuvius and Naples, and the shore,
and a sky that, unpolluted, would be blue.

   Deathbed scene.

Mimmo Perrella non è piu.
Mimmo Perrella is no more.

   *Cemetery gates. Tony Harrison reads from death
   notice.*

Mimmo Perrella non è piu.
Mimmo Perrella is no more.
This gate his body will be carried through
he walked past into work not days before.

Mimmo Perrella non è piu.
Let's follow Mimmo Perrella's fate,
or, rather, not one single fate but two,
that of the body brought in through this gate

and put under marble in a dark, dry hole
where Vesuvius's soil makes it like leather,
and that other fate, meanwhile, of Mimmo's soul
exposed to an uncertain, otherworldly weather.

   White marble tombs.

Mimmo's corpse stays here; his soul's set free
from the confines of its clay-stained cage
to struggle upwards, first to Purgatory
and after, Paradise, the final stage.

Stage one is when a man like Mimmo's died
and gets buried. Elsewhere that would be it.
But here in Naples when the body's dried
it gets dug up again out of its pit.

Poggioreale Cemetery.

Death, burial, exhumation, and then wound
in a winding sheet and put away
into a marble locker till the sound
of trumpets calling all to Judgement Day.

'Street' in cemetery.

It's only here in Naples that they do
the sorts of things at death that we'll see done.
Mimmo Perrella non è piu.
It's starting now, his funeral. Stage one.

Black horses and carriage.

Baroque black coach, six horses from the stable
of Gaetano Bellomunno, undertaker.
In Naples only Bellomunno's able
to send you in such style to meet your Maker.

How many million *lire*? The one-point-five
the family spent on such panache and state
they'd think a waste on Mimmo when alive
but once he's dead they never hesitate.

Coffin loaded onto coach.

A coach with gold rosettes and fleur-de-lys,
black and baroque, not British and discreet.
A funeral here's for everyone to see.
A Naples funeral brings out all the street.

Some get close, but others aren't so brave.
Some cope by unconcern. That man in grey,

while others maybe touch the box or wave,
can't face up to death, and turns away.

Coffin taken into church.

The censer swinging on the creaking chain,
the sobbing of a loved one half-suppressed,
commend the corpse of Mimmo freed from pain
to the care of God, and everlasting rest.

Coffin arrives at Poggioreale cemetery.

Vesuvius, now calm since it erupted
in '44, when Mimmo was a boy.
Sirens, war, volcanoes never interrupted
the sort of sleep these 'dear deceased' enjoy.

And only one sound penetrates that sleep
though families come here frequently to pray
for their repose, have conversations, weep,
and that's the trumpet call to Judgement Day

The Naples traffic scarcely ever stops.
They speed through green lights and ignore the red.
An ambulance with siren whining, cops,
might bring it to a halt. So will the dead.

Confraternity Chapel: burial.

Interred in *terra santa* for a span
of twenty or so months until it's dried
and what goes under marble as a man
comes out as Mimmo still, but mummified.

Then the desiccating soil is shovelled in,
when the marble slab's slid back in place,
that's the moment Mimmo's spirit must begin
its lengthy journey to the Lord's embrace.

And the family have to help to get him there.
Their love and care must will him on his way.

Spirit and corpse need suffrage and need prayer
and though he's more than missed he mustn't stay.

Slab slid back into place.

Though there's no sham about it when they grieve
and Mimmo's death broke everybody's heart,
the prayers they make encourage him to leave.
They need their 'dear departed' to depart.

Flower sellers.

Souls make demands in dreams, but don't ask much,
a *rifresco*, a refreshment, some small treat,
flowers, a few words, to keep in touch
until that day when all of them will meet.

Basement of S. Francesco Bonifaco Risorgeremo.

RISORGEREMO carved above the door
by which the dead announce: *We shall arise.*
Though those the living visit are 'no more',
neither wants to break their family ties.

The conversations look a bit one-sided
but they seem to think their words get understood,
the phrase of love, the secret wish confided.
The dialogue's one way but does them good.

People tending graves and sitting quietly.

'You've left our world and go towards another.
Though we're sorry that you've left us, we're afraid
that what we loved as father, or grandmother,
might still turn back and haunt us as a shade.'

Lockers where corpses crumble, skulls go hollow,
while the spirit labours slowly to its goal.
'Blaze a trail,' she prays, 'for me to follow'.
'Show me the way when Death unlocks my soul.'

*S. Giovanni a Carbanara, Confraternity Chapel of
Santa Monica.*

The confraternity, the family and friends
and Monsignor Petrone, the same priest
who commended Mimmo's body, now commends
the *soul* of one less recently deceased.

Giuseppe Venturelli non è piu.
He's between his burial and exhumation.
His journey's almost two-thirds through
and the mass will help him to his destination.

The confraternity is gathered for a mass
to help Giuseppe's spirit, and unite
their prayers and will to urge his soul to pass
from fire and darkness to the final light.

   Italian, with subtitles:

> '*We offer to God our supplications and the
> sacrifice of his own Son so that, if there remains
> in Giuseppe any debt of sin, Divine mercy will
> absolve it to let him reach the holy presence of
> God.*'

Priest, maestro, cello, keyboard, violin
urge Giuseppe's soul to new endeavour.
Once the hovering spirit's purged of sin
it won't be long before it's safe forever . . .

   Cemetery office: Giovanni Errico picks up tools.

Giovanni takes the irons he needs to prise
the marble slab back open, dig, and bring
the body back before its loved ones' eyes,
not what went under but some other thing,

still with a person's features here and there,
a wizened replica of what they knew

with clothes that have rotted and with ragged hair,
the marks of one now many months *non piu*.

If when it's exhumed the body's wet
Giovanni's going to put the corpse back in.
It means the soul's not made it up there yet:
moistness, as of blood and sex, means sin.

Exhumation.

Vincenzo Cicatiello non è piu.
He's been underground about two years.
When Mimmo Perrella's exhumation's due
his wife will greet him from the earth with tears.

He always took such trouble with his hair,
Even towards the end he kept it trim.
He was a natty dresser, took great care
over his appearance. Now, look at him!

First alcohol's sloshed on to wash him clean,
then disconnected bones are put to rights,
then liberal sprinklings of naphthalene,
then DDT to keep off flies and mites.

Was this the Vincenzo who I slept beside?
Vincenzo Cicatiello non è piu.
Now, now I know you've really died.
Till now I only half-believed it true.

Being seen in such revolting tatters
wouldn't suit him. He was much too proud!
Although he's dead, she still believes it matters
that they make him feel he looks right in his shroud.

It took Vincenzo sixty years of life
and twenty months of death to look like this.
When they exhume her husband, Mimmo's wife
will gaze on a flaking skull she used to kiss.

Giovanni carries body covered with black cloth.

Under a blanket with a yellow cross
he clutches a crucifix in leather claw
and leaves a wife and sister with the wounds of loss
that won't heal till they too are 'no more'.

Puts body into locker.

Family mourning now's allowed to cease.
The 'dear departed' 's really left the scene.
The soul's in Purgatory, the corpse at peace
in his locker, talced with naphthalene.

Giovanni stacking coffins into incinerator.

Though his father dug up bodies in the past
and generation hands it down to generation,
Giovanni hopes that he's the last
and Neapolitans accept cremation.

Though cremation has no popular approval
and might take years of work to win their hearts
when even after surgical removal
they won't incinerate the cankered parts;

a hysterectomy, an amputation,
a liver or a kidney cut away,
even these aren't given a cremation
but get put into the soil till Judgement Day,

when everything that's rotten is restored,
soul, head, body, arms, legs, feet.
No one expects to limp up to the Lord
or be resurrected only half-complete.

Coffins burning.

In Naples only coffins get cremated.
As the corpse's empty box goes in the flame,
to reach that Paradise so long awaited
the soul in Purgatory goes through the same.

Skulls and bones in the Fontanelle.

With family help Vincenzo's made it there
and in Purgatory his soul will get its purging.
But what of those who get no family care,
who got no mass, no prayers, no loved ones' urging?

Mimmo, Giuseppe, Vincenzo, all those three
have wives and families who'll do their best
to ensure that they'll get through to Purgatory,
and after a brief purging, join the blessed.

Perhaps the plague or epidemic dropped
so many bony orphans in one place
for Neapolitans to pity and adopt
and for refreshment given get back grace.

These are souls who don't have Mimmo's luck
and are abandoned and so can't aspire
to Blessedness above, and they stay stuck
in transit in the Purgatorial fire.

If prayer can ease the purifying blaze,
give balm to the abandoned where they burn,
their gratitude to someone when he prays
comes back as graces granted in return.

And those who grant such grace might get a niche
to keep the favours flowing, for repose,
though which old rib bone once belonged to which,
which skull to which stray hip, nobody knows.

Pray for the dead, the Catholic priests exhort,
but these popular beliefs are thought to border
on black magic, not what the Church has taught.
So the ossuary got closed by priestly order.

Rafaelle's tomb, Enzo praying.

Those abandoned souls in Fontanelle
are unreachable with bonehouse entrance bricked,

but there's the famous tomb of Rafaelle
that Enzo Borelli discovered derelict.

To show what abandoned souls can do
when given favours, let's look at the story
of one over a century *non piu* –
Rafaelle Liberatore . . .

Enzo Borelli restored his tomb and gates
and heaps the once neglected spot with flowers
and Rafaelle, pleased, reciprocates
by transmitting through Borelli healing powers.

Italian with subtitles:

BLONDE WOMAN
> *'I've come here for fifteen years and had many
> requests granted. A few days ago, my husband
> couldn't piss – the doctor wanted to do tests –
> but that night I put a photo of Rafaele on his
> stomach and next morning, he did 800 grams of
> urine . . . without doing the tests, or taking pills.'*

GREY-HAIRED WOMAN
> *'I wanted a job for my son: within a year he
> found one.'*

BLONDE WOMAN
> *'Enzo is very important, he makes requests for
> us and receives signs. He explains them and
> everything he says is true. That's why Enzo is
> so important.'*

Enzo praying, women praying and watching.

All these flowers, this *rifresco* giving
earned for Enzo Rafaelle's first known grace –
Enzo's sick mama continued living
when doctors had pronounced a hopeless case.

Enzo the rubber prays to Rafaelle
who's been 'no more' since 1853.
His photo on an ailing hubby's belly
guarantees 800 grams of pee;

work for a son, fiancé for a daughter,
a once-abandoned soul grants all this grace –
making money, making progress, making water
come from rubbing Rafaelle's marble face.

Women rubbing marble face.

He wrote verses too. I wouldn't mind
being like Rafaelle when I die,
a woman stroking me then her behind,
first fingering my face, and then her thigh –

Enzo kisses marble face of Rafaelle.

but I wouldn't fancy smackers from this guy!

Mimmo Perrella non è piu,
the years will pass, his soul get nearer heaven.
His corpse put in its locker after two
will still get visits after six or seven.

*Giovanni Errico takes bodies of Vincenzo and Titina
Genovese out of marble 'locker', unwraps winding
sheet, cleans and dusts bones.*

My father died some seven years ago
and once he'd gone my Mama couldn't wait
for the marble slab that Babba lay below
to be slid back for her to share his fate.

Souls make demands in dreams but don't ask much,
a *rifresco*, a 'refreshment', some small treat,
the locker opened for a loved one's touch,
a dusting down, a change of winding sheet.

It's not the Church but love says that I must.
And it's something that I'll always come to do,
till either they've both crumbled into dust
or I'm in the locker with them and *non piu*.

Portions of a person gnawed by mites,
this carcase crumbling limb by leather limb,
the leather liver, leather lungs and lights . . .
I still find my father in what's left of him.

   Picks up hand.

This hand that patted me, or, once or twice,
gave me an angry clout across the head.
My parents' spirits, safe in Paradise,
still like to see their bits in the same bed.

   Wraps bodies in clean sheets, replaces in locker.

I've had, you'd think, quite long enough to grieve.
They've both been dead for almost seven years.
I find it hard to take a final leave
or notice that they're missing without tears.

Two medallions in marble, some loose bones,
where parents whose embrace made me had been.
But a son can't show his love if he disowns
these fragments bundled up in naphthalene.

To know we'll meet in Heaven makes me glad.
Babba, Mama, are both now *non piu*
but we'll be back together when they add
non è piu to their son Enzo too.

And when Enzo Genovese *non è piu*
this is the locker he will go inside
and his spirit will be smelling the *ragu*
his mother made each Sunday till she died.

   All Souls' Day.

The afterlife means family, hugging, kissing,
the table set for everlasting dinner
with all their loved ones round it, no one missing
and no one diseased or sick, or still a sinner.

And All Souls' Day's a carnival of caring
for all those who've gone before and for their tombs.
Remembering bereavements, they come bearing
bunches of gladioli and bright blooms

for all their loved ones, and a few
for graves no one's brought flowers for.
Three million in this place are *non piu*
and before the day is over there'll be more.

   Procession and crowds.

But though people die today, because of crowds
there'll be no funeral coaches at the gate,
there'll be no burials, no change of shrouds
and souls bound for beyond will have to wait.

And the Cardinal will come arrayed in red
to walk past in procession and to pray
and give his blessing to three million dead
who wait as bones and dust for Judgement Day.

The All Souls' Day traffic's far too thick,
the ambulance we hear just can't get through.
Before it manages to reach whoever's sick
another Neapolitan's *non è piu.*

Relax in your marble lockers, you who wait
the call to Judgement Day, this isn't it.
Another man, like Mimmo, 's met his fate
and soon he'll start to dry out in his pit,

while his soul has other voyages to start
towards a place you can't get to alive,
and though most souls seem reluctant to depart
they're happier than here once they arrive.

So Neapolitans believe with few exceptions.
I'm the odd one out in disbelief.
But if they fool themselves, then the deception's
at least a healing way to handle grief.

And all these visitors this All Souls' Day
bringing their flowers to honour those who've gone
will come to the cemetery one day to stay
and start the journey Mimmo's started on.

And if you were a believer, unlike me,
and you looked towards Vesuvius, Capri,
the curving bay, the ocean, would you see
the souls of the departed passing through
the pall of pollution over Napoli,
through chemicals and clouds into the blue . . .

And beyond maybe? All I know is true:

Espedito Saggiomo non è piu

Vincenzo Genovese non è piu

Titina Genovese non è piu

Rafaelle Liberatore non è piu

Vincenzo Cicatiello non è piu

Giuseppe Ventorelli non è piu

Mimmo Perrella non è piu

Cheating the Void

Oblivion is darkness, Memory light.
They're locked in eternal struggle. Which
of these two forces really shows its might
when death's doors are thrown open by a switch?

Archive film: workers coming out of factory, 1895.

These people are all dead, and yet they walk,
the first in fact to move on celluloid.
Though they are silent and won't ever talk
their very movements seemed to cheat the void.

Death's no longer absolute, wrote the reviewer
having seen this film in 1895.
Do our TVs and videos make that truer
and help to make the dead seem more alive?

Paris: Père Lachaise.

Out of the *Metro* to the upper air
the dead brought back from underneath the ground,
and a century since the film of Lumière
out of the *Metro*, coloured, and with sound.

Napoleonic Paris cleared its plague-filled tombs
and first showed Europe more hygienic ways.
They stacked the dug-up bones in catacombs
and opened a green place called Père Lachaise.

Paris pushed, promoted and PRed
to induce the city's dead to settle there
and re-buried Héloïse with Abelard
and brought in La Fontaine and Molière,

and by process of promotional exhumation
of endorsing heroes long ago decayed
lured both great and small to emulation –
and now draws TV crews and tourist trade.

Tour starts.

The tour starts here with voices in your head.
Hear one corpse sing what another corpse composes.
Follow their music, let yourself be led
to where the shell of genius reposes.

Composers rot but their recorded notes
are all we need to make them seem alive.
The singers buried here have crumbled throats
but the voices they vibrated with survive.

And that, what's that? . . . A bird?
Follow the leafy paths to track the sound
and maybe find it's not a thrush you heard
but Mez Mezzrow's clarinet from underground.

Chopin's tomb, with tourists.

The Muse, one of Memory's nine daughters,
looks and doesn't like what she beholds,
the lyre finally unstrung when Lethe's waters
took Chopin underneath her chilly folds.

Drawn down into Oblivion and drowned
in Eternity's white noise and endless hiss
from where the waves wash up the surfaced sound
of divas from the same dark depths, like this.

Bellini's tomb.

Adelina Patti, Callas and the former
from scratchy wax before the First World War
sings 'Casta Diva' from Bellini's *Norma*,
then Callas, on hissless tracks, gives an encore.

Offspring of Edison's first phonograph,
intended by him only for dictation,
enables us to listen to Piaf
and engineer her vocal exhumation.

Oblivion that all our art defies.
Oblivion where all of us must go.
Oblivion that's gazed on by the eyes
of this graveyard's greatest painter, Géricault,

   Géricault's tomb.

who went on painting till the very last
defying the dark void through his last days
till he changed his pain-racked body for one cast
in bronze still painting here in Père Lachaise.

   Bronze relief of The Raft of the Medusa.

His masterwork *The Raft of the Medusa*,
blown by the wind and battered by the waves,
reproduced in metal but its sculptor/reproducer
believing no male organ much suits graves,

   Jim Morrison's tomb.

made the dying man more modest for the frieze
and gave the death-offending member a bronze veil.
But *Jim* who doesn't, *didn't*, care who sees,
for unveiling his on stage, got thrown in gaol.

'Death and my cock are the world,' said Jim.
That may have been but now I rather doubt
there's much left of that vaunted part of him
or nothing that he'd feel like pulling out.

   London: Kensal Green, Nunhead.

The void may well be cheated by a voice,
composer's quill, the artist's brush or pen,
but memory might only have one choice:
a stone in Kensal Green – eleven pounds ten.

Mr Kemp, the mason, Kensal Green,
professional friend to loving memory,
of the firm of J. S. Farley who have been
naming the void since 1833:

MR KEMP
> 'Here are some of the books which were used in
> those days as catalogues with hand-painted
> drawings of the various memorials. These are
> round about the 1850s. There is a tomb there,
> £55, inscription extra. There's one here in Portland
> stone, a solid tomb, £11 10s, inscription extra.
> There's a six-foot headstone there, curbing and
> foot stone, £11 11s. Another one for £11 10s,
> £6 15s 6d.'

Memory puts up names in chiselled letters
meant to last beyond the mourners' day;
Oblivion makes descendants soon forget us
and lets the weather wear the names away.

The spider spinning on the holly bough,
the moths that spiral in the shafts of sun
are all the visitors the dead get now
where Memory's strangled by Oblivion.

The stone that still reads WATSON's going green.
Lichen furs the letters of each word.
Crevasses to be crossed are all they mean
to millipede and ant and ladybird.

The first Oblivion is death, the next
neglect, and finally the third
where moss and ivy blank out mason's text
and no one cares whose body is interred.

Vandals might strip tombstones of their lead,
jerk ring or jewelled bangle off a bone,
of value to the living not the dead,
but Oblivion can do such work alone.

MR KEMP (*echoed*)
    '£11 11s . . . £6 15s 6d . . . £55 . . . £11 10s . . .
    Inscription extra.'

Bodies with breeding, a better class of bone
first drew dead clientele to Kensal Green
which claimed a royal corpse to set the tone.
A princess made it *the* place to be seen.

This, as Mr Kemp would say, 's a 'solid tomb',
one of the first and solidest erected here
and the deferential swish of worker's broom
keeps common dust from settling on Sophia.

Sophia, daughter of King George III
(though 'precedence beneath the earth's a jest!'),
by choosing Kensal Green to be interred
gave it the cachet to attract the best.

Lords and Ladies, late and early nipped
beneath heartsease, forget-me-not and yew.
What are they now, a stone with chiselled script
saying SIR WILLIAM CASEMENT – who?

Late of Bengal but now of Kensal Green,
Sir William Casement oversees these kids,
jobless for a year, employed to clean
his lichen-encrusted caryatids.

Chuprassie, sepoy, subahdar,
used to serve Sir William's slightest whim.
Now, things being in Britain what they are,
these have no choice but bow and scrape to him.

The circus owner joins the social set.
Though the nobs are no doubt snubbing him in Heaven
Ducrow's bones are rubbing shoulders with Debrett
for three hundred times '£11 11s'.

(*Inscription extra*'.)

Pegasus the winged horse helps him fly,
this 'Colossus of Equestrians' Ducrow
without his hat and gloves into the sky,
and angels from the next tomb watch his show.

Before the Blesseds' astonished saintly faces
Ducrow still cracks his circus master's whips,
putting God's chariot horses through their paces
and the spangled Horsemen of the Apocalypse.

   Genoa: Staglieno.

Ducrow dismounts where bourgeois Genoese
made monuments more lavish than his own,
the chiselling bankers' chiselled effigies,
the solid burghers even solider in stone.

Mazzini buried here serenely stated
(before he died) that Death did not exist.
Others hedge their bets and get translated
from flesh into marble by a realist.

Flesh perishes but marble's meant to last.
They squandered money they'd amassed by trade
to cut a dash in death, not be outclassed
by competition in the colonnade.

Not just a hat and gloves as with Ducrow
but *them*, their face, their limbs, and what they wore,
not just on top but all the frills below
and every detail etched cried out for more –

the delicate brocade, the flimsy lace,
the widow's teardrop falling from a lash,
every feature Memory could trace
provided the remembered had the cash.

   Tomb of nutseller.

I didn't have it, but I swore I would.
I'd save my *lire* so that when I died

I'd stand among the nobs. I'm just as good
though they sniff a bit to see me at their side.

They don't like hawkers in the colonnade
and I sold necklaces of nuts and rings of bread.
Though alive they might despise my lowly trade
they can't feel quite so snooty when they're dead.

Coin by coin commissioned, head to toe,
the nutseller enshrined among the rich,
not sorry to take my rest from life below,
glad that my marble twin still works my pitch.

I worked too hard to have kids of my own
and having kids is all I'd say I miss.
I feel a wee bit jealous when that child of stone
gives her mamma a long, lingering kiss.

South of France: Marseille, Nice.

Sunshine is life and here the sunny Med
with honeymooners, beachballs and blue sky
seems an unlikely landscape for the dead,
but even the idle rich have got to die.

The best of life so close, so out of reach.
How tantalising to be good and dead
with all those sunburnt bodies on the beach
when you're mere marble, and no eyes in your head.

The sun, the sea, the half-clad shapes,
topless torsos, thighs lapped by the waves,
all have a date with death, no one escapes,
stretched out, as if to sunbathe, in their graves.

They see them sunbathe, and they see them swim
if a dead man's eyesight can survive.
So much *joie de vivre*, and yet, says Jim,

JIM MORRISON (*sync.*)
NO ONE HERE GETS OUT ALIVE!

OK Jim, but there's no need to shout.
Go back and rest your bones in Père Lachaise.
Everybody knows they won't get out
of here alive, but like their holidays.

These waters, so inviting in the sun,
that people dip their toes in, swim in, float,
can darken any day into Oblivion
and a farewell sail in Charon's ferry boat.

Venice: San Michele.

This island of the dead's so short of space,
most graves in Venice have a ten-year lease
then each cross with the dead's ceramic face
gets moved, and those who want to rest in peace

get their bones collected for the common pile
to make room for another boat-borne box.
The dead spared exhumation on this isle
are the famous and the Russian Orthodox

which include Stravinsky and Diaghilev.
Our sound machine exhumes their *Rite of Spring*
to summon flowers up. The dead are deaf
to music, birdsong, boats, to everything;

to these drums that shake the earth down to its core,
invoking spring to turn the dug soil green,
to the furiously following First World War
shaking all the cemeteries we've seen.

Milan: Cimitero Monumentale.

Time running out for Europe and for man,
Oblivion in our century overtaking
Memory, pursued here to Milan
where men of stone bring God's heart close to breaking.

What does Christ gaze down on from his cross?
A century where innocence has died

and mankind finds no meaning in the loss
of millions almost worse than crucified.

Child (Mia) alongside tomb sculpture of child.

Film machines exhume the ones who've died
and bring this baby Mia back to view
but Oblivion with his bombs and genocide
is almost neck and neck since World War Two.

Innocence all unaware how time
can make her smiling playmates petrified.
Graves are fun to play on and to climb,
she doesn't know the meaning of 'they died'.

Locked in eternal struggle which one wins,
Oblivion or Memory, Darkness, Light?
Maybe Oblivion and Memory are twins
like here on this gravestone, left and right.

Photos of twins.

Machines have maximised Oblivion's slaughter
that Memory films on Lumière's machine
and this Muse in Milan here, Memory's daughter,
doesn't seem to care for what she's seen.

That emotion in the Muse's face is fear
that shows itself through her half-covered eyes
as the century darkens over baby Mia
and Oblivion's smoke-stacks blacken Europe's skies.

Hamburg: Ohlsdorf.

Herr Blümke walking in cemetery, shooting rabbits.

This bloke in case you think so's not recruiting.
Graveyards don't have problems keeping full.
It's not a human enemy he's shooting,
it's Herr Blümke's early-morning rabbit cull.

The dead don't register the rifle's sound,
though once for days on end that's all they heard,
burrowing for their lives into the ground.
Now rabbits burrow down where they're interred.

Herr Blümke, rabbit-culler, takes the prize –
Two thousand killed a year here, but the War
when it came rabbiting to Hamburg from the skies
in just one day bagged fifty thousand more!

   Archive film of charred bodies lying in street.

We'd sooner that Oblivion destroyed
some memories like these Hamburg streets.
Some film we'd sooner pitch into that void
that Lumière's invention sometimes cheats.

In 1943 the Allied raid
intended to subdue the German nation
caused fires that reached 800 centigrade,
Two hundred more than needed for cremation.

The lawns of Ohlsdorf, where still mourning mothers
search level grass, where every loved one shares
a common grave with fifty thousand others
but want to claim one blade of it as theirs.

'Remember me, but, ah, forget my fate!'
Impossible in Hamburg. History refuses
to have that motto carved above her gate
as she's the least forgiving of the Muses.

   Gates of Bombenopfer monument open to reveal
   Charon's ferry.

The gates of death are opening once more
not to let souls out, as in the Lumière,
but into Charon's ferry for the farther shore.
He starts the outboard with a stony stare.

Why do the ferried close their chiselled eyes?
What do you passengers not want to see?
Their destination where dark Oblivion lies
or what they leave behind in Germany?

Charon's ferry's chugging at the wharf
for those who do not care for what they've seen
from this landing stage of stone here at Ohlsdorf,
from Venice, Genoa, Milan, and Kensal Green,

from Nunhead, Menton and from Père Lachaise,
but Charon's eyes are never known to close.
He sees the sad processions and his gaze
pierces Oblivion's depths like Géricault's.

Tours go back to where they started,
always A to A not A to Z,
but in this ferry boat once you've departed
Charon chugs back empty for more dead.

Letters in the Rock

LADY ROSE HARE
*'We don't really know what sort of person she
was, what her interests were or anything like that.'*

VICKY NAISH
*'I mean he's, he's still my dad as far as I'm
concerned, he'll never be any different.'*

MYRA DAVEY
*'They loved their garden, they really did, and
after they died the natural thing to do was to
scatter their ashes in their garden.'*

THE HON. SIMON HOWARD
*'They'd put a lot back into Castle Howard and
so it was a logical conclusion to their lives to be
buried here in the Mausoleum.'*

MAUREEN STREET
*'I mean he was only ten months old, he was
quite fond of soft toys.'*

Master Masons' Conference, Blackpool.

In Blackpool August 1936
Dad planted me inside my mother's womb.
The fact of my conception's hard to mix
with letters etched by chisels on a tomb.

My father's favourite place for holidays
isn't the first place I'd expect to see
such mournful graveyard furniture displays,
the mason's trappings of mortality.

This stone that's aptly carved with Blackpool Tower
isn't just display, it waits the name
of one who's reached the inevitable hour
and thinks that Heaven and Blackpool are the same.

> *'In Loving Memory of Thomas Gray' on computer
> screen.*

'In Loving Memory of Thomas Gray.'
Good job the letters in it are a few –
sandblasted and then squirted with gold spray
each letter costs you £1.32.

TONY HARRISON
> *'Now we've got Thomas Gray, could we have a
> verse from Gray's* Elegy?'

TONY MILLS
> *'Yes, in that style?'*

TONY HARRISON
> *'In that style, fine, if I can remember it.'*

TONY MILLS
> *'Yes, we clear that one, quite logically from line
> one we can select this style and the text and the
> size that we need and quite simply type it in, so
> if you tell me what to type in, away we go.'*

TONY HARRISON
> *'Right, "The Boast of Heraldry . . ." '*

SALES PERSON
> *'You see, if you've got a very windy cemetery
> then you're going to find that that will stay
> within the container, no problem. Something like
> that in a very windy area with tall flowers and
> it's just going to blow over and you're not going
> to keep them there at all. That's the whole idea
> of the weight.'*

CUSTOMER
> '*I see that . . .* '

TONY HARRISON
> '*. . . the Pomp of Pow'r*
> *And all that Beauty, all that Wealth e'er gave,*'
> – *new line* –
> '*Awaits alike th'inevitable Hour.*
> *The Paths of Glory lead but to the Grave.*'

It's shock enough to know your loved one's gone
but the mason estimating that the rock
your dear departed's name gets lettered on
will cost eight hundred pounds compounds the shock.

If memorials are raised the words are terse.
In Memory's sometimes shortened to I.M.
and almost no tombs now get lines of verse.
The paths of glory lead but to the crem.

In fire and molten magmas mountains started
and turned into granites ebony, red, grey,
that bear the chiselled names of our departed
that several lifespans shouldn't wear away.

> *Rock factory.*

Sugar and syrup at 300 Fahrenheit –
poured on to metal plates this boiling mix
of Blackpool magma cools to brilliant white
coloured and lettered, cut into sweet licks.

The fates, those three that measure, spin and sever
on ancient looms or something up to date,
allot us all a span that's not for ever –
from the start life's lettered with our final fate.

VICAR (*in crematorium*)
> '*Jesus said, I am the resurrection and the life,*
> *whoever believes in me will live, even though he*

*dies, and whoever lives and believes in me will
never die. Do not be worried and upset, he said.
Believe in God and believe in me. There are
many mansions in my Father's house and I am
going to prepare a place for you.'*

'Burning Burials', said Sir Thomas Browne,
stop 'our skulls being used as drinking bowls',
the puny and the portly rendered down
to about five pounds of powder, and their souls.

But there's the rub, for many are afraid
that souls don't stand much chance of coming through
a chamber where 600 centigrade
makes windblown ash of all the rest of you.

What Americans have christened 'the cremains'
poured through a plastic funnel to return
to nature, and tomorrow's autumn rains
wash away what's shaken from the urn.

'Slow thro' the Church-way Path we saw him borne'.
Gray's *Elegy*'s a mine of apt quotation
but an Elegy on a Crematorium Lawn
wasn't what fired Gray's imagination.

This is where they lead, the paths of glory,
and the British, on the whole, don't seem to care,
but let's let some who do tell us their story
of who they want remembered, how, and where:

MYRA DAVEY (*Myra's house, Taunton*)
*'When my father's parents both died they both
wished that they should be cremated so we did
this. The service I thought was much nicer and
afterwards the question of the ashes. I said to
father, well, what shall we do with the ashes and
you really didn't want anything to remind you,
did you?'*

ERNIE HILLBURN
> 'No, and my mother and father used to spend
> a lot of time in the garden and Myra suggested
> scattering them in the garden which I thought
> was a good idea.'

MYRA DAVEY
> 'They loved their garden, they really did, because
> Grandma always used to refer to the bottom
> part of her garden as a "little bit of Heaven",
> and she always said that she felt nearer to God
> there than anywhere else, so when Grandpa died
> to me the natural thing was to put them together.
> I did it totally by myself. I did it late afternoon.
> It was an emotional thing for me because I felt
> I'd brought them home again and there, that is
> where they were going to stay.'

ERNIE HILLBURN
> 'You see, the cemeteries in the course of time
> they get very neglected and there comes a time
> when I'm gone and probably my daughter's
> gone, and nobody else will ever go to the grave
> or to care for it and then it just goes derelict.'

MYRA DAVEY
> 'Of course at Taunton Deane they've got the
> facility of the Book of Remembrance and both
> my grandparents' names are there and my
> mother's name will be put there.'

ERNIE HILLBURN
> 'We go out every anniversary to read – to look at
> the book – to read their names.'

MYRA DAVEY
> 'To read their names, yes. We found that most,
> well everyone wishes cremation more than

anything else. I myself, I would want it and I know that Dad certainly wants it.'

ERNIE HILLBURN
'Oh yes, yes, I should definitely want to be cremated.'

MYRA DAVEY
'Yes.'

ERNIE HILLBURN
'And I don't mind what they – '

MYRA DAVEY
'What's done with you. (Laughs.) You'll probably end up in the garden. Oh, you like your garden, Dad. (Laughs.)'

VICKY NAISH (*Nunhead Cemetery*)
'We much prefer burials, this is our way of thinking. My father's wish was always to be buried, always. He always said never burn me, Vicky, you know, because he was burned enough in the War, you know, and he never ever approved of cremations, always burials, much preferred burials. And he's got his wish. This is not a private grave, it's a public grave, which was my mother's wish, to have an ordinary common grave, for the simple reason before my father died at the beginning of 1982 Nunhead Cemetery was in the news quite a lot about vandalism, people coming into the cemetery and opening the old graves. Because many years ago, and it still sticks in my mum's mind, if you had a big headstone and a private grave and so forth that meant you had plenty of money and you were actually buried with all your jewels etc. So we much prefer to have it this way and to

*have a wooden cross and not only that, there's
not just my father buried here, there are five
others, because normally a common grave has
six coffins, you know, six people in it. I mean,
I don't know who the other five are.'*

Vicky tidying grave.

*'When I first used to visit, the first Christmas
there was somebody else attending to this grave
as well, but unfortunately I haven't seen anybody
now for at least two years that come up here to
see to it, just my family, my mum and myself and
my husband. And that's all.'*

*'You never forget someone who's so important
to you, I mean every day there's something that
goes on that clicks through your mind that, oh,
you know, even if you're on a bus or something
like that, you'll just look out of the bus window
or even your home, you look out of the window,
and you'll see sort of a thing, like a car or
something like that – oh, my dad used to have
one of those. Every day there's always something
in life that reminds you of the dead.'*

SIMON HOWARD (*Castle Howard Mausoleum*)
*'Well, here we are in the Chapel of the
Mausoleum, which is in the main drum behind
the columns and sits above the crypt. As you can
see it's a very light and spacious and airy room.
It was from here in front of the altar that the
service was conducted for my father's funeral,
with the clergy either side, whereas for my
mother's funeral the service was conducted from
inside this stall here. I think a rather more
impressive position. And then the family would
have sat in these pews either side – stalls. And*

they have a certain amount of depth to them and one really gets a feeling of space.'

Simon enters crypt.

'Well, this is the crypt which houses sixty-three niches and of these sixty-three, nineteen are permanently occupied by my forebears. It's down here in the crypt that the committal takes place and the body is in the coffin which is put into the niche, and once in the niche when everyone has gone the stone is put in place, and on that stone will be carved the name of the occupant, and the date of birth and death, and more often than not whose son or daughter they were.'

Simon and his mother's and father's niches.

'Previous to this century the last person to be interred in the Mausoleum was the eighth Earl of Carlisle. He was interred in 1889 and it wasn't till my mother died in 1974 that the practice was started again. Both my mother and father felt very strongly that they had contributed a great deal to the resurrection of this estate and they both felt that they wanted to be buried together here in the Mausoleum. My father died in 1984 and was interred below my mother.'

'In the future it is hoped that all the family will continue to be buried here at the Mausoleum, certainly myself.'

MAUREEN STREET
(*Nunhead cemetery, teddy-bear grave*)

'My dad did say to me, will you have him cremated, and I just said yes, yes, 'cause it was only sort of the day or the day after, and I'm *really really pleased that Stephen, he just said no, no, and I didn't argue with him. I said, all right, if that's what you want. I just wanted it over and done with, but now I really am so glad that he's been buried rather than cremated. Can't imagine burning a baby's body, no matter if he's dead or what, you know.'*

'We felt that a teddy bear would have been more appropriate for his age, because he was only a baby. An ordinary headstone, they cost so much money, and it wasn't what we wanted. I mean, they could have done us one on granite, as a headstone four or five inches thick with a teddy bear carved on it, which is not what we wanted. We wanted something that looked cuddly, that looked solid.'

STEPHEN STREET

'Every time I look at it it breaks my heart, but if I went up there and looked at a lump of granite I don't suppose it would mean anything to me.'

MAUREEN STREET

'I think it's made with love, where granite's made for profit. That teddy bear is made because I wanted to make it, I wanted to do something for him, and it's filled with love. I mean, to me that teddy bear is him really. He was cuddly and that's just how the teddy bear looks to me, you know. I mean sometimes I go up there and I expect it to be soft, but he's, I mean, it's hard as stone . . . (Laughs.)'

'I made it myself in an adult institute during the day, on a Monday afternoon, which took me quite some time, but I felt I was doing something for him and it kept me going. It really did keep

me going. We thought the verse was very very
appropriate, especially for a cot-death baby.
It was.'

"We were not there to see you die to hold your
hand or say goodbye but we'll remember our
whole lives through those ten short months we
spent with you."

'– and then I just put "God Bless". He's my son,
you know, and I feel very strongly about it, that
I should give him some of my time, and an hour
out of every two weeks doesn't hurt anybody.
And I like him to have fresh flowers, it's the least
I can do for him. The thought of him having
dead flowers, you know, if they've been up there
for a month or two, it really upsets me, so I like
to go and replace them. Perhaps in years to
come, when I'm over it a bit more, perhaps I'll
plant flowers and then I'll know that he'll have
fresh flowers, plants, and I won't need to go so
much, but at the moment I still need to go that
much. It's almost as if he's still with me, perhaps
that's how I feel, you know, I won't let him go.'

SIR THOMAS HARE (*Stow Bardolph Chapel, Norfolk*)
   'Well, the Chapel was built at the end of the
   sixteenth century and it's really the only thing
   that's left here which was contemporary with the
   first settlement of our family in the area.'

Children at Sunday School.

'I often wonder what the people buried
underneath would think about a lot of children
running about over their corpses, but I like to
think that they were all, nearly all of them were
members of very big families, and I just hope

*that they would like the idea of the new life
continuing.'*

*'Quiet, quiet now, everybody, and let's all be
quiet and remember where we are and we start
as usual by saying the Lord's Prayer together:
"Our Father which art in Heaven . . ."'*

LADY ROSE HARE (*monuments in Chapel*).
*'We wanted to start a Sunday School and it was
the only place that we could start it. We're very
fond of the Chapel and especially since we've
had the Sunday School, it's all come alive in a
way.'*

SIR THOMAS AND CHILDREN
*'". . . and deliver us from evil, for the Kingdom,
the Power and the Glory are yours, now and for
ever, Amen."'*

SIR THOMAS
*'Now, it's Catherine's turn this week to read a
prayer, and when she's said it the response is,
"Dear God, we believe in you."'*

CATHERINE
*'Dear God, thank you for all our friends and
relations who have died, we are glad that you
have made Heaven so that we don't have to be
so sad. We know that you have room for every
one who believes in you.'*

SIR THOMAS AND CHILDREN
'Dear God, we believe in you.'

SIR THOMAS
*'I should like the tradition of monuments to
continue, in a simple form, but perhaps showing
something about the person and their interests on*

them, as well as just the bare facts of when they were born and died. The only specific instruction I've left in my own will is that I should have a Christian burial because you never know, you might die in some part of the world where that wouldn't happen. I thought that was important.'

LADY ROSE
'Yes, I agree with Tom. I think I'd like some sort of memorial and I should like my interests shown on that memorial, maybe in some sort of decoration, just to show what sort of person one was a little bit. Not just one's name and age.'

Door opens to reveal wax effigy.

'Now, we're going to open the cupboard and see who's come back. Shall we open it very slowly and see who's in there?'

CHILDREN
'Oooooooo!'

LADY ROSE
'Now who can remember her here before?'

CHILDREN (*arguing*)
'No . . . yes.'

LADY ROSE
'What do you think's been happening to her while she's been away?'

SIR THOMAS
'Well, this is the wax effigy of Sarah Hare, there are no other wax effigies as far as we know in parish churches in this country.'

LADY ROSE
'She does look a bit different, doesn't she?'

CHILD
'She looks much different, she had longer hair . . . '

LADY ROSE
'Do you think her hair looks different?'

CHILDREN
'Yes.'

SIR THOMAS
'She left very specific instructions in her will. She says, "I desire to have my face and hands made in wax, with a piece of crimson satin thrown like a garment in a picture. Hair upon my head and put in a case of mahogany with a glass before and fixed up so near the place where my corpse lies as it can be, with my name and time of death put upon the case in any manner most desirable."'

LADY ROSE
'Do you think she's glad to be back? She died in 1744, so how old does that make her?'

CHILD
'About a thousand . . . '

LADY ROSE
'No, not quite as much as that.'

Clown laughing, Blackpool.

'The Boast of Heraldry, the Pomp of Pow'r
And all that Beauty, all that Wealth e'er gave,
Awaits alike th' inevitable Hour.
The Paths of Glory lead but to the Grave.'

Blackpool for me's this clown convulsed with laughter
and how people on their holidays behave,
not the paraphernalia of the hereafter
and lettered rock that marks a person's grave,

The heraldry of Howard and of Hare,
the crem that burns up power, beauty, fame,
the baby's grave with home-made teddy bear,
and the tomb with Blackpool Tower that waits a name.

Blackpool Tower on gravestone of Harold Marsden.

Harold loved his Blackpool all year round
and what he loved in life he wanted after,
Blackpool Tower, the pier, the prom, the sound
of waves and gulls and fun and seaside laughter.

LADY
'Give over, will you . . .'

OTHER LADY
'No, you've got to laugh . . .'

Sings.

'. . . with my little stick of Blackpool rock,
Along the promenade I stroll . . .'

Harold's gone to his Blackpool in the sky
and if, like him, my Blackpool-loving dad
had believed here's where we go to when we die
he wouldn't have thought that dying was too bad.

If when getting near the inevitable hour
my dad like Harold Marsden had have thought
that he'd need his pumps for foxtrots in the Tower,
he'd have packed less glumly for the last resort.

Life's stick of rock's still got a few sweet licks
and death lettered right through life can't make it sour,
so lick your skullicious lollies down to sticks
and scorn for now the inevitable hour.

THE BLASPHEMERS' BANQUET
(1989)

The Blasphemers' Banquet was first broadcast on BBC1 on 31 July 1989.

Music Dominic Muldowney
Sung by Teresa Stratas

In *The Misanthrope* of Molière (trans. Tony Harrison) Edward Petherbridge was Philinte, David Horovitch was Alceste, and Donald Pickering was Oronte

Voltaire's Follies (Paris) featured Jean François Prevand, Gerard Maro, Yves Pignot and Remy Kirch

Voice of Rev. Wallace Brian Cox

Photography Mike Fox, Paola Ribeiro
Sound Recordist Fraser Barber
Additional Photography Colin Clarke
Additional Sound David Keene
Dubbing Mixer Stuart Grieg
Special Sound Andrew Wilson
Dubbing Editor Stuart Napier
Videotape Editor Peter Belcher
Designer Edward Lipscombe
Graphic Designer Andrew Hunter
Production Secretary Teresa Watts
Production Assistant Sally Corfield
Researchers Harriet Bakewell, Amanda Barrett
Film Editor Peter Simpson
Executive Producer David Pearson
Director Peter Symes

Int. Omar Khayyam Restaurant, Bradford

The blasphemers' banquet table: there
on mirrored cushions will sit Voltaire,
me, Molière, Omar Khayyam, Lord Byron
and that, that's Salman Rushdie's chair.

It's perfect for tonight's blasphemers' meeting,
this place renowned in Bradford for good eating
that used to be a church and gets its name
from the poet who loves *this* life, however fleeting,

Omar Khayyam, who also loved his wine and had no care
for those cascade-crammed castles in the air
the Koran promises to those who sacrifice
'this fleeting life' for afterlife up there.

Often called the 'Voltaire of the East',
Omar Khayyam will pour wine at our feast
and I'll propose the toast to Salman Rushdie
and all those, then or now, damned by some priest.

SALMAN RUSHDIE
     *'And frankly I wish I'd written a more critical
     book.'*

Demonstrations.

     *'Kill the bastard, burn him . . . kill the bastard . . .
     burn him to death.'*

When I see bigots wanting Rushdie dead
burning a book I'm sure they've never read,
marble bust or not, Voltaire's got stored
a much more critical book in this old head.

Voltaire bust with book burning projected on it.

I too heard bigots rant, rave and revile
books of mine which, after a short while
were canonised as classics, which is why
you always see Voltaire with this wry smile.

A boy in Abbeville for having sung
a mildly blasphemous ballad had his tongue
ripped from its roots, and on his blazing body
my *Philosophical Dictionary* was flung.

Comédie Française foyer.

And I whose books got flung into the blaze
of Inquisitorial *auto da fés*
am now a monument with Molière
in the Crush Bar of the *Comédie Française.*

*Voltaire's statue reflected in TV monitor dissolves to
reveal funeral of Ayatollah Khomeini.*

Superimposed quotation, Ayatollah Khomeini:

> *'I know that during my long life I have always
> been right about what I said.'*

TERESA STRATAS (*sung refrain*)
> *'Oh, I love this fleeting life.'*

The Koran denounces unbelievers who
quote 'love this fleeting life' unquote. I do.
I'm an unbeliever. I love this life.
I don't believe their paradise is true.

*Sparkling water (Bradford fountain near site of book
burning).*

The afterlife for which that chilled corpse prayed
was a paradise of fountains and green shade
and dark-eyed houris and a garden
where roses bloom forever and don't fade,

unlike this world of ours where things fade fast.
In a place where nothing changes and things last
the *fatwa* Fascist lolls in Paradise
and waters full of stars go flowing past.

Superimposed quotation, Ayatollah Khomeini:

> 'These are things which are impure: urine,
> excrement, sperm, blood, dogs, pigs, unbelievers,
> wine, beer and the sweat of the excrement-eating
> camel.'

And as a righteous man he'll be arrayed
in richest silks and delicate brocade
and be served sherbets by chaste virgins,
he, whose *fatwa* made the world afraid.

And while the Ayatollah, at a fountain's side,
chooses some dark-eyed virgin for a bride,
down here where life is fleeting and time flies
a man I've asked to dinner has to hide.

Tony Harrison sitting in Bradford square.

This isn't paradise but the Bradford square
where Rushdie's book got burnt, just over there.
By reading it, where fools had it cremated
I bring it whole again, out of the air.

The Satanic Verses *appears out of thin air and into his
hands.*

Near where the National Theatre does a play
by one priests smeared as Satan in his day
I read a book by one dubbed Satan now
whose work, like Molière's, is here to stay.

And of the afterlife I have no heed.
What more could a godless mortal need
than a samosa and a can of beer
and books, like Rushdie's, to sit here and read?

Crane shot, Bradford city centre.

And I've asked its hidden author out to eat
with five blasphemers he might like to meet
at the OMAR KHAYYAM Tandoori
not far from here near Bradford's Paradise Street.

At this blasphemers' banquet I've set up
Omar Khayyam will cry 'Come Fill the Cup'
and Molière, Voltaire, Lord Byron and myself
will toast *The Satanic Verses* when we sup.

Omar Khayyam, the poet of Iran
whose quatrain I'm using here, as best I can,
will pour for us his choicest flask of wine
while I pass round the Peshawari nan.

Queen Victoria statue, Bradford; statue and Alhambra
Theatre.

Blasphemers sharing Bradford bread and wine
are due to rendezvous at half past nine
after blasphemer Molière at the Alhambra
in a blasphemer's English version – mine.

PHILINTE

> *'Your black philosophy's too bleak by half.*
> *Your moods of black despair just make me laugh.*
> *I think by now I know you pretty well . . .*
> *We're very like Ariste and Sganerelle,*
> *the brothers in that thing by Molière,*
> *you know,* The School of Husbands, *that one*
> *where. . . '*

ALCESTE

> *'For God's sake, spare us Molière quotations.'*

Superimposed quotation, Ayatollah Khomeini:

> *'There is no humour . . . in Islam*

There is no laughter . . . in Islam
There is no fun . . . in Islam'

ORONTE
        '. . . but still I'm at a loss to know what's in my
        poem.'

ALCESTE
        'Jesus wept! It's bloody rubbish . . .'

Int. theatre.

Priests may turn to piety and prayer,
I turn to poetry and plays by Molière.
'Theatre,' said Hugo, 'is a place for forming souls,'
but the only gods it knows are those up there.

Theatre lights fading.

Believing only in this life below,
these are the only gods I'll ever know.
We live and die and only time destroys us,
falling forever into the big 'O'.

That great big O of nothingness that swallows
poets and priests, queens and Ayatollahs
not only infidels but fundamentalists
whether in black turbans or dog collars.

Molière bust in Comédie Française.

In Molière's own time these pious frauds
thought it a blasphemy to tread the boards.
He'd be gratified to see his 'blasphemies'
doing slightly better business than the 'Lord's'.

Int. theatre: lights fade out.

Because he died and no priest heard him swear
that he abjured the stage, this Molière
was buried without candles at the dead of night,
a fate the Church made many actors share.

Sung refrain:

'*We live and die and only time destroys us.*'

Charles Rice's tomb, Undercliffe cemetery, Bradford.

Bradford, when Charles Rice was alive,
saw the Church and theatres both thrive;
now the churches have new uses and of the theatres
only the Alhambra managed to survive.

Track from tombs to wide shot, Bradford.

And of the many churches Charles Rice knew
of those left standing there are very few
with singing Sabbath congregations; mosques
are the only sacred houses now built new.

One church where some of these at rest come from's
long since flattened by Luftwaffe bombs,
the Four Square Gospel Church is auction rooms,
the Presbyterian purveys crisp popadums.

The golden dome and muezzin's minaret
as panoramas on his panto set
for *Ali Baba* or *Aladdin* at the Royal
were all the Orient that Charles Rice met.

Gravestone with Omar Khayyam quotation.

The only influence then out of Iran,
before the fanatic Ayatollah, was a man
who praised wine and despised the Paradise
promised to Moslem *men* by the Koran.

But this Bradford tomb with Rubai'yat quatrain
faces the half-built mosque in East Squire Lane,
its gold dome shining, and so new
it's still not felt a drop of Bradford rain.

Still domeless girders open to the sky,
an even bigger mosque goes up nearby,

our church/tandoori rendezvous, named after
the poet who penned this gravestone's gold *rubai*:

'Lo some we loved the loveliest and the best
that time and fate of all their vintage pressed
have drunk their cup a round or two before
and one by one crept silently to rest.'

> *Sung refrain:*

> > *'Oh'*

> > *'Oh, I love this fleeting life.'*

> > *'Oh'*

> > *'Omar Khayyam'*

Camera moves from graveyard down to restaurant/
church.

REV. ALEXANDER WALLACE
(quoted from sermon of 1853)
> *'Oh, that I could but rightly speak of the practical*
> *influence which the life of Christ ought to exert*
> *upon us all. He went about doing good that he*
> *might influence us to do the same.'*

St Andrews built in 1849
nourishes Bradford under a new sign

Int. restaurant.

and beer and Bombay special biryani
oust Bible bombast from the Scots divine.

And imbibers have a few months' grace before
these girders get their gold dome on next door
and muezzin's call sours Omar's ruby vintage
curdling the stomach of the currievore.

Where there was passionate preaching and packed pews
are King Prawn Rogan Josh and Vindaloos.

For Bradford devotees of Indian food
the OMAR KHAYYAM restaurant is 'good news'.

The blasphemers' banquet table, there
on mirrored cushions will sit Voltaire,
me, Molière, Omar Khayyam, Lord Byron
and that, that's Salman Rushdie's chair.

REV. WALLACE
'A *wine bibber, oh that we could imbibe that
spirit, oh surely . . .*'

Ruined or altered Bradford churches.

They sing of time that bears us all away
and how God alone's resistant to decay.
But his congregations and his churches aren't;
where's the pulpit, where's the cross, and where are they?

Abandoned graveyard.

Where some of Bradford's past already lies
life flowers in these bright affirming eyes,
though her forehead rests on some old grave
she thinks that time stays still, and never flies.

It won't be long before she knows
that everything will vanish with the rose
and then she'll either love life more because it's fleeting
or hate the flower and life because it goes.

Indian children.

Beautiful sisters in their white and green
innocent of what these crude words mean
but maybe they will soon discover beauty
is inescapably bound up with the obscene.

Track from obscene graffiti on wall to new mosque:

'*Scarface bumbed his dad upside down. He
licked his mum Fanny out 200 Time a minute*'

Various creeds attempt to but can't split
the world of the spirit from the world of shit.
Crude scrawls and sacred scrolls come from one mind.
Scarface subverts the saint and won't submit.

This message LEAVE NO LITTER in Urdu
seems to have some problem getting through.
Man's fear of his own filth makes him go seeking
the unblemished beautiful in the untrue.

The thorny whys and wherefores, awkward whences,
things that seduce or shame or shock the senses
panic the one-book creeds into erecting
a fence against all filth and all offences.

Feeling that life seems blasted by some blight
we keep on yearning for some purer light
but this, as Bertrand Russell wrote, is born
from our deep fear of everlasting night,

*Undercliffe cemetery, tomb – move down to auction
rooms in town.*

fear of that big O that swallows whole
both the human body and the soul,
fear of time that makes us live and die,
fear of transience that takes its daily toll,

Southend Hall Auction Rooms.

fear of living, fear of being dead,
fear that what we love most's soonest fled,
fear of loving what is fleeting for itself
our fear of what false prophets make us dread,

of doomsday with its dreadful but false dooms,
of time that bustles men back into tombs,
of that fleeting transience that can transform
the Four Square Gospel Church to auction rooms,

145

Int. auction rooms.

the transience that makes this life-warmed ring
dangle for buyers from a numbered string
and numbers us, knick-knacks of nothingness,
the going – going – gone of everything.

DAVID BISHOP (*auctioneer*)
> '*Start me at a pound for the lot, I've a pound,
> two, have we two now, have we one, are we
> done now? Couldn't you take something at fifty
> quid? Who was it? Mrs Bennett. One-five-four.
> One-five-four is the gold ring. One-five-four.
> Where shall we have a tenner, a fiver then. A
> gold ring is this. Must be at scrap value at this
> sort of money. Start me at a fiver. Three pounds
> then. Have we three? Right we haven't. Put it
> down, Brian.*'

> '*Silver frame, one-five-five. One-five-five, the
> silver frame. Forty pounds for it . . . twenty
> then.*'

Bishops once burned books (and people!), here
it's Mr Bishop, Bradford auctioneer,
who has them boxed and bundled in job lots
with wedding rings and repro jardinière.

Sung refrain:

> '*Oh, I love this fleeting life.*'

Camera pans across room and television sets.

> '*Thirty-five, now, you can't beat tuning into the
> mass media, fount of all knowledge is that. Are
> we all done at thirty-five pounds then? Is that it?
> And it's Mr Capstick at thirty-five pounds.*'

> '*Lot two-six-seven are three bundles of books.
> Many tomes of ancient knowledge there. Here*

we go. Where shall it be, at twenty pounds, I've
a tenner, a fiver, only bid at seven. Tenner you're
trying, twelve, at fourteen now, at fourteen,
sixteen, eighteen, are we done at sixteen?'

Marble bust of Voltaire.

'All right, we've two-fifty-three now which is . . .
what is it made of? Marble? It's marble, isn't it,
Brian? This marble bust. Right, two-fifty-three,
where do we start this? Unusual item, quickly
then . . . sixteen, eighteen, twenty, I've twenty
bid. Are we all done at twenty pounds? Mr
Nicholson at twenty pounds, Harrison at twenty
pounds. Well, there's one thing that can be said,
your fame's not travelled before you, is that
correct, sir? Thank you. Right . . .'

Time, that gives and takes our fame and fate
and puts say, Shakespeare's features on a plate
or a Persian poet's name on a Tandoori
can cast aside all we commemorate

HM Queen on biscuit tin.

and make Lot 86 or Lot 14
even out of Cardinal and Queen
and bring the holy and the high and mighty
to the falling gavel, or the guillotine.

Voltaire bust.

Paris: Place de la Republique (news footage and
actuality).

When a small boy bellows *Mort! Mort! Mort!*
for Salman Rushdie and fanatics roar
Death to the imagination a revival's due
of work I wrote two centuries before.

When I have to watch this Paris square
packed with murderous protest, then with prayer
at the feet of the Republic, then it's time
that France (and even Britain) read Voltaire.

London demonstration against Rushdie, 27 May 1989.

Sung refrain:

> *'Oh, I love this fleeting life
> Oh, I love this fleeting life.'*

War memorial.

Byron statue in Hyde Park.

Lord Byron heaves a bronze Byronic sigh
to see familiar bigotry march by
but being dead since 1824
and cast in bronze he casts a colder eye.

Robert Southey, Poet Laureate and fool,
said Byron headed the 'Satanic School'
of poetry, which, he thundered, undermined
all religious faith and moral rule,

Byron cartoon.

and a Satanic poet, so Southey said,
goes on accumulating guilt when he is dead
as long as copies of his verses circulate
and go on, unlike Southey's, being read.

Statue.

My Satanic poems, Satanic play
made bigots brand me Satan in my day.
Have patience, brother Satan, you might be
a bronze, like me, in Bradford or Bombay.

Crowd.

> *'Kill the bastard . . .'*

And down the river, just a little way,
the National Theatre's done a matinée
of a three-hundred-year-old piece by Molière
branded by bigots the Satan of his day.

Paris fountain.

And those condemned in God's or Allah's name
may end up statues in the Hall of Fame.
'The most irreligious man who ever lived'
some priest called Molière. I got the same.

Comédie Française: Molière statue, Voltaire statue.

Molière's *Tartuffe* the first French play
to strip hypocrisy's sour mask away
was the one most hated by fundamentalists
till my play about the prophet: MAHOMET.

Sequence from Mahomet.

'Allah, Allah, Allah . . .'

Play develops into extended sequence of fundamentalist religions.

Though not much played since 1742.
a revival of my play's long overdue.
By MAHOMET I meant all fundamentalists
Moslem, Catholic, Protestant and Jew.

REV. IAN PAISLEY
'We have to preserve and maintain in this island true Protestantism, and the Protestant way of life. And I have news for the Roman Catholic church in Ireland today, we Protestants are here in Ireland to stay.'

RABBI MEIR KAHANE
'. . . you know someone who wants to, who wants to kill you . . . get up first and go and kill

him first, that is Judaism, that is Judaism, that is sanity.'

MOTHER ANGELICA
'It is without question the most blasphemous, the most disrespectful, the most satanic movie that's ever been made.'

Image of Ayatollah Khomeini.

US PREACHER
'. . . the world passeth away.'

Sequence ends on bleeding boy and fountain in Hyde Park at end of demonstration.

Sung refrain:

'Oh, I love this fleeting life . . .
Oh, I love this fleeting life . . . '

There's me, and one-two-three-four-five!
Four of them can't come, they're not alive,
and one who can't because the *fatwa* Führer
forced him into hiding to survive.

Restaurant.

Right from the beginning I'm afraid I knew
you'd never make our Bradford rendezvous.
But my invitation was a way of showing
things you still might like to but *can't* do,

say, stroll round Bradford like I did today,
watch the *Comédie Française* perform a play,
a child pilot a chopper on a roundabout,
applaud the Voltaire Follies' MAHOMET.

The Ayatollah forced you to decline
my invitation to share food and wine

with poets branded as blasphemers
including Omar, now our restaurant sign.

Omar Khayyam, the poet of Iran,
the 'Voltaire of Persia' and a man
who praised wine, and despised the Paradise
promised to Moslem *men* by the Koran.

* The Ayatollah in his rich brocades
sucking sherbets by shimmering cascades
nods approval to the theologian
who wants the world to kill all those with Aids.

* Note the new name: Abdullah-al-Mashad,
the latest mullah, dangerous and mad –

SALMAN RUSHDIE
    'Frankly, I wish I'd written a more critical book' –

Sadly, Salman, I sometimes wish you had!

The dead don't dine, those under threat
are not at liberty to come here yet.
But when you're free you're welcome and meanwhile
I toast your talent on your TV set.

Where you're in hiding, tuned to the BBC,
I hope you get some joy in watching me
raise my glass to *The Satanic Verses*,
to its brilliance and, yes, its blasphemy.

It's blasphemy enabled man
to break free from the Bible and Koran
with their life-denying fundamentalists
and hell-fire such fanatics love to fan.

* Under legal pressure the BBC removed these two quatrains from
the film, though the *Independent* had published a Reuters report
from Sara-el-Gammal quoting the head of the Fatwa Committee of
Al-Azhar University.

Omar loves 'this fleeting life' and knows
that everything will vanish with the rose
and yet, instead of Paradise, prefers
this life of passion, pain and passing shows.

Omar writes how nothing stays the same
and it's an irony of fleeting fame
that this Tandoori, OMAR KHAYYAM today,
tomorrow will be called another name.

Ext. restaurant.

*Sung refrain of the letters coming down as the
workers dismantle the restaurant sign.*

THE GAZE OF THE GORGON
(1992)

'To the same degree, though in different fashion,
those who use force and those who endure it
are turned to stone.'

Simone Weil
The Iliad, or the Poem of Force

'Art forces us to gaze into the horror of existence,
yet without being turned to stone by the vision.'

Friedrich Nietzsche
The Birth of Tragedy

Ask General Schwarzkopf who Goethe and Schiller
and Heine were. He would be well advised to answer
if he wants to go on addressing Chambers of Commerce
at $50,000 a pop. "Were they the outfield of the
St Louis Cardinals in 1939?"'

Kurt Vonnegut

The Gaze of the Gorgon was first broadcast on BBC2 on 3 October 1992.

Composer Martin Kiszko
Soprano Angela Tunstall
Photography Mike Fox
Sound Recordist Trevor Gosling
Dubbing Mixer Peter Hicks
Dubbing Editor Sue Goodsall
Research Gail Taylor
Additional Research Gerald Lorenz
Production Secretary Anita Gol
Production Manager Valerie Mitchell
Film Editor Liz Thoyts

Directed by Peter Symes

[Lines within square brackets were not included in the broadcast film.]

Exactly a hundred years ago, in 1892, the marble statue of a dissident German Jewish poet, rejected by his fatherland, was taken by Elizabeth, Empress of Austria, to a retreat in Corfu. This film poem follows its fortunes through the century from its eviction from the island by the German Kaiser, who bought the palace after the Empress was assassinated in 1899, to its present resting place at Toulon in France.

Once established in Corfu, the Kaiser claimed that while Europe was preparing for war he was excavating the fifth century BC pediment which featured a giant Gorgon. The film poem takes this terrifying creature of legend who turns men to stone as a metaphor for what the Kaiser unearthed on to our century, and finds her long shadow still cast across its closing years.

Clutched in the left hand of the marble Heinrich Heine the Kaiser evicted from Corfu is the manuscript of '*Was will die einsame Träne*', a *lied* set to music by Schumann. The song in various transformations makes the same journey as its hounded author.

Gulf: Tank Gorgon / Golden Sea.

From long ago the Gorgon's gaze
stares through time into our days.
Under seas, as slow as oil
the Gorgon's snaky tresses coil.
The Gorgon under the golden tide
brings ghettos, gulags, genocide.

*ECU-Land (Frankfurt).**

That's maybe the reason why
so many mirrors reach so high
into the modern Frankfurt sky.

ECU-land seems to prepare
to neutralise the Gorgon's stare.
But what polished shields can neutralise
those ancient petrifying eyes?

Goethe statue, Frankfurt.

Great German soul, most famed Frankfurter
on his plinth, the poet Goethe.
Born Frankfurt but deceased Weimar
where his mortal remnants are.
The old Cold War used to divide
where he was born from where he died
but now they're once more unified.

Schiller statue.

* ECU was the original name for what is now the Euro.

And once more it doesn't seem so far
from Frankfurt-am-Main back to Weimar.
And but an amble down an avenue
to Friedrich Schiller on full view
and I suppose I ought to say
it's right they're put on proud display
(though often scorned although their scale
's, say fifty times this can of ale).
It's proper that the Fatherland
should give them monuments so grand,
but there's another German who
is quite the equal of those two
(and greater in some people's eyes!)
whose monument's a fifth their size.

Heinrich Heine memorial.

There are, I think, three reasons why
my statue's not so bloody high:
one, I was subversive; two,
(what's worse to some) I was a Jew;
and three, I'm back here almost hidden
because I was ten years bedridden
with syphilis; this keep-fit freak
scarcely suits my wrecked physique.
This monument that's far more humble
's to the voice you're hearing grumble
that he's less on public view,
Heinrich Heine, poet and Jew.

Two grander monuments were planned
but turned down by the Fatherland,
though to the horror of the Habsburg court,
both had the Empress's support,
Elizabeth of Austria, Sissy, who
felt inspired by the soulful Jew
(but to be frank I wouldn't quote

the poems she claimed my spirit wrote!).
In eighteen ninety-two
Sissy took me to Corfu,
and statues Germany rejected
found safer spots to be erected
and with a more appealing view
of sea and cypress in Corfu
and, like many another hounded Jew,
the second statue found its way
to safe haven in the USA.

Your average Frankfurt-am-Mainer
doesn't give a shit for Heine
(nor, come to that, the young mainliner!)
So elbowed to one side back here,
surrounded by junked junkies' gear,
I, Heinrich Heine, have to gaze
on junkies winding tourniquets
made from the belt out of their jeans,
some scarcely older than their teens.
The Gorgon has them closely scanned,
these new lost souls of ECU-land.
The Gorgon's glance gives them their high
then, trapped in her gaze, they petrify.

   Schumann lied (*soprano*).

Ach, meine Liebe selber
Zerfloß wie eitel Hauch!
Du alte, einsame Träne,
Zerfließe jetzunder auch!

Schumann set those words I wrote
that might bring lumps into your throat
(unless you grabbed for the remote!)
And even if you turned away
you could still hear the sung *lied* play.
The marble Heine Deutschland banned

had this *lied* held in his hand,
a manuscript whose crumpled folds
a war-cracked index finger holds.
Where the statue goes the song goes too.
I took it with me to Corfu.
And wish to God I was still there
not here with bloodstains in my hair.
Europe's reluctant to shampoo
the gore-caked coiffure of the Jew,
the blood gushed from a botched injection,
in case it gives it some infection,
or maybe Europe doesn't care
there's junkies' blood in Heine's hair.

The gaze of modern Frankfurt's glued
to this glassy-eyed high altitude.
The Europe of the soaring cranes
has not seen fit to cleanse these stains
or give new hope to the stainer.

   (*Soprano.*)

Was will die einsame Träne?

What is the music that redeems
desperate kids in such extremes?
Do those I hope you're watching need
Schumann's setting of my *lied*?
'This lonely tear what doth it mean?'
we might well ask in such a scene.

Gaze and create. If art can't cope
it's just another form of dope,
and leaves the Gorgon in control
of all the freedoms of the soul.

[I can do nothing, even cry.
Tears are for the living eye.
So weep, you still alive to shed

the tears I can't shed, being dead.
And if I could I'd shed my tears
that in the century's closing years
the nations' greatest souls preside
over such spirit-suicide,
and that in 1992
Schiller, Goethe, Heine view
the new banks rising by the hour
above a park where chestnuts flower
whose canopies you'd think might cover
lunch-time lounger, reader, lover,
but for one who wrestles on his own
against the Gorgon who turns men to stone,
the tree with white May blossom sways
like snakes that fringe the Gorgon's gaze,
the serpents that surround her stare.
Spring blossom hisses like her hair,
as this young junkie tries to choose
which vein today is best to use.]

    Frankfurt police.

The junkies' early evening high
is cut short by the *Polizei*,
who read the law they half-enforce,
and let some shoot-ups take their course.

The regular police routine
is shift the junkies in between
Schiller and Goethe every day
and pass by Heine on the way.

From Schiller's statue back to Goethe's
watching smartly dressed Frankfurters
enter the theatre, and dogs divide
the opiate from the Opera side.

The horns tune up, the dogs bark *'raus'*,
the precincts of the opera house,

the maestro's rapturous ovations
kept safe by *Polizei* alsatians.
They glimpse a shoot-up then they go
for their own fix of *Figaro,*
see heroin addicts then go in
to hear heroes sing in *Lohengrin,*
and evening junkies grouped round Goethe
hear distorted *Zauberflöte.*
Music is so civilising
for the place with new banks rising.
The main financial centre
of the EEC has to present a
fine *Turandot, Bohème, Così,*
for the European VIP.
Traviata, Faust, Aida,
even Schumann's setting of my *lieder,*
just to show, although it's mine,
I can put my own work on the line
and ask as the opera's about to start
what are we doing with our art?

Are we still strumming the right lyre
to play us through the century's fire?

['Bankfurt' they call it; by the way,
I was a banker in my day
and had a somewhat brief career
as Harry Heine banker here,
but the banks have grown and rather dwarf
the Jewish poet from Düsseldorf.
Not only me. Banks in the skies
cut even Goethe down to size.]

With clouds of coins, cash cumuli
floating in the foyer sky
gliding guilder, hard ECU,
dream clouds of 1992,

you'd think this Opera House foyer's
a long way from the Gorgon's gaze.
Escape, they're thinking, but alas
that's the Gorgon in the glass.

The ECU bank-erecting crane
reflected in van windowpane,
where, afraid of Aids, the youngsters queue
to trade old needles in for new,
though higher and higher into the blue
new banks to house the hard ECU
rise into the Frankfurt skies,
piece by piece, like Gorgon's eyes
or polished shield of one who slays
the Gorgon, but can't kill her gaze.

    Schumann lied (*soprano*).

Was will die einsame Träne?
Sie trübt mir ja den Blick.
Sie blieb aus alten Zeiten
In meinem Auge zurück.

Sie hatte viel leuchtende Schwestern,
Die alle zerfloßen sind.
Mit meinen Qualen und Freuden,
Zerfloßen in Nacht und Wind.

Wie Nebel sind auch zerflossen
Die blauen Sternelein,
Die mir jene Freuden und Qualen
Gelächelt ins Herz hinein.

Ach, meine Liebe selber
Zerfloß wie eitel Hauch!
Du alte, einsame Träne,
Zerfließe jetzunder auch!

Corfu, shrine of Heinrich Heine.

Isn't this a somewhat finer
monument to Heinrich Heine?
Banished from the Fatherland
with pen and *lied* still in my hand.
The *lied* that Schumann makes so touching
is in this manuscript I'm clutching,
and though war breaks round the manuscript
my hand will always keep it gripped.
But I'll have ten years of peace
with my Empress here in Greece
from this year 1892,
when Sissy brought me to Corfu.
[It was fun to have the Empress fawn
on one so much more lowly born
and so notorious a despiser
of King and Emperor and Kaiser,
those Krauts in crowns who used to squat
on Europe's thrones but now do not,
wherever history's been rewritten,
that's everywhere but backward Britain,
but then I always found the English mind
compared to Europe's lagged behind.]

My shrine was in the forest glade
and up above she had displayed
Apollo with the lyre that plays
the darkness out of our dark days
in old times when Apollo's lyre
could save men from the petrifier.

For Sissy these weren't mere antiques,
these Muses of the ancient Greeks.
All the human spirit uses
to keep life's colour were the Muses,
or at least to Philhellenes like her
and many of her age they were.

[She retired from the Imperial Court
into art and poetry, music, thought,
though I really wouldn't care to quote
the poems she claimed my spirit wrote,
most of her lines are deadly dull
but in all her soul is 'like a gull'
or 'swallow' like the ones that flew
around her Muses in Corfu
and though a palisade of peace
surrounded Sissy and myself in Greece
it was nonetheless a palisade
where Sissy thought and wrote and played.]

Music Room: Schumann lied (*piano*).

How would all these Muses fare
when dragged screaming by the hair
to gaze into the Gorgon's stare?

Dying Achilles *by Ernst Herter* (*1884*).

The fatal wound, the calf, the thigh
of Achilles who's about to die.
This hero of Homeric fame
gave Elizabeth's retreat its name.
This Achilles of 1884
foresees the future world of war
and shows the Empress half-aware
of horrors brewing in the air.
Her presentiment and pity shows
in the Achilles that she chose,
helpless, unheroic, dying,
watching clouds and seabirds flying
and not one so-called 'Eternal Being'
the Gorgon gulls us into seeing.
First the dead man's gaze goes rotten
then flies feast, then he's forgotten
after those who used to shed

their tears for him are also dead,
unless a bard like Homer brings
the dead redemption when he sings.
Along with me the Empress/versifier
revered blind Homer and his lyre,

Triumph of Achilles *by Franz Matsch.*

the ancient poet whose *Iliad*
was the steadiest gaze we'd ever had
at war and suffering Sissy thought
before the wars this century's fought.
Though melancholic, steeped in grief,
the Gorgon was a mere motif
for Sissy who was unafraid
to have the Gorgon's face portrayed
on ironwork or balustrade,
and this almost charming Gorgon stares
from wardrobe doors and boudoir chairs,
but unwittingly they laid the track
that brought the grimmer Gorgon back.

Schumann lied (*piano only*).

[The palace style based on Pompeii's
might warn us of the Gorgon's gaze
but as her century drew to its close
still found poems in the rose,
the lily of loss and grieving hearts
until this closing century starts.]
The Empress posed above those roses
vanishes as her century closes
and the Muses she believed in threw
their roses to . . . I don't know who.
All the century's fresh bouquets
decayed beneath the Gorgon's gaze,
the grimmer Gorgon simply waited
till Sissy was assassinated

in the century's closing year,
which brought the German Kaiser here.
And when the Kaiser's gaze met mine
contemplating in my shrine,
the Kaiser's eye began to harden:
I don't want his kind in my garden.
He said straightaway: *Get rid*
of Sissy's syphilitic Yid!
Dammit! the man's a democrat,
I've got no time for shits like that.
So once more the poet-refugee
was crated up and put to sea.
The crating up I had to face
the Kaiser wished on all my race.

And as the Kaiser wasn't keen
on Sissy's sentimental scene
of Achilles dying he'd make him stand
and represent the Fatherland.
He didn't like this sculpture much.
He liked his heroes much more butch,
more in his own imperious style.
He'd build an Achilles men could *heil*!

'Build my Achilles armour clad,'
the Kaiser said, 'and confident in steel,
not some mama's little lad
with an arrow in his heel.

Make the wounded warrior stand,
regrip his spear and gaze
through Sarajevo to the Fatherland,
the Lord of all that he surveys.

And put a Gorgon on his shield
to terrify his foes
wherever on Europe's battlefield
the Kaiser's Gorgon goes.'

Triumphant Achilles (*statue*) *by Johannes Götz* (*1909*).

And that is almost everywhere
as gazers freeze in stony sleep
seeing her eyes and coiling hair
hissing like chlorine gas at Ypres.

Doors opening. Triumph of Achilles (*painting*).

The Kaiser, though a Homer freak,
despised the victim and the weak
and looking at Sissy's picture saw
Achilles riding high in war.
For him the focus of the painting
was triumph, not some woman fainting,
but Sissy always used to see
Hector's wife, Andromache,
who has to gaze as Achilles hauls
her dead husband round Troy's walls.
The soon-to-be-defeated rows
of Trojans watch exultant foes
who bring the city to the ground
then leave it just a sandblown mound,
but the Greeks who'll watch Troy blaze
are also in the Gorgon's gaze,
the victims and the victimiser,
conquered and the conquering Kaiser,
Greeks and Trojans, Germans, Jews,
those who endure and those who use
the violence, that in different ways
keeps both beneath the Gorgon's gaze.
A whole culture vanished in the fire
until redeemed by Homer's lyre.
A lyre like Homer's could redeem
Hector's skull's still-echoing scream.

Statue of Achilles.

Not like Sissy's Achilles' sculpted dying
this one's triumphant, time defying.
The crane has hauled into the skies
the Kaiser in Homeric guise
(though not that you would recognise!)
Not only does this monster dwarf
the dissident from Düsseldorf
now newly banished from Corfu,
it dwarfs all Sissy's Muses too.
What can lyre play or bard recite
the same scale as such armoured might
to face his gaze and still create?
Boxed up again inside a crate,
and forcibly reshipped
but still with pen and manuscript,
the shore receding, my last view
of my brief haven in Corfu,
hearing as cypresses recede
a fading phrase of my faint *lied*,
was Achilles' spear whose gilded tip's
the Kaiser's signpost to Apocalypse.
Which of us, the marble Jew
the Kaiser kicked out of Corfu,
or armoured giant, him or me,
would make it through the century?

The founder of the 'master race'
put this inscription on its base.
Those cavities in secret braille
say: *All the Kaiser's work will fail!*
but, wrought in characters of weighty lead,
these pockmarks in the plinth once read:
'The greatest German to the greatest Greek.'
Though not quite equal in physique
the Kaiser's there in his creation,
emblem of his warlike nation,

this bellicose, Berlin-gazing totem
has hornets nesting in his scrotum.
Envenomed hordes have gone and built
their teeming nests in Prussia's kilt,
and perforate the scrotal sac
of the tutued 'Teutomaniac'.

Kaiser excavation stills.

But while all this trouble's brewing
what's the Prussian monarch doing?
We read in his own writing,
how, while all Europe geared for fighting,
England, Belgium, France and Russia
(but not of course his peaceful Prussia),
what was Kaiser Wilhelm II
up to? Excavating in Corfu,
the scholar Kaiser on the scent
of long lost temple pediment,
not filling trenches, excavating
the trenches where the Gorgon's waiting
there in the trench to supervise
the unearthing of the Gorgon's eyes.

This isn't how warmongers are,
this professor in a panama,
stooping as the spades laid bare
the first glimpse of her snaky hair.

The excavator with his find,
a new art treasure for mankind.

The patient Kaiser, piece by piece,
prepares the Gorgon for release,
the Gorgon he let out to glower
above us all with baleful power.

Barbitos.

The *barbitos,* the ancient lyre,
since the Kaiser's day,

is restrung with barbed wire.
Bards' hands bleed when they play
the score that fits an era's scream,
the blood, the suffering, the loss.
The twentieth-century theme
is played on barbed-wire *barbitos*.

Terpsichore – Achilleon.

Terpsichore, the muse who sees
her dances done by amputees.
How can they hope to keep her beat
when war's destroyed their dancing feet?
Shelled at the Somme or gassed at Ypres,
they shuffle, hobble, limp and creep
and no matter what old air she plays
they can't escape the Gorgon's gaze.

Melpomene with tragic mask.

The tragic mask of ancient days
looked with eyes that never close
straight into the Gorgon's gaze
and sang Man's history through its throes.

But now where is she when she sees our need?
Tragedy's masks have changed their style.
Lips like these won't sing my *lied*.
They've forgotten how to smile.

What poems will this mouth recite?
There'll be no Schumann sung from this.
Before these Germans went to fight
they'd been beautiful to kiss.

This is the Kaiser's Gorgon choir,
their petrifaction setting in,
grunting to the barbed-wire lyre,
gagging on snags of *Lohengrin*.

Gorgon pediment.

With glaring eyes and hound-like snarls
from the maze-bound Meanderthals,
the Kaiser's Gorgon will preside
over ghettos, gulags, genocide.
Mankind meanders through the maze
made rigid by the Gorgon's gaze.
Following a more flowing shape
might find us freedom and escape
from the Gorgon and her excavator
who gears his kind for horrors later.
The Kaiser couldn't stand one Jew
in marble near him in Corfu
but the Kaiser's not uncommon views
were just as vicious on all Jews:
'A poison fungus on the German oak'
(to quote the bastard makes me choke!)
This is how the Gorgon blinds
her henchmen's eyes and rigid minds.

Arrow motif on pediment.

The Gorgon worshippers unroll
the barbed-wire gulags round the soul.
The Gorgon's henchmen try to force
History on a straighter course
with Gorgonisms that impose
fixities on all that flows,
with Führer fix and crucifix
and freedom-freezing politics.
Each leader on his monstrous plinth
waves us back into the labyrinth
out of the meander and the maze
straight back into the Gorgon's gaze.

Gorgon motif into swastika.

The Kaiser in his notebook drew
where the Gorgon leads us to,
step by step and stage by stage
he steers the Gorgon through our age.
Her hand on his unlocks the door
that never will quite close on War.

The junkie and the nationalist
both get their fixes with clenched fist.
And even in the ECU-world
the Kaiser's flag's once more unfurled.

Ocean-borne bodies and Nazi flag.

My statue, meanwhile, got away
with swastikas daubed on my face
out of Hamburg to Marseilles
to Toulon and a new safe base.

Statues of Gorgon's henchmen being demolished.

And apart from finger, nose and pen,
my statue's pretty much intact
but those that let the Gorgon out on men
are totally broken and cracked.

Heine's statue in Toulon.

My statue, meanwhile, got away
with swastikas daubed on my face
out of Hamburg to Marseilles
to Toulon and a new safe base.

And apart from finger, nose and pen
my statue's pretty much intact,
but those that let the Gorgon out on men
are totally broken and cracked.

Banished from the Fatherland
still with my *lied* in my hand,

though the pen the poems flowed from
was shattered by an air-raid bomb,
so being without it I recite
as I do now what I can't write.
The *lied* that Schumann makes so touching
is in the manuscript I'm clutching.
This manuscript with faded writing
survived a century of fighting.
Though war broke round this manuscript
my broken hand has kept it gripped.

    Toulon – lied, *Schumann arr. Kiszko.*

[No longer hunted or hounded
and safe and far from fear.
If all the dogs are silenced
why do my eyes shed this tear?

The tears I let fall on the journey
were falling for all I saw.
Today I gaze on the ocean
so far from the fear of war.

The gloom that surrounds those frozen
beneath the Gorgon's gaze
now falls as the century's shadow
to darken our hearts and days.

And though I gaze in sunlight
on springtime's brightest hues,
no longer hunted and hounded,
I weep for six million Jews.]

    End lied.

But when through dappled shades of green
I catch glimpses of a submarine,
and across the ocean have to face
through waving palms a naval base,

it's then I'm reassured to know
that just a hundred years ago
when this rejected marble Jew
escaped with Sissy to Corfu
my other monument made its way
to safe haven in the USA,
safe from Europe's old alarms
into the New World Order's arms.

The Bronx, New York.

The Gorgon who's been running riot
through the century now seems quiet,
but supposing one who's watched her ways
were to warn you that the Gorgon's gaze
remains unburied in your day
and I've glimpsed her even in the USA,
you'll all reply he's crying wolf,

Gulf War.

but in the deserts of the Gulf
steel pediments have Gorgon's eyes
now grown as big as tank-wheel size
that gaze down from her temple frieze
on all her rigid devotees.

Skull – lied, *Schumann arr. Kiszko (soprano).*

The closing century's shadow
has darkened all our years
and still the Gorgon's filling
my empty sockets with tears.

The tears I let fall in the desert
the sand has all soaked away.
My eyes and all that they gazed on
are gone from the light of day.

175

They've gone with these palls of blackness
the smoking desert blaze.
Will all of our freedoms and glories
end up in the Gorgon's gaze?

O so much life has vanished
in smoking fiery skies.
The closing century's shadow
is cast across all our eyes.

End lied.

'Triumph of Achilles' (detail).

The empty helmet of one whose eyes
have gone to feast the desert flies,
the eyes of one whose fate was sealed
by Operation Desert Shield.
They gazed their last these dark dark sockets
on high-tech Coalition rockets.

Tourists.

Soon, in 1994,
in this palace Greece starts to restore,
in this the Kaiser's old retreat
Europe's heads of state will meet,
as the continent disintegrates
once more into the separate states
that waved their little flags and warred
when the Kaiser's Gorgon was abroad.
So to commemorate that rendezvous
of EU statesmen in Corfu
I propose that in that year
they bring the dissident back here,

Painter in the Achilleon singing.

and to keep new Europe open-eyed
they let the marble poet preside . . .

BLACK DAISIES FOR THE BRIDE
(1993)

*To the staff and residents
of Whernside Ward*

Black Daisies for the Bride was first broadcast on BBC2 on 30 June 1993.

Therapist Elaine Hallam
Young Maria Maria Bovino
Young Kathleen Cathryn Bradshaw
Young Muriel Maria Friedman
Hospital Entertainer Richard Muttonchops

Music Dominic Muldowney
Director Peter Symes
Producer Fiona Finlay
Camera Mike Fox, John Daly
Editor Peter Simpson
Researcher Harriet Bakewell

Staff of Whernside Ward, High Royds Hospital

Day: John Tennison (Acting Senior Charge Nurse); Steve Toal (Charge Nurse); Bob Moran (Acting Charge Nurse); Angela Fielding (Senior Staff Nurse); Robert Maginnis (Senior Staff Nurse); Liz Young (Staff Nurse); Irene Kirk (Enrolled Nurse); Mand Morland (EN); Kamla Suarez (EN); Maria Withy; Joan Ambler; Peter Stott; Rita Jefferson; Sarah Haley; Christine Miller; Pilar Haney; Sheila Brown; Audrey Robinson; Heather Dalton; Christina Acebal; Olive Watson

Night: Denis Stanley (EN); Anita Johnson (EN); Ann Miller; Jenny Roe; Audrey Wilton; Joyce McIntosh; Pat Renton; Paddy Suraweera

Christine Davey (Cleaner); Joyce Cockroft (Housekeeper)

Choir of St Mary's R.C. Comprehensive School, Menston

Philip Blackledge; Clair-Marie Bloomer; Terrenia Brosnan;
Naomi Chetterley; Deborah Clark; Elena Claughton;
John Connor; Natalie Davis; Duncan Hall; Sadie Hassell;
Helen Lewis; Catherine Reynolds; Christina Rigby;
Catherine Rowan; David Stead

Choirmaster David Mountford

MUSICAL NOTE

*The dialogue and songs in this script are modelled on the
following music:*

1 'Daisy, Daisy, give me your answer do!'
(Words and music: Harry Dacre)

2. 'Oh! You Beautiful Doll'
(Music: Nat D. Ayer. Words: A. Seymour Brown)

3. *'Vogliatemi bene'* from Act I, *Madame Butterfly,*
by Puccini

4. 'In the Bleak Midwinter' (arr: Holst)

*In the script the following abbreviations are used to
indicate which model of pre-existing music a particular
line follows:*

DD	'Daisy Daisy' (a verse of 6 lines)
BD	'Beautiful Doll' (a verse of 7 lines)
BMW	'Bleak Midwinter' (a verse of 4 lines)

1. EXT. HIGH ROYDS HOSPITAL, DAY

A Yorkshire dry-stone wall. The clock tower of High Royds Hospital, Menston, near Ilkley, is first glimpsed through a crack in the dry-stone wall, then seen in the distance as the central feature of a large Victorian psychiatric hospital, opened in 1888 as the West Yorkshire Paupers' Lunatic Asylum.

Soundtrack: a recording from c. 1950 of Maria Tobin singing 'Vogliatemi bene' from the end of Act 1 of Madame Butterfly, *in an English translation:*

'Ah, love me a little,
Oh just a very little,
As you would love a baby.
'Tis all that I ask for . . .'

> *Old recording fades down on high note, and Maria Tobin, the resident of Whernside Ward, 1992, fades up singing what might be regarded as her one surviving note from* Madame Butterfly.

2. INT. WHERNSIDE WARD, HIGH ROYDS HOSPITAL, DAY

Beginning with Maria Tobin, five residents of Whernside Ward, all victims of Alzheimer's disease in its various stages, address us directly, like newsreaders or storytellers, but in their own form of progressively disintegrating English. They are:

MARIA TOBIN (*b*. 1912)
DOROTHY CHAPLIN (*b*. 1927)
with MURIEL ALLEN (*b*. 1927) IN THE BACKGROUND
MURIEL PRIOR (*b*. 1913)
IRENE CLEMENTS (*b*. 1920)
KATHLEEN DICKENSON (*b*. 1908)

MARIA TOBIN

O murals, the babble of ewes,
beautiful Jews.
I said 'Oo . . . Mm . . . I'll come and buy another two.'

Laughs.

He said, 'Everything is right!'
I said, 'Oo, that's good!'
Yes, it would be better.
It's nicer when they come in
and they're not worrying all the day.

DOROTHY CHAPLIN

Oo flippin' 'eck it . . . it's like . . .
Oo 'eck . . . 'eckykyeck.
And then . . .
t'bloomin' clegs have to come a down a bit
and, er . . .

Claps.

Oh get downstairs, them . . . them bloody steps!

Laughs.

Muriel Allen drums her feet rhythmically in the background.

MURIEL PRIOR

I love you!
I love you!
I love you!
I love you!

IRENE CLEMENTS

The only poory, poory, poory, poory
lickit in the Andes.
Take it over they're playing it then.

Laughs. Maria Tobin's one note is heard.

Come alongdong then, darling doggy!
Dindin, and you'll gettyget.

*Kathleen Dickenson utters stream of untranscribable
consonants and vowels, apparently meaningless but
with much of the intention, rhythm and ghostly
structure of communication.*

3. EXT. HIGH ROYDS HOSPITAL, DAY

A reflected cloud passes through a hospital window.

*Sound track: Maria Tobin's one trilled surviving note
from* Madame Butterfly *is gradually obliterated by the
distant sound of an electric tug used for carrying waste
and meals down the long hospital corridors. Its sound is
like that of the chilling wind of a gathering winter storm.
Both cloud and tug forebode the blizzard of forgetfulness.*

4. INT. WHERNSIDE WARD, DAY

*Rhythmical montage begins with two patients – Mabel
Frost, eating at a table, and Gladys Middleton, seated –
calling out their characteristic repetitive cries.*

MABEL FROST

Come! Come! Come! Come! Come! . . .

GLADYS MIDDLETON

Tell us!

5. INT. HIGH ROYDS HOSPITAL, MAIN HALL

Intercut with Whernside Ward (continuing montage).

The Therapist arrives through the main door, and walks down tiled corridor over mosaics of black daisies dating from the earliest period of the hospital.

The Therapist's walking rhythm is intercut with patients' cries, beating hands, feet, the swaying of nurses' watches, etc.

6. INT. LONG CORRIDOR LEADING TO WHERNSIDE WARD, DAY

The Therapist walks the length of the corridor towards Whernside Ward door with its red sign.

An electric hospital tug, carrying yellow and blue waste bags, overtakes the Therapist.

A Male Patient, probably from a ward for schizophrenics, walks in a black raincoat down the long corridor, smoking. His clouds of smoke hang in slanting shafts of sunlight.

The Therapist passes a seated Woman Patient sitting on one of the fold-down seats provided in the long corridor. The Woman Patient takes a puff from a cigarette in her right hand. The Woman Patient takes a puff from a cigarette in her left hand.

The Therapist approaches the door of Whernside Ward.

7. INT. WHERNSIDE WARD, DAY

The Therapist arrives and is greeted by Maria Tobin singing her 'one note out of Butterfly'.

MARIA TOBIN
(*voice-over*)

But it has to be told!

The Therapist and Maria Tobin walk together towards Nursing Office, with Maria Tobin again giving voice to her note.

8. INT. WHERNSIDE WARD NURSING OFFICE, DAY

The Therapist greets Senior Charge Nurse John Tennison in the Nursing Office. They look at the board of residents' names and discuss one of them, namely Muriel Allen.

Close-up: name board and name: MURIEL ALLEN.

They turn and look out of the window of the Nursing Office onto the ward.

9. INT. WHERNSIDE WARD. DAY

The Therapist sings 'Daisy, Daisy' to Muriel Allen.

Muriel Allen stops her repetitive moans and listens briefly, but does not respond.

THERAPIST
(*sings*)

Daisy, Daisy, give me your answer do!
I'm half crazy all for the love of you!
It won't be a stylish marriage,
I can't afford a carriage,
But you'll look sweet upon the seat
Of a bicycle made for two.

Daisy, Daisy . . .

The Therapist tails off in disappointment.

11. INT. WHERNSIDE WARD, DAY

Muriel Allen, having disengaged herself from the efforts of the Therapist, wanders within reach of the seated Eleanor Bellerby, who makes to grab her.

12. INT. WHERNSIDE WARD, NURSING OFFICE, DAY

The Therapist sits in the office with John Tennison.

THERAPIST [DD 6]
She sang Daisy two weeks ago!

John Tennison looks from his work to the Therapist, acknowledging the disappearance of the very last song in Muriel Allen's dwindled repertoire. He then hears a scream from Muriel Allen, being attacked by Eleanor Bellerby outside the Nursing Office. John Tennison leaves to deal with the fracas.

13. INT. WHERNSIDE WARD, DAY

JOHN TENNISON [DD 1A]
Ladies! Ladies!

14. INT. NURSING OFFICE, DAY

The Therapist looks out at John Tennison separating the squabbling women.

THERAPIST [DD 1B, 2]
(*voice-over*)
Thinking what they've all been
makes Alzheimer's horrible . . . obscene.

15. INT. WHERNSIDE WARD

Wordless music [DD 3, 4]. Maria Tobin sings her one note out of Butterfly'.

16. INT. NURSING OFFICE

John Tennison, returning from separating the two women, pauses to register Maria Tobin's note, and offers it as some comfort to the disappointed Therapist.

JOHN TENNISON [DD 5A]
She always sings –

John Tennison passes Therapist and sits at desk.

THERAPIST [DD 5B, 6]
but everything's
her one note out of *Butterfly*!

Maria Tobin sings her note again.

THERAPIST [DD 1–6]
Listen! Listen! You remember that time before
I tried Maria with the Puccini score.
But every bar that I was playing
had only her one A in,
the one trilled A she sings all day
and she never remembers more.

The phone on John Tennison's desk rings. John Tennison answers it.

JOHN TENNISON [DD 1A]
Whernside! Hold on!

John Tennison places his hand over the receiver and turns to the Therapist, who is preparing to leave.

THERAPIST [DD 1B]
. . . Next session's Muriel Prior.

The Therapist looks through the glass window of the Nursing Office towards Muriel Prior being seated by nurses in the ward.

THERAPIST [DD 2]
(*voice over, thinking*)
She could be one who music might inspire!

JOHN TENNISON [DD 3–6]
With Christmas about to happen
We've got that banjo chap 'n
He might get through with one or two.
After him there's St Mary's choir.

John Tennison turns back, takes his hand off the
receiver, and speaks to his caller.

The Therapist leaves the Nursing Office.

17. INT. WHERNSIDE WARD, ENTRANCE CORRIDOR, DAY

The Therapist presses the four numbers on the electronic
access security pad that operates the door out of
Whernside Ward into the long hospital corridor.

Close-up of the digits 6288, the numbers which open the
door. The four numbers are synchronised to the first four
notes of the tune of 'Daisy, Daisy', which forms the basis
of the Therapist's Song. The door opens.

THERAPIST
(*voice-over, speaking on opening door*)
(6–2–8–8) Today brought me no success!

The door slams behind the Therapist and her song
begins.

18. INT. LONG HOSPITAL CORRIDOR, DAY

The Therapist walks down the corridor singing the
Therapist's Song, exiting over the entrance hall mosaic
of black daisies, with the main door finally slamming
behind her.

BLACK DAISIES FOR THE BRIDE

*She passes the Male Patient in black raincoat making
a telephone call on the corridor payphone.*

THE THERAPIST'S SONG

(6–2–8–8) Today brought me no success!
Muriel Allen stayed locked in her deep distress.
The monstrous misadventure
of Alzheimer's dementia
has struck one who, who used to do . . .
well, what *did* she do, try and guess?

Muriel Allen, a therapist like me
now beyond all forms of therapy.
And if Alzheimer's doesn't spare a
lifetime professional carer,
and destroys a mind of Muriel's kind,
and a therapist . . . no one's free!

Muriel Allen's days have all gone astray,
life's bright blossoms clutched in one black bouquet.
The music in her still lingers
in twisting, twitching fingers,
and in the beat of sneakered feet
that she drums in the ward all day.

Daisies! Daisies! Their petals black and thrown,
thrown on paths where memories turn to stone.
A black bouquet of these is
for brides Alzheimer's seizes.
The groom beside each white-clad bride
wears a black daisy buttonhole . . .

19. EXT. HIGH ROYDS HOSPITAL, MAIN DOOR

A yellow sign reads PLEASE KEEP THESE DOORS SHUT. *The Therapist exits past the sign with the door slamming behind her, cutting off the last note of her song. She stops to savour the world outside the hospital beneath a black sign which reads* WELCOME TO HIGH ROYDS HOSPITAL. *She looks at the bare winter trees with rooks' nests in their branches, suggesting the pattern of the brain's blood supply with the sections damaged, as an Alzheimer's patient's brain might be revealed through positron emission tomography. An X-ray of forgetfulness.*

In the Therapist's mind a choir of schoolchildren begin to sing to a tune based on 'In the Bleak Midwinter'.

CHOIR [BMW 3]

Songs seem last to leave the brain, leave the brain.

The Therapist crosses to her car parked outside the dormitory of Whernside Ward. We see reflections of the leafless trees in the window of the ward and the shape of a hospital iron bedstead. She pauses by the open door of her car and looks again at the bare brainscan trees on the horizon.

THERAPIST [BMW 4A]
(*voice-over, speaking*)

But in Muriel Allen . . .

The Therapist gets into her car and, when she is seated, sings [BMW 4B].

. . . none remain.

Soundtrack: the sound of a hospital electric tug moving down the long corridor, like the sound of an ominous wind. It is the beginning of the blizzard of forgetfulness. The blizzard starts with a few flakes of wedding confetti in the shapes of bells, hearts, loveknots

and horseshoes of various colours falling onto the
windscreen of the therapist's car.

CHOIR [BMW 3, 4]
(*voice-over*)

All life's brightest moments filling hearts and heads,
Alzheimer's, like a blizzard, rips up into shreds.

The blizzard of confetti builds in intensity, obliterating
the Therapist's view of the outside world. As the
blizzard intensifies we hear more sounds of the electric
tug passing down the corridor and the voices of the
Chorus of Relatives of residents of Whernside Ward
recollecting the first stages of the Alzheimer's disease
which afflicts their loved ones. She switches on the
windscreen-wipers, whose rhythm recalls the rhythmical
montage which first introduced us to the hospital.

CHORUS OF RELATIVES

It takes everything away from you, dun't it?
It's the stripping away of all present memory.
The person that you knew is no longer there, but the
   shell is there.
He put his pants on back to front.
Auntie got doubly incontinent.
He couldn't find even simple words for *Scrabble.*
He started ringing me up in the night.
He was always getting lost.
He couldn't sign his name; he couldn't write or anything.
Apple cores in vases, stuck amongst plants.
He was aggressive with his own reflection.
All the ornaments started being painted gold.
It's like a bereavement.
It *is* a bereavement. It's horrible.
She started being lonely and she started losing things,
   hiding things and forgetting things.
She put her windscreen-washer on when I said indicate.

She got a pair of scissors and just cut through an electric
    cable.

20. INT. WHERNSIDE WARD NURSING OFFICE, DAY

*The Ward Cleaner with the same rhythm as the
windscreen-wipers erases writing from the board where
the residents' names are listed.*

*A Nurse (whom we will later see singing as the young
bride Maria Tobin) writes in a space in the list of names
the name* MARIA TOBIN *in red marker ink.*

CHORUS OF RELATIVES
(*voice-over*)

My mother could put a dress together in two minutes,
    absolutely fabulous, she was a fantastic woman.
The way she made friends was amazing.
She helped people who were in trouble, she comforted
    them.

21. INT. WHERNSIDE WARD, DAY

*Maria Tobin seated in a chair beneath a decoration of
white plastic roses and lilies of the valley.*

MARIA TOBIN

We're all happy, we're all knotting.
I went in the other day and pushed the . . .
. . . my knitwell for the two . . .
two men and the bends at the back,
that were dying, crying, almost crying . . .
Christ had said to him, 'You're mine!'
and I put the receiver on.
He'd made it all himself.
I didn't like it at all.
And then the Queen Mary came up and sat on top of me.

I went down to see her, and she said . . .
mmm . . .
(*Imitating Queen Mary.*) 'Oh hello dear, how are you?
How are you? Can you help me?'
So I said, 'Well, what are you selling for?'
He says, 'I am charging a change of heel . . .
of *heel*!'
You've got to watch your watch as . . . as stead.
So this poor lad had to wait . . .
wait for his lotchester.
So I went and locked it in,
left it in, and he came in.
He just had it in today.
I put it on my head. (*Laughs.*)
I said, 'Oo God! I can't lose my lids now.'

> *Touches hair as if to prepare herself for some
> important occasion.*

I'm going to get all my colls today,
Yes, milk core . . . milk call and my crepe silk paws.

> *She hears her young self singing 'Ah, love me a little'
> from* Madame Butterfly. *She sighs.*

Cosi fai?
Che besogna?

> *The camera tilts from Maria Tobin up to the bouquet
> of white plastic roses and lilies of the valley.*

> *Mix to:*

22. ROSTRUM CAMERA SHOT

*Rostrum camera shot of the wedding photograph of
Maria Tobin. The bride carries a bouquet identical to the
arrangement of white plastic roses and lilies of the valley
in the ward.*

The photograph is seen through the mesh of the window of the door out of Whernside Ward, framed by the cream-coloured door. To the right of the window a blue and white circular sign reads FIRE DOOR KEEP SHUT. *The camera pulls focus from the window mesh to Maria Tobin in all her bridal glory.*

Soundtrack: the Puccini aria in the young Maria Tobin's recording continues.

23. INT. ENTRANCE CORRIDOR, WHERNSIDE WARD, DAY

The Nurse (who is to sing as the young bride Maria Tobin) walks towards the door of Whernside Ward and presses the 6288 access code to exit. As the numbers are pressed, Maria Tobin's song is cued by four notes synchronised to the nurse's finger on each digit. The song is an arrangement of the original Puccini aria recorded by the young Maria Tobin c. 1950.

24. INT. LONG CORRIDOR OUTSIDE WHERNSIDE WARD, DAY

The door opens. The door slams behind the Nurse, who is transformed into the young Maria Tobin dressed in all her wedding finery and carrying a bouquet of roses and lilies of the valley. Everything about her appearance matches the original photograph. She begins to sing the once-familiar but now forgotten Puccini aria, and as she does so she moves down the corridor, away from the presentiment of her future residence on Whernside Ward, represented by the Voices of Nurses in her head.

THE SONG OF THE BRIDE I
MARIA TOBIN

MARIA TOBIN

My name's Maria Tobin!
Yes, half of Leeds was gawping and throwing confetti,
ooing that I'm so pretty,
but now the cloud I'm under, dark'ning my mem'ry,
buries my piano with *Butterfly* score on.

Following the musical line where Butterfly's lover,
B. F. Pinkerton, responds to her in the original Puccini
score, the Voices of Nurses are heard cajoling or
cautioning Maria Tobin, the present resident on
Whernside Ward.

VOICES OF NURSES
(*voice-over*)

Breakfast, Maria, put your pinafore on!
Maria, NO! That's an electric cable!
Sing us a song, Maria!

MARIA TOBIN
(*distancing herself from the voices*)

I knew so much Puccini
Bohème and *Butterfly*
Now I've forgotten and my flutt'ring Butterfly's on . . .
on a dark'ning horizon.

VOICE OF NURSE
(*voice-over*)

Maria, come and sing!

MARIA TOBIN
(*voice-over*)

That bloody 'Daisy' song!

VOICE OF THERAPIST
(*voice-over, singing*)
'Give me your answer do.'

MARIA TOBIN
(*voice-over*)
My answer's NO then!
That bloody 'Daisy, Daisy!'

MARIA TOBIN
Maria!
I've lost Maria!
Maria!

25. INT. END OF LONG CORRIDOR. AUTOMATIC DOORS

The young bride searches for her lost self, singing her own name, and as she approaches the doors marked with blue and yellow signs AUTOMATIC DOORS – KEEP CLEAR *they open onto a dark oblivion through which a blizzard of confetti blows, obliterating the torn poster on which can still be read* MARIA TOBIN, ITALIAN OPERA STAR.

As the automatic doors close they trap the train of the wedding dress, crushing the silver appliquéd shape of what might be both loveknot or butterfly. The image recalls the exchange between Madame Butterfly and Pinkerton on the fragile nature of the butterfly, and Butterfly's fears of suffering a similar fate to the delicate, pierced creature whose name she bears.

PINKERTON
Mia Butterfly
Come t'han ben nomata
Tenue farfalla . . .

BUTTERFLY

Dicon ch'oltre mare
Se cade in man dell'uom
Ogni farfalla d'uno spillo
E trafitta
Ed in tavola infitta!

26. INT. WHERNSIDE WARD, DAY

Darkness on the entrance corridor. It is early morning.
The Housekeeper, Joyce Cockcroft, switches on a light,
and then another.

Close-up of rows of tea mugs. From a large metal teapot
the first of the mugs are filled.

Maria Tobin is given a mug of tea by the Nurse (who we
have just seen singing the Song of the Bride 1).

Another Nurse gives a mug of tea to another resident.

From the door marked FEMALE DORMITORY, *Muriel*
Prior, supported by Nurses Steve Toal and Maria Withy,
emerges, shuffling with difficulty. She is helped to sit at a
table.

Kathleen Dickenson is seated at a table, drinking tea.
Irene Clements is seated at a table, staring ahead,
seemingly lost in concentration. On her left the former
therapist Muriel Allen is seated and begins to scream in
her characteristic way. The Choir sings throughout.

CHOIR [BMW 1, 2]
Muriel Prior's scarcely able still to walk,
only says 'I love you' if and when she'll talk.

[BMW 1–4]
Slowly they're forgetting everything they've been,
accordionist like Kathleen, crooner like Irene.

197

Songs that Irene used to croon, used to croon,
though the words are garbled still have tune.

[BMW 1,2]
Irene hates such noises, Muriel Allen's shriek,
they disturb her music fading week by week.

IRENE CLEMENTS
(*sync*)
Shut up you, you bugger and deggarad.

CHOIR [BMW 1–4]
Kathleen played piano, played accordion too,
sometimes her hands remember what they used to do.

But mostly Kathleen cleans and cleans, cleans and cleans
as though the home she lives in's still Kathleen's.

[BMW 1–4]
And it's bustling Kathleen's most repeated chore
to wipe and clean and polish Whernside Ward's locked
    door.

Kathleen Dickenson tries the door and finds it locked.

Kath's caressing fingers coaxed, coaxed accordion chord
but can't press the door-code that opens Whernside Ward.

*Kathleen Dickenson spends a good deal of her day
bustling energetically around Whernside Ward, cleaning
almost every object she comes into contact with,
licking her forefinger and index finger, and applying
the spittle to the object intended to be cleaned and
polished. She is seen going through this daily routine.*

27. INT. WHERNSIDE WARD NURSING OFFICE, DAY

The Ward Cleaner (who is to sing the Song of the Bride II)
writes on the board of residents' names the name
KATHLEEN DICKENSON *in green marker ink.*

CHORUS OF RELATIVES

(*Kathleen Dickenson's niece, voice-over*)

Auntie was very kind and gentle; loved children. Danced
with 'em, sang with 'em.

She used to play the piano for 'em, play the accordion
for 'em, learn 'em how to knit and crochet.

She used to grow all her own flowers, vegetables. She
never bought a vegetable. I don't think there were
anything she couldn't do, you know, when she was
all right.

She was ever so clever . . . Yes . . . yes . . .

28. INT. WHERNSIDE WARD, DAY

*Kathleen Dickenson, after her seemingly endless cleaning
chores, is resting in a chair beneath a shelf with an
arrangement of white plastic lilies. She looks up and is
apparently thinking. The camera tilts up to the flowers.*

Mix to:

29. ROSTRUM CAMERA SHOT

*Rostrum camera shot of the wedding photograph of
Kathleen Dickenson with her husband Harold. The bride
carries a bouquet identical to the arrangement of white
plastic lilies in the ward.*

*The photograph is seen through the mesh of the window
of the door out of Whernside Ward, framed by the
cream-coloured door. To the right of the window a blue
and white circular sign reads* FIRE DOOR KEEP SHUT.
*The camera pulls focus from the window mesh to the
photograph of the married couple.*

30. INT. ENTRANCE CORRIDOR, WHERNSIDE WARD, DAY

A Ward Cleaner in blue overalls walks towards the door of Whernside Ward and presses the 6288 access code to exit. As the numbers are pressed the Song of the Bride II *is cued by four notes from the tune of 'Oh! You Beautiful Doll' (Ayer, arr. Muldowney). The door opens and the blue overall passes through the frame.*

31. INT. LONG HOSPITAL CORRIDOR

The flaring hem of the cream silk wedding dress of Kathleen Dickenson, and a pair of white high-heeled shoes, emerge through the bottom of the open door.

The door slams shut. Kathleen Dickenson in her wedding dress begins to sing the Song of the Bride II.

She moves down the corridor with the kind of energy that is still apparent in her older self, but her relish and energy are shadowed by a presentiment of her future and she sees through a corridor window the continuous blizzard of forgetfulness.

THE SONG OF THE BRIDE II
KATHLEEN DICKENSON

Yeah, a motorbike bride, I'm Kath the motorbike bride.
Harold and me we used to court on
a BSA and then a Norton,
Harold, him steering, and me, me in the car at the side,
motorbiked to mountains, me and Harold went
up Mickle Fell, and up Penyghent,
c . . . c . . . c . . . can't you still tell from my stride?

And together we'd bike to every good mountainous scene.
Wrapped up well in warm windjammers,

gazed at peak-top panoramas,
those long vistas of green, those great long vistas of green.

Climbed up Whernside, Yorkshire's toughest peak,
that out of puff we couldn't speak

Three breaths.

. . . till Harold said   'I love you, Kathleen!'
                         'I love you, Kathleen!'
                         'I love you, Kathleen!'

Nothing, nothing of that, nothing, none of it stays,
motorbiking, mountaineering,
lost in mists I won't see clearing,
lost in the blizzard of days, the burying blizzard of days.
From the Whernside tramped up in our mountain gear
to this Whernside wandered with no Harold here,
and . . . and . . . and . . . those . . . long green vistas all
   greys.

Voice-over camera track around Kathleen Dickenson,
the present resident on Whernside Ward.

. . .
. . .
. . .
. . .

If I hadn't lost the power to reminisce
these are the moments that my heart would miss,
m . . . m . . . m . . . m . . . moments on mountains with
   him.

The bride on the corridor drops her bouquet.

(And my fingers were green, won every gardening prize.
No one's fingers could be greener
than Kathleen's, our restless cleaner.
Feasts for the lips as well as feasts for the eyes –

pies from home-grown rasps, pies from home-grown
   straws,
pies out of bil'bries off of Ilkley Moors,
g . . . g . . . g . . . garden-grown gooseberry pies!)

If you want to know who, you really want to know who,
who she's been then cast your eyes on
cloth she crocheted butterflies on,
fish Kath caught with her rod, these fruits that Kathleen
   once grew.
Kathleen was, before Alzheimer's cruelly struck,
an angler, climber, dancer, gardener, cook –
now . . . now . . . now . . . now . . . Kath knows nothing
   she knew.

All I remember is four or, at the very most, five
words that still've got some meaning
spending days on Whernside cleaning,
not much memory left, soon even less'll survive.
With Alzheimer's shredding all remembered time,
the blizzard's blowing, but Godammit I'm . . .
g . . . gl . . . gla . . . glad . . . I'm still Kath and alive!
                              I'm still Kath and alive!
                              I'm still Kath and alive!

32. INT. END OF LONG CORRIDOR, AUTOMATIC DOORS

Before the automatic doors, on which can be read the
blue and yellow signs reading AUTOMATIC DOORS –
KEEP CLEAR, *is set a table covered with a white*
tablecloth with crocheted butterflies and vine leaves
made many years before by the Kathleen Dickenson who
is now a resident on Whernside Ward. On the table are
laid plates and bowls filled with the products of Kathleen
Dickenson's gardening and angling. There is a bowl of
raspberries, a bowl of strawberries, some sticks of
rhubarb (the most commonly grown fruit in Leeds),

*a bowl of gooseberries and a number of runner beans.
There is a blue plate patterned with butterflies with four
trout freshly caught by Kathleen Dickenson herself as a
young champion angler. There is a vase of blue and
yellow flowers from her garden.*

*The bride circles the table, trailing her fingers along the
edge of the plate with the fish. Her white-clad reflection
passes across the shiny wet bodies of the fish. Her
wedding veil snags briefly on a protruding stick of
rhubarb.*

*As a final affirmation of an undiminished relish for
existence, the bride, Kathleen Dickenson picks up the
bowl of her home-grown strawberries, and savours their
scent and deliciousness. She turns with the bowl and the
automatic doors open. They open onto a dark oblivion
with a blizzard of confetti. The bride disappears slowly
into the darkness swirling with confetti.*

Cut to:

33. INT. WHERNSIDE WARD, DAY

*A table with a plastic bowl of strawberry yoghurt and
a spoon. The spoon, full of yoghurt and spilling over,
is lifted to the mouth of Kathleen Dickenson. Yoghurt
drops from the spoon to the floor.*

*Kathleen Dickenson sits at the table to finish her yoghurt.
Nurse Sheila leaves frame to feed another patient and
speaks to the Ward Cleaner (who is under the table
cleaning up Kathleen Dickenson's spilled yoghurt).*

> SHEILA [BD 1A]
Oo, our Kath likes her food!

> WARD CLEANER [BD 1B]
> It's remarkable how they all eat!

SHEILA [BD2, 3A]
Odd, how men all end up needing,
more than women do . . .

WARD CLEANER [BD 3B]
(*voice-over*)
. . . Spoon feeding!

SHEILA [BD 4A]
(*voice-over*)
But then isn't that men!

John Tennison enters with a plate of meat stew
intended for Mathew Paul. He places the plate on the
table.

JOHN TENNISON [BD 4B, 5, 6]
. . . though some aren't admitting defeat.
Like Mathew Paul . . . who'll soon forget
what a fork's used for, but not yet . . .
. . . proud he still can manage his meat.

CHOIR [BMW 3, 4]
All his soul says '*Go away, go away!*'
To the blizzard worsening every day.

[BMW 1–4]
Two more months of mealtimes left for Mathew Paul
before the fork he fights with makes its final fall.

And Mathew Paul he kept his pride, kept his pride,
for two more months of mealtimes, then he died.

The last note is cut off by Mathew Paul's fork falling
from his hand onto his plate. The sounds of a hospital
tug, like the distant gusts of a blizzard.

34. INT. WHERNSIDE WARD ENTRANCE CORRIDOR, DAY

The face of Maria Tobin appears at the glass panel of the door of Whernside Ward, gazing down the long corridor.

35. INT. LONG CORRIDOR LEADING TO WHERNSIDE WARD, DAY

The Therapist arrives on another visit to Whernside Ward, this time for a session with Muriel Prior.

36. INT. WHERNSIDE WARD, DAY

Muriel Prior, supported by Nurses Irene Kirk and Sheila Brown, shuffles slowly towards a table.

CHOIR [BMW 1–4]
(*voice-over*)

Muriel Prior's scarcely able still to walk,
only says 'I love you' if and when she'll talk.

Two names though are still entwined, still entwined
in a loveknot deep in Muriel's mind.

37. INT. WHERNSIDE WARD, NURSING OFFICE, DAY

A Nurse (who will sing the Song of the Bride III*) writes on the name board the name of Muriel Prior.*

38. INT. WHERNSIDE WARD, DAY

The Therapist sits close to Muriel Prior. She writes on a pad the names MURIEL *and* JIM.

THERAPIST
(*pointing to first name*)
What does this say, Muriel?

MURIEL PRIOR

Muriel.

Therapist now points to the name JIM *written on the pad.*

MURIEL PRIOR
(*reading*)

Jim!
My husband!

Soundtrack: the first two notes of the Song of the Bride III – *based on the Therapist's 'Daisy, Daisy' (Dacre, arr. Muldowney) – seem both to attract Muriel Prior's attention and to activate the 6–2 of the Whernside Ward door's access code: 6288.*

39. WHERNSIDE WARD ENTRANCE CORRIDOR, DAY

Close-up of a finger pressing the final digits 8–8 of the access code 6288. The 8–8 is synchronised to the third and fourth notes of the Song of the Bride III.

A blue nurse's uniform passes through the frame. The door opens.

40. INT. LONG HOSPITAL CORRIDOR, DAY

The Nurse emerges as the young bride Muriel Prior.

Close-up of the young Muriel Prior's eyes, which remind us of the characteristic eye movement of the old Muriel Prior. She sings and is revealed in all her wedding finery, and she walks down the long corridor singing the Song of the Bride III.

On the line: 'but me the bride stays locked outside / and can't walk into Whernside Ward', the Bride turns towards the door of Whernside Ward, and is seen in

*reverse angle through the mesh of the window of the
door out of the Ward, framed by the cream-coloured
door. To the right of the window a blue and white
circular sign reads* FIRE DOOR KEEP SHUT.

*After the lines: 'Muriel! Muriel! Some moments when
I call / I feel you hear me but mostly not at all', the
Bride makes a characteristic eye movement left, where
she sees through the open fanlight of a corridor window
gusts of the blizzard of confetti and forgetfulness.*

*Cut to: close-up of the bouquet of fresh anemones, on
which a few flakes of confetti fall. As she moves out of
frame we cut back to her older self on Whernside Ward.*

THE SONG OF THE BRIDE III
MURIEL PRIOR

Mem'ry! Mem'ry! There's no access code or key
into memories old Muriel shared with me,
but something I started saying
survives until today in
her 'I love you', that's when us two
are together as we should be.

(Muriel! Muriel! Behind those big blue eyes
mem'ry's dying before the person dies.
It's like old Mother Hubbard
with memory as the cupboard.
It's been stripped bare of what was there
though you'd stocked up a life's supplies.)

Muriel! Muriel! We should have a great hoard
of life's best moments gathered with love and stored.
We should have a mem'ry brimming
with scenes with us and Jim in

but me the bride stays locked outside
and can't walk into Whernside Ward.

Muriel! Muriel! Some moments when I call
I feel you hear me but mostly not at all.
There's a blizzard now dividing
the day you were a bride in
from these you'll spend until the end
watching burying flurries fall.

(Muriel! Muriel! Sometimes when I call
I feel you hear me but mostly not at all.
Your steady blue-eyed gaze is
through blizzards to black daisies,
where once there grew of every hue,
life as full as a flower stall.)

Muriel! Muriel! I'm the Muriel who wed
but your memories of being me are fled.
You've forgotten when you married
the anemones you carried,
the sad thing is, anemones
stand unnoticed above your head.

Getting quieter.

Muriel! Muriel! My voice in your ear grows less,
fading into the storm of forgetfulness.
If life gave you back tomorrow
our memories, joy and sorrow,
not just the best, but all the rest,
would you want to relive them . . . ?

MURIEL PRIOR
(*the resident in Whernside Ward*)
YES!

41. ROSTRUM CAMERA SHOT

Rostrum camera shot of the wedding photograph of Muriel Prior with her husband Jim. The bride carries a bouquet identical to the arrangement of anemones in the ward.

The photograph is seen through the mesh of the window of the door out of Whernside Ward, framed by the cream-coloured door. To the right of the window a blue and white circular sign reads FIRE DOOR KEEP SHUT. *The camera pulls focus from the window mesh to the photograph of the married couple (cf. Scene 22).*

42. INT. WHERNSIDE WARD, DAY

Muriel Prior, seated in a blue chair beneath the arrangement of plastic anemones, as if hearing some verses of the song. As the camera moves from the plastic anemones to her face she answers the final question of the young bride Muriel Prior with a whispered 'Yes!'

MURIEL PRIOR
(*sync*)

'Wh . . . wh . . . what about that . . . that thing that
   I wanted to do?'

CHOIR

Muriel Prior's 'I love you' used to fill the air.
Now she's a nurse's memory and an empty chair.

43. INT. WHERNSIDE WARD NURSING OFFICE, DAY

CHOIR [BMW 1, 2]

Muriel braves the blizzard with her big blue eyes.
In a few more weeks, though, Muriel Prior dies.

   Cut to: the plastic anemones on a shelf above the blue chair in the ward where Muriel Prior always sits.

Behind these shelves the Nurse who sang the Song of
the Bride III *enters from a maroon door marked*
FEMALE TOILET, *wearing white rubber gloves and
carrying a yellow plastic waste sack. She stops to
remove her gloves, and as she does so the camera pans
down from the anemones to the now empty blue
chair.*

*Camera pans down the board of residents' names. We
hear the Choir begin to sing.*

[BMW 1–4]
For the men and women written on this board
Death's got the only door-code out of Whernside Ward.

And till Rene Parker died, Rene died,
her husband's weekly kisses consoled his bride.

[BMW 1–4]
Only eight more kisses then he'll lose his dear,
swept off in the blizzard where brides disappear.

Eight more weeks for Mathew Paul, who says GO AWAY
to the blizzard worsening every day.

[BMW 1, 2]
Though the blizzard's blowing, right until the last
he'll sing 'Daisy, Daisy' through the stormy blast.

44. INT. WHERNSIDE WARD, DAY

*Cut to: a pianist on the ward piano playing 'Daisy,
Daisy'. The camera tracks to discover the Therapist with
Mathew Paul in mid duet:*

. . . It won't be a stylish marriage,
I can't afford a carriage,
But you'll look sweet upon the seat
of a bicycle made for two. (*Etc.*)

Cut to: the sneakered feet of Muriel Allen leaving the frame.

45. INT. WHERNSIDE WARD, ENTRANCE CORRIDOR, DAY

The face of Maria Tobin appears at the meshed glass panel of Whernside Ward door, gazing down the long hospital corridor.

She sees Richard Muttonchops, the hospital entertainer, who enters Whernside Ward with his banjo.

46. INT. WHERNSIDE WARD, DAY

Irene Clements in her fractured English signals the arrival of Richard Muttonchops.

Muttonchops begins to play 'Oh! You Beautiful Doll' to Maria Tobin, who is hand in hand with the Nurse, Joyce McIntosh.

MUTTONCHOPS

Oh! You beautiful doll, you great big beautiful doll!
Let . . . me put my arms about you,
I could never live without you.
Oh! You beautiful doll, you great big beautiful doll!
If you ever leave me how my heart will ache,
I want to hug you, but I fear you'd break,
Oh, oh, oh, oh,
Oh you beautiful doll!

Maria Tobin dances in response, but when she sings she utters the familiar 'one note out of Butterfly'. She says to Muttonchops, 'Well, you are a beautiful doll!' and continues dancing.

Muttonchops serenades seated residents, most of whom show little response until he reaches Irene

*Clements, sitting with Nurse Angela Fielding, who has
her arm around Irene's shoulder, beating time to the
music.*

*Irene Clements begins to sing along with Muttonchops,
though the words are incomprehensible. Nonetheless
the energy and tone of the rendition remind us that
Irene spent many years as a pub crooner.*

*Muttonchops passes on to serenade Kathleen
Dickenson, who is cleaning a central heating radiator
with her fingers. At the sound of the music she turns
and begins to sway in time to the song. It is as if she
is moving to the rhythm of and reclaiming the* Song
of the Bride II *her young self sang in the corridor. It
seems that she's 'glad she's still Kath and alive'.*

47. INT. WHERNSIDE WARD, DAY. CLOSE TO CHRISTMAS

*Maria Tobin, swathed in green Christmas tinsel as if she
were wrapped in furs for the opera, utters her familiar
one note.*

*The ward is being prepared for Christmas. A box of tinsel
decorations and Christmas-tree baubles is deposited on a
table. Five nurses begin to sort out the decorations and
decorate the Christmas tree. They are Maria Bovino,
Sheila Brown, Joyce McIntosh, Audrey Robinson and
Liz Young.*

SHEILA BROWN [BD 1–48]

I bet some memories'll stir, once we've put lights on our
    tree.
Bound to get some mem'ries stirring
with gold and frankincense and myrrh in.
Bound to stir up a few.

LIZ YOUNG [BD 4B]
I hope that's how it'll be!

JOYCE MCINTOSH [BD 5, 6]
When the kids sing carols, though I could be wrong,
I bet a few of ours'll sing along.

SHEILA BROWN [BD 7]
Christmas *always* sets some memories free!

LIZ YOUNG [BD 1–3]
Yes, for someone like you, without Alzheimer's, that's true!

*Liz Young sees Kathleen Dickenson bustling about the
ward, cleaning near another Christmas tree.*

Christmas can't have too much meaning
When you spend all year spring-cleaning!

MARIA BOVINO
Our Maria'll give a wobbly warble or two.
We might just get carols out of Mathew Paul,
a tune from Irene . . .

LIZ YOUNG
. . . but from most, damn all!

SHEILA BROWN
(*voice-over*)
Oh if only something of Christmas gets through!

48. INT. WHERNSIDE WARD NURSING OFFICE, DAY

*Nurse (Maria Bovino) leads Maria Tobin to the Nursing
Office board with residents' names which in the lower
right-hand corner reads:* CHRISTMAS 1992, MUSIC, ST
MARY'S SCHOOL.

MARIA BOVINO
What does that say, Maria?

MARIA TOBIN

Chris . . . mas . . . *la musica!* . . . *Santa Maria!*

CHOIR OF ST MARY'S SCHOOL
(*soundtrack*)

In the bleak midwinter, frosty winds made moan,
earth stood hard as iron, water like a stone;
snow had fallen, snow on snow, snow on snow,
in the bleak midwinter, long ago.

What can I give him, poor as I am?
If I were a shepherd, I would bring a lamb;
if I were a wise man I would do my part,
yet what I can I give him – give my heart.

49. INT. WHERNSIDE WARD, DAY

*The Choir of St Mary's School is singing the carol to the
assembled residents and some of their relatives. Mrs
Benford, the wife of a resident, Harry Benford, is sitting
between him and Irene Clements, who is delivering a
characteristically garbled address to a Ward Cleaner,
Christine Davey. Mrs Benford, thinking that Irene's
conversation is disturbing the carol, begins to conduct
Irene in the rhythm of the carol, and succeeds towards
the end of the verse in inducing Irene to join in the tune,
if not with recognisable words.*

*The camera then pans from Mrs Learoyd, wife of
resident Donald Learoyd, holding his hand, through the
gathered residents, and comes to a halt on Maria Tobin
sitting with Nurse Irene Kirk.*

*Cut to Muriel Allen, former hospital therapist, whose
songless but obsessively rhythmical presence haunts the
performance of the carol.*

*Cut to the face of Maria Tobin at the glass panel of
Whernside Ward door, gazing down the long hospital*

*corridor. She sees a procession of three brides: herself,
Kathleen Dickenson and Muriel Prior.*

The Three Brides begin to sing the Song of the Bride IV.

50. INT. LONG HOSPITAL CORRIDOR, NIGHT

*The Three Brides process slowly down the darkened
corridor until they disappear and Maria Tobin is left
gazing down the long corridor that seems to lead
onward and onward and onward towards oblivion and
forgetfulness. The long, empty hospital corridor finally
mixes to a long fire-break in a forest of forgotten
Christmases.*

THE SONG OF THE BRIDE IV
TRIO

CHOIR [BMW 1–4]
All three brides of Whernside . . .

MARIA
Maria . . .

MURIEL
Muriel . . .

KATHLEEN
Kath.

CHOIR
Who once walked the aisle now walk a stormy path.

KATHLEEN
Kath . . .

MURIEL
Muriel . . .

MARIA

Maria . . .

CHOIR

They've all lost their ways
bearing through the blizzard withering bouquets,

MURIEL [DD 1–4]

turned to daisies, their petals black and strewn,
strewn on paths where carols all lose their tune.
Though the music keeps on playing,
the notes won't stop decaying . . .

MARIA
(*Puccini*)

Though the music keeps on playing
the notes won't stop decaying.

KATHLEEN [BD4]

Lost with black daisy bouquets, in the burying blizzard
of days.

*The corridor is empty. The sound of the hospital tug,
like the gust of a blizzard, becomes almost tempestuous.*

Mix to:

51. EXT. A FIRE-BREAK IN A FIR PLANTATION, DAY

*The camera begins to track past fir tree after fir tree, and
discovers a dark gap in which can be glimpsed the
fluttering remnants of a wedding dress.*

CHOIR [BMW 1–4]
(*voice-over*)

Through these firs oblivion's blizzards blow and moan,
snuffing every Christmas they have ever known.

In the forest mem'ries blur, mem'ries blur
and the lost lose contact with the brides they were.

[BMW 1,2]
If we could give them voices, we would hear them say:
Gather all your mem'ries, savour every day.

And the bride who wore this glove, wore this glove,
bids us all remember songs and love.

*The white elbow-length kid glove worn by Maria
Tobin is wound around the base of a tree. The
blizzard of forgetfulness begins.*

*A· heart-shaped flake of confetti falls into the open
palm of the glove. The blizzard of forgetfulness
intensifies and obliterates the glove in drifts of
confetti. Intense flurries blow among the firs.*

52. EXT. WHERNSIDE WARD GREEN FIRE DOOR, DAY

*Through the blizzard of confetti and forgetfulness, and
the sounds of the hospital tug, now like a threatening
storm, the face of Maria Tobin appears at the glass panel
of the green fire door.*

53. INT. WHERNSIDE WARD, DAY

*Muriel Allen swings the curtains across the frame as the
blizzard sounds from the hospital tug seem to enter the
ward itself.*

*Various faces of residents who hear the blizzard
destroying their memories.*

*Muriel Allen keeps swaying the curtain as she did at the
beginning of the film.*

*The camera pans from the face of Doreen Mitchell up to
a plastic arrangement of carnations, but this time there is
no transformation into the resident as young bride. The
blizzard intensifies.*

54. INT. WHERNSIDE WARD, ENTRANCE CORRIDOR, NIGHT

Maria Tobin hovers around the Whernside Ward door, trying the handle, brushing her fingers over the access code security pad without understanding its function. Her hand passes over the blue and white circular sign that reads FIRE DOOR KEEP SHUT.

> MARIA TOBIN
> (*sync*)

Fire door *kept* shut.

55. INT. LONG HOSPITAL CORRIDOR, NIGHT

The face of Maria Tobin appears at the meshed glass panel of the Whernside Ward door.

> MARIA TOBIN
> (*sync*)

Goodbye darling, thank you very much, don't go far.

56. INT. WHERNSIDE WARD ENTRANCE CORRIDOR, NIGHT

Maria Tobin's point-of-view: a glow of blue and yellow through the meshed glass. The camera pulls focus from the wire of the mesh to discover a hospital tug laden with blue and yellow waste sacks. A blue one nearest the glass panel has a white label which reads GENERAL WASTE.

The tug pulls away with the sound we have associated throughout the film with the blizzard of forgetfulness. It proceeds down the long, darkened corridor.

Close-up of yellow and blue plastic waste sacks with one of the blue sacks bursting open to scatter flakes of confetti in the wake of the hospital tug.

The tug passes through frame still scattering confetti in its wake.

A scattering of still flakes of confetti.

The sound of the hospital tug recedes into the distance.

The sound of the four numbers 6–2–8–8 being pressed. The sound of Whernside Ward door opening, creaking closed, and slamming shut.

The scattered flakes of confetti jump in the gust from the doors and resettle into stillness.

Soundtrack: over the disappearing hospital tug, the voice of the young Maria Tobin is heard singing the lines from Madame Butterfly*:*

Ah, love me a little,
Oh just a very little,
As you would love a baby.
'Tis all that I ask for . . .

The sound of the Whernside Ward door closing cuts off the aria in mid-flow.

A MAYBE DAY IN KAZAKHSTAN
(1994)

A Maybe Day in Kazakhstan was first broadcast on Channel 4 on 1 May 1994.

Steadicam Operator Alekos Yiannaros
Camera Assistant Linos Meitanis
Sound Recordist Nikos Barounis
Telecine Grading Colin Peters, Luke Rainey
Rostrum Camera Ken Morse
Production Managers Ariane Cotsis, Paul Frift
Assistant Producer Alison Carter
Lighting Cameraman Alistair Cameron
Editor Julian Sabbath
Music Richard Blackford

Executive Producer Michael Kustow
Producer Andrew Holmes
Directed by Mark Kidel and Tony Harrison

Produced in association with the Foundation for Hellenic Culture

A city wall not quite sure where,
no May Day posters plastered there.

Flea market.

Although it's May Day no parade
disturbs the new free world of trade,
only the memory of a choir
and from it one voice rising higher

The lyra *man.*

out of a red doll standing near a
man who bows a Black Sea *lyra.*
I seek directions from the man
who welcomes me to 'Kazakhstan!'

What sometimes haunts these traders' looks
are dark nights and days in cattle trucks.

Cold dark deportation trains
still jolt and judder through their brains.

From Black Sea coast to Kazakhstan
cooped up in a cattle van.

Confined to Kazakhstan and far
from Sukhumi and Krasnodar.

May Day comes and haunts a man
with memories of Kazakhstan.

Flag-seller.

Red flags he flogs for what he can
once flew high in 'Kazakhstan!'

This flea market that's now free
from surveillance by the KGB,
though things to aid the human eye
take aim, survey or even spy
are all part of this pavement trade
police no longer keep surveyed.
The free market, seller/buyer
of tablecloths and *Stolichnaya*,
hats made of Siberian furs,
and surplus Soviet secateurs
we see flea-market browsers feel
to test the sharpness of the steel.

Maybe they once cut the wire
that put barbed confines round a choir,
not for pruning plants but man
collectivised in Kazakhstan.

   Red dolls.

They seem to sell these everywhere
as talismans against despair,
these little dolls on every stall
no force seems able to make fall.
The doll, no matter what the drop, 'll
come up trilling from her topple,
cling to her song and go on clinging
though Kazakhstan could crush her singing,
collectivised and forced by rote
to still the *lyra* in her throat.

   Tools and spare parts.

We see in these flea-market scenes
all the system's stilled machines,
the bit, the drill, the cog, the gear,
the technology of yesteryear.
The hammer once gripped in the fist

of Stakhanovite and Stalinist
or cast in gold as an award
for greater output quotas scored.
The Stakhanovites have all downed tools
and live by new free-market rules.
And no red flags to stitch or darn
means surpluses of scarlet yarn.

   Red Army uniform.

The people's flags of deepest red
novel coverlets to drape a bed.
And uniforms have been sloughed off,
redundant after Gorbachev,
mere novelties a trader peddles,
not in Red Square impaled with medals
bouncing on breasts as brass bands play
marchers and missiles through May Day.

This march-past's only shoppers' feet
browsing on flea-market street
in various shoes, high heels or suede,
not in black boots and on parade.

   Old woman knitting.

She sees their feet from where she's sitting
on the pavement, peddling, knitting.
And maybe all her bright bootees
will walk to better times than these,
not crash their heels to May Day brass
as medalled smilers watch them pass,
not keep in step, or form in ranks
and march as boots in front of tanks.
And maybe the head that wears this bonnet
won't ever need a gas mask on it . . .

   Gas masks.

The Kazakhstan these masks come from
was the test site for the Soviet bomb.
And choristers in gas masks gag
and can't perform the People's Flag.
The most you'll ever get from them
's a fearful muffled requiem.
The metronome these masks employ
gets sold here as a gruesome toy.

   Radiation meters.

These meters dumped in great amounts
measure radiation counts.

Army issue anti-gas
and army-surplus May Day brass
some Kazakh or Uzbek brigade
marched past with playing on parade.

They need a new tune to redeem
the redness of the old regime.

   Toy xylophone.

The tune we hear three browsers play
still haunts them though it's had its day.

Pavement peddlers trading trash
from Communism's fatal crash,
salvaging the washed-up cargo
from their ill-fated, shattered *Argo*,
spewing from its kitsch-crammed hold
debris to be bought and sold,
and all that spewed-up spillage sprawls
on these pathetic pavement stalls.

Doomed Argonauts condemned to peddle
the bric-à-brac of badge and medal
from that doomed voyage that maroons

   Lenin.

228

Lenin here with fork and spoons,
cast in bronze now cast away
to read *Das Kapital* all day.
Most stalls sell his statuette
(though I haven't seen one bought here yet),
this manikin time's mummified
in philosophical formaldehyde,
and behind bronze Vladimir Ilyich
(once you've pressed his little switch)
there, in strange surgical disguise,

   Trotsky.

Dr Trotsky rolls his eyes
drinking his prescribed solution,
only his eyes in revolution
and that by no means permanent
once Dr Trotsky's battery's spent.
And Trotsky drinks and drinks and drinks
because the new free market stinks.
Though New World Order mongers crow
that History's got nowhere to go
and make the socialist despair
it's ever going anywhere,
the New World Order thinks we're wiser
when every man's a merchandiser.
But Trotsky goes on making toasts
to *glasnost* and the gulag ghosts.
The foundered *Argo*'s former crew
now peddling here on pavements new,
marooned in free flea-market forces
with no sights fixed on future courses,
what new horizons do they scan,
these castaways from Kazakhstan?

They scan the market where they are,
not Sukhumi or Krasnodar . . .

and not Georgia, Tblis
(Thlisi, Georgia) but Greece –
not the Black Sea coast Sukhum
but to Athens, Greece, that they've all come.
This market wasn't Kazakhstan
but where democracy began

Acropolis.

two millennia and a half ago
which makes its progress pretty slow.

Athinas Street, Athens.

This flea-market Athens street
is where a dream and nightmare meet.
These peddlers, Greeks, once deportees
to Kazakhstan, call Kleisthenes,
democracy's first dreamer, kin
(a dream they want including in)
so come to Greece to reconnect
and salvage lives that Stalin wrecked
and get to feel like Greeks again,
though Greeks still call them Soviet men,
forced out of Georgia and displaced
from fertile farms to barren waste,
at two hours' notice packed in trains
to Central Asia's arid plains.

Archive. Song (tune: 'Red Flag').

'Forced from our farm in Sukhumi
though full of tears my eyes could see
the cotton glow, a golden fleece
cold in moonlight far from Greece.

Though long ago I've not forgotten
the moonglow on the Kazakh cotton
when we staggered from the cattle van
collectivised in Kazakhstan.'

Their nightmares in the old regime
have not quite dimmed the ancient dream.

  Tubas.

Two Soviet tubas, silver, brass,
struggle through the May Day mass,
tubas in whose bulled-up gleam
red flags blazoned the regime,
tubas in which bazookas shone
reflecting coats with medals on,
tubas with missiles mirrored in,
now, unregimented, can begin
to learn a new tune for today
and play a fanfare not for May
but Maybe Day and that maybe
's the future of democracy.

  Procession up Acropolis.

Two tubas join their band to blow
as jaunty a new *Jubilo*
as may be hazarded in days
when only a muffled fanfare plays.

This band of Greeks who get called Russian
with their strings, brass and percussion,
whatever they could buy or borrow
(and sell on their own stalls tomorrow)
will play a cautious fanfare blown
for democracy's foundation stone.

  Fanfare to Parthenon.

They'll wake what may be from the waste,
this makeshift band of the displaced.

Not marble but millennia weigh
on cables that maybe'll fray.
Depending how you calculate

democracy's foundation date
is 506 or 7 or 8
but once you've got it off the ground
with gleeful or more grating sound
and got it hoisted in the air,
it goes into which structure? Where?

With democracy the truth is this:
no final fanfared edifice,
only the crane however grating
continually recreating . . .

    Girl in Theatre of Dionysus. Lyra *player.*

The people's flags of deepest red
spread for tender feet to tread.
Those scarlet standards he saw fly
above his and other heads, held high
in Kazakhstan, when he was Russian,
now he's Greek he watches cushion
the girl's first cautious tread
onto the path of fallen red.

GIRL
(*song*)

'From Kazakhstan now back in Greece
I dream the maybe, piece by piece.
I dream with open eyes and see
the marble of maybe . . . maybe.'

    Wide shot, Theatre of Dionysus. Fade.

The scarlet banners she trod on
to find her red dolls have all gone
with all the instruments that played
back into flea-market trade,
the red flags back on pavement stalls,
folded, as May Day evening falls.

232

THE SHADOW OF HIROSHIMA
(1995)

The Shadow of Hiroshima was first broadcast on Channel 4 on 6 August 1995.

Sound Programmer Glenn Keiles
Research Assistant Sarah Bhathena
Assistant Producers Alison Carter, Diane Holmes
Telecine Grading Colin Peters, Luke Rainey
On-line Editor Adam Grant
Dubbing Mixer Nick Rogers
Hiroshima Location Manager Keiko Ogura
London Location Manager Dan Leon
Camera Assistant Jack Holmes
Film Editor Luke Dunkley
Sound and Music Richard Blackford
Lighting Cameraman Alistair Cameron
Executive Producer Michael Kustow
Producer Andrew Holmes

Written and directed by Tony Harrison

I heard a sound I thought was birds
but then I swear I heard these words:

'This voice comes from the shadow cast
by Hiroshima's A-bomb blast.
The sound you hear inside this case
is of a man who fans the face
he used to have before the flash
turned face and body into ash.
I am the nameless fanning man
you may address as Shadow San.

The inferno flayed me as I fanned,
gold fan with cranes on in my hand.
In that fierce force but one degree
of quicker combustibility
separated fan and me,
but that one degree meant that the man
was stamped on stone but not the fan.

My shadow's fading and I fear
I may not make centenary year,
and so before I finally fade
give one last outing to this shade,
and you will be my eyes to see
this fiftieth anniversary.'

He bowed. I bowed, and then began
one day's parole for Shadow San.

*

237

Radio exercises.

The Shadow said, 'I recognise
this pre-war tune for exercise.
Not only here but through Japan
this was how each day began
with music from the NHK
(our BBC) to start the day.
This Radio Tai-chi's been broadcast
before and since the A-bomb blast.
Radio Tai-chi's brought the nation,
ruined and wrecked, regeneration
of weary flesh and hopeless soul
and got the flag back up the pole.

My shadow's eighty, so is this
devastated edifice,
built 1915 by a Czech –

A-Bomb Dome.

now A-Bomb Dome, symbolic wreck
left standing for our meditation
on nuclear death and devastation.

Though the river by the name
of Motoyasu's just the same
and though the old sun emblem flies
there's nothing else I recognise
in all this city I called home
but this gaunt husk, this gutted Dome
opposite the Peace Park where
they'll loose the doves into the air
tomorrow at 8.23
too late, alas, for me to see.
At 8.15 the Peace Bell's chime
means my fiftieth burning time.

*

KOBAISHI SAN

Kobaishi San,
Hiroshima's champion pigeon man,
does Radio Tai-chi exercises
beside his pigeon-racing prizes
and cooing and flapping up above's
a loft full of symbolic doves
his pigeons are called on to be
tomorrow at 8.23.
August 6th, 8.23's
the time tomorrow that makes these
flapping pigeons VIPs.
Kobaishi San's cohort
of colombophiles, apart from sport,
every August 6th supply
doves of peace to fill the sky
at 8.23: eight minutes past
the time of Hiroshima's A-bomb blast.
And all the homing pigeons home
back to their lofts past A-Bomb Dome.
He'll be there to count them back and by
about 8.30 he can scan the sky
and at 8.40 can begin
to whistle his flock of pigeons in.

*

The Flame of Peace burns just behind
the ten green cages where, confined
until tomorrow's special day,
the pigeon fanciers' peace doves stay,
kept unfed, till they're set free
tomorrow at 8.23,
and, in about ten minutes, speed
back to their lofts to get their feed.

*

SAKAMOTO SAN

And this is Sakamoto San,
proud his birds can help Japan
make tomorrow's plea for Peace,
who crates a score for the Release.
And he'll be at his loft to count,
if twenty go, the same amount
come home. Though the flight back's short
peace doves can get lost, or caught.

*

Hara San paints the A-Bomb Dome.

While pigeon fanciers prepare
others start the day with prayer.
Like Hiroshi Hara who each year
begins his own peace ritual here.
'Hiroshi Hara, did you say?'
said Shadow San, 'Alive today?
How come a man now sixty-three
survived the Bomb blast and not me?'

Because, by chance, he was away
at his grandmother's that fatal day,
Hara San has lived to see
this fiftieth anniversary.
Hara San, lucky to survive
and live to 1995,
is a painter and his way
of commemorating A-Bomb Day
and all his friends lost in the war
is on the 5th, today, to draw
and paint the A-Bomb Dome with water from
the river those flayed by the Bomb,
including all his friends from school,
jumped in, hoping it would cool

their burning and bomb-blackened skin,
here where he dips his bottle in.
His schoolmates' shrieks from blackened lips
haunt Hara San each time he dips
his brush in water from the stream
to give relief to those who scream,
all his dying schoolmates, those
whose skin slid off their flesh like clothes.
Like clothes, three sizes oversize,
their flayed skin loosens from their thighs.
Burns and blisters, bloated blebs
burst as the Motoyasu ebbs,
the tidal Motoyasu trails
black flaps of flesh like chiffon veils.
Like kimonos with their belts untied
black sloughed-off skin floats on the tide.
This water mixed with children's cries
paints the Dome, green trees, blue skies
and in that way, he hopes, redeems
something from his schoolmates' screams.
'The force that blew the Dome apart,'
said the Shadow, 'makes short work of art.'

*

Baseball stadium.

Close to the Dome on soil where heat
burnt the soles off people's feet,
on Saturdays, close to Ground Zero,
crowds cheer the current sporting hero.

Tomorrow they may pause in play
to watch the peace doves pass that way.

Shadow San stood, head on one side,
listening, and then he cried:
'You'd need a stadium five times higher

to seat all those who died by fire.
Where you see baseball I can hear
all those thousands who can't cheer.
Listen, can't you hear the choir
of those who perished in the fire?'

'I hear a baseball being hit
or thudding into catcher's mitt!'

Shadow San, exasperated
I heard no chorus of cremated,
deaf to all the humming dead,
turned to me again and said:

'Dead men's mouths make only M,
the M in Do*m*e, the M in Bo*m*b,
tuned to the hum that's coming from
the A-Bomb Dome that I hear hum
all round this baseball stadium,
still after all these fifty years
reverberating in my ears.
Can you *not* hear it? Or the choir?'

'No, only a baseball hitting wire!'

And you, in front of your TVs
which are, no doubt, all Japanese,
all you sitting there at home
can you hear the humming Dome,
the M, the M? As one of those
who always haunts where water flows
Shadow San, destroyed by heat,
drew me away to this retreat.

*

    Shinto shrine.

'This,' said Shadow San, 'this shrine,
though I'm not certain, seems like mine.

The fiery fountain dragon felt
the same fierce force that made me melt
and melted but can be remade
to spout cool water in the shade.
Burnt red banners and bamboo,
orange arches all made new.
That character carved on this trough
was blackened but not blasted off.
This lion though its jaw got cracked
has all the rest of it intact.

I came here to this Shinto shrine
most mornings between eight and nine,'
the Shadow told me, 'and the day
I was to die I came to pray,
to pull the bell rope, throw the yen,
bow twice, clap twice'. . . He broke off. Then
Shadow San, although he fanned
obsessively, grabbed at my hand
and with a more than shadow squeeze
made my blood and spirit freeze.

    Sonoko.

'I see my Sonoko returning.
It was her who I was yearning
on the steps for, burning, burning.
Ah those tender, tender fingertips
the memory of those lips, those lips.'
At that moment no dead man
can have longed for life like Shadow San,
who, hoping love could break through time
thought he watched his loved-one climb
the blasted but now rebuilt shrine
to seek the help of powers divine.

But once he'd seen her throw the yen
hope left him when he spoke again.

'No! No!' he said, 'Not Sonoko,
we both died fifty years ago.
And if she *had* survived she'd be
a scarred and shrunken seventy-three.
But that girl, head bowed at the shrine
wrings my heart, she's so like mine,
so like the girl I was to meet
that August 6th and go and eat
sushi and drink *sake* and . . .
the night of love we'd also planned.
And I sat longing, planning
on the bank steps, fanning, fanning
in a hundred Fahrenheit
longing for my girl and night . . .
when all my flesh was set alight.'

*

NHK and A-Bomb Dome.

Above this shrine where he had seen
the girl like his, the workers clean
windows at the NHK
(their BBC) for Peace-Dove Day
and clean the windows so they'll see
to film the peace-doves being set free
or point out to visitors the view
the Shadow keeps returning to:
'The A-Bomb Dome I never can
quite lose from view,' said Shadow San.
'It's as if,' he said, 'these views were by
my favourite painter Hokusai,
and if he re-did his hundred views
instead of Mount Fuji now he'd choose
as Hara San, his painter heir
still painting on his folding chair,
chose, the A-Bomb Dome, the eye

always gets recaptured by.
I take my city bearings from
that fellow relic of the Bomb.'

Elementary school.

The school where all the pupils died
stands rebuilt near this riverside.

*

When Shadow San set eyes on these
he began to sing in Japanese:
'*Misu, misu kudasai,*
Water, water, they'd all cry
burned and blackened, soon to die
if these pupils here had been
in this same room at 8.15
the 6th of August '45.

None of them would be alive.

And none would see another star
if they'd been where now they are,
and me, this shadow Rip Van Winkle
for whom all stars have lost their twinkle,
came here to school before the War
and also learned to use a saw.

I hear my own voice in this choir
I hope the world will spare from fire.
I learned this song, it's one you sing
to calm little pigeons panicking.'

*

Mitsufuji San.

The A-Bomb Dome and all the rest
make Mitsufuji San depressed.
He wouldn't mind if it was made

into a vast pinball arcade,
a game that millions will play
even tomorrow, A-Bomb Day.
He's never been to see you yet,
I told the sullen silhouette.
He thinks it's better to forget.

He likes to sing, to play, to laugh,
never goes near the Cenotaph,
unless, like now, delivering doves.

He only does the things he loves,
what makes him happy, and doves do.
He sings to them to make them coo;
his girlfriend does, and he'd prefer
to sing this little song to her,
a pigeon song he'd sooner use
to calm her flutters into coos.
Shadow San who said he'd seen
birds in flames at 8.15
with a dead man's closed mouth M
hummed the pigeon song with him,
then said quietly, 'Which burns quicker,
birds or basket, wings or wicker?'

   Tram crosses the Aioi Bridge.

As the sun-drenched streetcar crossed
the centre of the Holocaust,
the Aioi Bridge the Enola Gay
took focus from that fatal day,
I heard the fanning Shadow say:
'The trams of Hiroshima ran
always on time,' said Shadow San,
'but at 8.15 were blasted black
along this then bomb-buckled track
and all the passengers, like me,
were fanned into eternity.'

Mitsufuji San phones Sonoko.

The Shadow melted into shade.
I thought the phone made him afraid,
I thought the booth put him in mind
of that place he'd been confined
until this morning in and must return
when the Peace Bell chimes to burn
and to resume at 8.15
his most uncarnal quarantine.
Though Mitsufuji hates to dwell
on why and how the A-bomb fell
the Dome's dark hellish silhouette
summons up his dove, his pet.
The fanning shade stood flabbergasted
that the Dome the Bomb had blasted
could now so magically summon,
from waste and wilderness, a woman.

I asked the Shadow to translate:
'The A-Bomb Dome makes him a date
but he's got some hours to wait.
He'll leave his peace-doves first and then
go to play pinball until ten.'

*

Hara San paints the A-Bomb Dome.

Hara San hears scorched throats croak
where now new thirsts get quenched by *Coke*.
'And *Coke*,' sighed fanning Shadow San,
'has come to conquer new Japan.'

The forecast from the NHK
predicts another scorching day
tomorrow and the shops will sell
scores of ice-cold crimson cans
of *Coke*, and scores and scores of fans

to cool the watchers waiting for
the liberated doves to soar.

*

Tomorrow morning, 8.15,
he'll give the trees their August green
and the sky its final blue,
then what Hara San will do
at the very moment the Bomb fell
and he hears the tolling of the bell
is seal and sign it with the date . . .
'The date that also sealed my fate,'
added the watching Shadow San
who, as the day cooled, closed his fan.

  Sunset.

The setting sun forecast as stronger
tomorrow made my shadow longer,
but Shadow San's stayed just the same
as when first cast by flash and flame.

The sun tomorrow that's forecast
as hot as when the A-bomb blast
exploded fifty years ago
will make the fans flap to and fro
and sell a fortune in iced drinks
but now, turns fiery red, and sinks.

*

  Hiroshima by night. Neon lights.

Except when nightworld neon threw
his outline out in red or blue,
or he made another bitter joke
about the crimson conqueror, *Coke*,
he stayed unseen and silent in the night
until he stopped me at this sight:

Parlor Atom pinball arcade.

'Parlor Atom, look this sign
must mean another A-bomb shrine
with shadows in it just like mine.
Perhaps I'll find a fellow shade.'

'It's a mere pinball machine arcade
I'm sorry to tell you, Shadow San,
there are thousands like it in Japan
there are thirty million Japanese
spend their nights in "shrines" like these.'

'I thought Mitsufuji came to pray!'
'No, Shadow San, to play, to play
A pinball addict I'm afraid.'

We watched him enter the arcade.
The sound unleashed made Shadow shrink.
He shouted out: 'It makes me think
of Hiroshima shattering, and me
a shadow showered with bomb debris.'

*

Mitsufuji San meets Sonoko.

Shadow San drew me ahead
half-excited, half in dread,
and when Mitsufuji came he said:
'Mitsufuji's little dove
's so like my own cremated love,
and maybe all my dead man's yearning,
still undiminished from the burning
has made Mitsufuji San,
the Hiroshima pigeon man,
and the *sake* girl he's met unite
to commemorate my final night.'

249

The thought consoled him for a while.
But Shadow San soon lost the smile
I'd imagined that he'd had
and stopped me in the night to add:

'Like men condemned to hang or fry
get favourite meals before they die,
the man who fanned his way to hell
wills them to the Love Hotel.'

*

Mitsufuji San and Sonoko in Love Hotel.

'Seeing Sonoko asleep
could even make a shadow weep.
Girls as beautiful, as young, as sweet
were seared to cinders by the heat.

Sayonara, Sonoko,
I love you but I have to go
back to my museum case
with no body and no face,
back to a world where none embrace
nor do the things I did before
our hawks and jingos joined the war,
and you're so lucky to do after –
drinking *sake,* singing, laughter,
even Parlor Atom, but above
everything on earth, to love.

Sayonara, I must return
back to the bank steps where I'll burn.
Tomorrow morning, 8.15,
only this flimsy paper screen,
flammable as a fan, 's between
your sleeping body and the man
who'll be cremated, Shadow San.

When you hear the Peace Bell chime
that's 8.15, my burning time.
First the conflagration of the fan
then after it the fanning man.

Before my eyes burst from the heat
a blazing dove falls at my feet.'

Shadow San departs.

I saw the saddened shade retire
to face again the flash and fire.

*

Radio exercises. Mitsufuji San wakes in Love Hotel.

Mitsufuji San's alarm
that his doves may come to harm
makes him run past A-Bomb Dome
to catch a tram to take him home
across the bridge they call Aioi,
the bomb-aimer of 'Little Boy'
high up in the Enola Gay
fifty years ago today
took focus from where now we see,
walking the upright of the T,

Peace ceremony begins.

two survivors' shadows but
shadows still fixed foot to foot,
two survivors here to find
the special seats they've been assigned
to hear the speeches, pray, and see
precisely at 8.23
all the doves in the release
making their winged plea for peace.

*

The cicadas' dry tattoo
gets quicker towards 8.22.
Fans, like a chorus of quick sighs,
will the doves into the skies.
A white glove poised against the blue
signals it's 8.22,
only one minute now before
the liberated doves will soar
above the fans and the cicadas –
Sakamoto San's, Okada's,
and champion Kobaishi San's
and carefree Mitsufuji San's,
flying above the sighing fans.

Once the signaller's white glove
gives the signal, every dove
will rise and fly as cage-doors fall,
crash to the ground, and free them all.

And fanciers wait at home to greet
their hungry peace-doves home to eat.
Normally each fancier's flock
's back and fed by nine o'clock.

Release of doves, 8.23.

*

Last dove.

The peace-doves have been freed but why
won't this last shaking straggler fly?
Perhaps he's seen what's in the sky.

Hawks.

Where peace-doves are the birds of prey
are never very far away.
These hawks cruising the skies

don't care what peace-doves symbolise.
These emblems are mere morsels, meat,
their ripped-out innards good to eat.
Since yesterday the hawks have waited
to see their lunches liberated.
Hiroshima hawks are glad to glut
and gorge themselves on peace-dove gut.

It's not inappropriate birds of prey
are also present on Peace Day.
They could well stand for Japanese
who forced other Asians to their knees.
They stand for a spirit from the past
that moved Japan before the blast,
the old Japan that took Nanking
under its dark, blood-spattered wing,
Japan in her aggressive guise
taking Pearl Harbor by surprise,
the prison camps that made us pray
for any means to bring VJ.

Many doves freed on this day
fall victims to these birds of prey

Mitsufuji San back at pigeon loft.

and Mitsufuji fears his may.
A dove he sang to might this minute
have a hawk's beak thrusting in it.

Or, turned scavenger, join other strays
from all the former Peace Dove Days,
from ninety-four, three, two, one.
The Peace Park's almost overrun
and the symbol of man's peace-seeking soul
is a matter for city pest control.

And peace-doves of the recent past
could end up sterilised, or gassed.

Those symbolic doves that flew
in ninety-one or ninety-two.
in ninety-three or four survive
by fighting these from ninety-five . . .

A-Bomb Dome and pigeons.

Pigeon/Peace-doves brawl and fight.

Is the world at peace tonight?

Fan.

Or are we all like Shadow San
facing inferno with a fan?

PROMETHEUS
(1998)

'Fire and Poetry, two great powers
that make the so-called gods' world OURS!'

Prometheus (1998)

'To make films is to be a poet.'

Pier Paolo Pasolini

Fire and Poetry

I

As a child I learned to dream awake before the coal fire in our living room. Staring into the fire, with its ever-changing flames, shifting coals, falling ash, and what were called 'strangers' – skins of soot flapping on the grate – evoked in me my first poetry. My first meditations were induced by the domestic hearth, I have always associated staring into flames with the freedom of poetic meditation. It has been proposed by Gaston Bachelard that it is from brooding before flames that early man developed his interior life. It was also my job to light the fire, and to fetch the coal up from the cellar. With a bucket from the dark dank cellar that had been our shelter from German air raids and incendiary bombs, I brought the black coal that fuelled my dreaming. I later learned that the Latin for hearth is *focus*. And fire is what I focus on in *Prometheus*. And I remembered my Latin when, filming *Prometheus* on the roads of Romania, I saw on a forest-fire sign the word FOC: FIRE.

II

The myth of Prometheus, who brought fire to mankind, keeps entering history at significant moments. One of the sources of my film is the *Prometheus Bound* of Aeschylus (525–456 BC) Most Greek tragedy shifts its time scale from immediate suffering to some long-term redemption through memorial ritual or social amelioration, or simply through the very play being performed. The performed suffering was old, the redemption contemporary. The

257

appeal to futurity is not simply that 'time heals' because it brings forgetfulness and oblivion, but because creative memory is at work, giving the suffering new form, a form to allow the suffering to be shared and made bearable across great gaps of time. And who continually cries out across millennia to present himself to 'later mortals' as a θεαμα (something to be looked at), especially in his final words, more than Prometheus? Who calls from a remoter past than the bound Prometheus, and yet who still manifests himself when history moves in directions where defiance and unfreedom cry for help? It is a myth because of its time scale that encompasses many generations of mortals, which continually makes us reassess our history. It might give the disappointed Utopian a refuge from despair. And maybe these days the Socialist.

No play in the ancient repertoire works over a longer time scale than *Prometheus Bound*. Or deals with more unbroken suffering. Its span is not, as in the *Oresteia,* the ten fateful years of the Trojan War, but thirty millennia: thirty millennia of tyrannical torture, thirty millennia of defiance. And so it is not surprising that at times of the collapse of ideas that might have created liberty and equality the figure of the chained Titan, Prometheus, is remembered. Nor is it surprising that for those who dramatise history as dialectical struggle Prometheus has come to embody the tyrannically restrained champion of the downtrodden and oppressed. When men feel themselves in chains, the myth of the Titan re-enters history. Out of hopelessness comes a new need for the chained martyr's undiminished hope, though every day Zeus's eagle tears the liver from his body:

> To suffer woes which Hope thinks infinite;
> To forgive wrongs darker than death or night;
> To defy Power, which seems omnipotent;
> To love and bear; to hope till Hope creates

From its own wreck the thing it contemplates;
   Neither to change, nor falter, nor repent;
This, like thy glory, Titan, is to be
Good, great and joyous, beautiful and free;
This is alone Life, Joy, Empire, and Victory.

So Shelley concludes his own *Prometheus Unbound*, when the wreck that Hope had to contemplate was the failure of the French Revolution to deliver liberty, equality and fraternity. But hope is also created out of the contemplation of the wreck of tyrannies, earlier despotisms demolished over a long period of time, not overthrown by revolution, with Nature running riot over ruined imperial stones. It was precisely this spectacle that Shelley had all around him as he composed his *Prometheus Unbound* in Rome in 1819. Shelley found this everywhere in the ruins of the imperial city:

> Rome has fallen, ye see it lying
>   Heaped in undistinguished ruin:
> Nature is alone undying.
>   'Fragment: Rome And Nature'

And specifically in the Baths of Caracalla, which he chose as his alfresco study in which to write his play. These grandiose baths, built by the Emperor Caracalla (211–217) on the Aventine hill of Rome and enlarged by Elagabalus (218–222) and Alexander Severus (222–235), were in use until AD 537, when the Goths of Vitgis cut the aqueducts of Rome. The famous Farnese Hercules, the hero who finally killed the tormenting eagle of Zeus and freed Prometheus, stood in the colonnaded passage between the *frigidarium* and the *tepidarium*. The ruins of the ideals of the French Revolution turned Shelley to the myth, and the famous posthumous painting by Joseph Severn, now in the Keats-Shelley House in Rome, shows him working on his *Prometheus Unbound* in 1818/19 in the ruins of the Baths of Caracalla. Such ruins revealed to Shelley the proof that even the greatest of powers come to an end, a suitable ambience in which to compose his *Prometheus Unbound*. And the Baths of Caracalla is still an appropriate place in which to contemplate the ruins of time and the collapse of empire, with their braced brick molars, thirds of arches, seagulls on the jagged rims fenced off with hazard tape, or with a red-and-white warning hurdle. The bricks abraded back to rock and dust. Signs which give you a clue to the vast ruins: APODYTERIUM; NATATIO. The whole vast collection of fragmentary walls braced and netted, sometimes held together, by the roots of briar and blackberry, laurel, yew, fig. And fennel – perhaps the most appropriate plant to preside over this preface as it was in a stalk of fennel that Prometheus hid the fire he stole for Mankind. This preface to my *Prometheus* film was sketched there, as Shelley's *Prometheus Unbound* was a hundred and eighty years ago, in the Terme di Caracalla, Rome. The whole of Shelley's great poem, which I had in my pocket, seems to end back in the Baths of Caracalla when, as Richard Holmes writes, 'the vision has dissolved and Shelley is sitting within the blossoming labyrinths of the Baths of Caracalla'. These ruins helped Shelley to give the struggle between Zeus and the chained Titan a millennial scale. Zeus or a Roman Emperor, or a regime intended for all time, could also be like Ozymandias:

> 'My name is Ozymandias, king of kings:
> Look on my works, ye Mighty, and despair!'
> Nothing beside remains. Round the decay
> Of that colossal wreck, boundless and bare,
> The lone and level sands stretch far away.
> 'Ozymandias' (1817)

It is the time that dealt, again in Shelley's words, with Bonaparte:

A frail and bloody pomp which Time has swept
In fragments towards Oblivion.
                    'Feelings of a Republican
                on the Fall of Bonaparte' (1816)

Everything toppling into the 'dust of creeds outworn'
(*Prometheus Unbound*, 1.697). The 'vast and trunkless
legs of stone' of the ruin of Ozymandias could well refer
in 1989 to the dismantled and toppled statues of Lenin
and various Eastern European Communist leaders in
bronze or stone all over the Eastern bloc. Ozymandias and
the ruins of the Baths of Caracalla for Shelley, as the
toppled Berlin Wall for us, were evidence of time overturn-
ing the tyrannies, an assurance that Prometheus would not
suffer for ever.

Byron has similar reactions to Rome and the triumph of
time:

Oh Rome! my country! city of the soul!
The orphans of the heart must turn to thee,
Lone mother of dead empires! and control
In their shut breasts their petty misery.
What are our woes and sufferance? Come and see
The cypress, hear the owl, and plod your way
O'er steps of broken thrones and temples, Ye!
Whose agonies are evils of a day –
A world is at our feet as fragile as our clay.
            Childe Harold's Pilgrimage, Canto IV, LXXVIII

Cypress and ivy, weed and wallflower grown
Matted and mass'd together, hillocks heap'd
On what were chambers, arch crush'd, column strown
In fragments, choked up vaults, and frescos steep'd
In subterranean damps, where the owl peep'd,
Deeming it midnight: – Temples, baths or halls?
Pronounce who can; for all that Learning reap'd
From her research hath been, that these are walls –

Behold the Imperial Mount! 'tis thus the mighty falls.
Childe Harold's Pilgrimage, Canto IV, CVII

Byron's statue by the Danish sculptor Thorvaldsen in the
garden of the Villa Borghese has a thoughtful poet seated
on a fallen fragment of column and beside it a human
skull, imperial might and fragile clay made one in time's
momentum. The momentum that crushed hope and Pro-
metheus who kept it burning like a torch of liberty. The
Titan has been described as 'a primordial figure in the
history of hope'. In Shelley and Byron's time the 'history
of hope' had met its obstacles, and if Prometheus was, as
he was for Shelley, 'the saviour and the strength of
suffering man' (*Prometheus Unbound,* 1.817) and the
patron saint of the overthrow of tyrannical power, then he
too was tormented by that shrivelling of hope in Man.
One of the things that Prometheus is tortured by, apart
from the eagle eating his liver, is the vision sent to him of
what is in fact Shelley's own anguish, the failure of the
French Revolution:

> Names are there, Nature's sacred watchwords, they
> Were borne aloft in bright emblazonry;
> The nations thronged around, and cried aloud,
> As with one voice, Truth, liberty, and love!
> Suddenly fierce confusion fell from heaven
> Among them: there was strife, deceit, and fear:
> Tyrants rushed in, and did divide the spoil.
> This was the shadow of the truth I saw.
> > *Prometheus Unbound,* 1.648–55

Byron also writes with Shelley's bitterness about the effect
of the failed French Revolution on Europe's struggle for
freedom:

> But France got drunk with blood to vomit crime,
> And fatal have her Saturnalia been
> To Freedom's cause, in every age and clime;

Because the deadly days which we have seen,
And vile Ambition, that built up between
Man and his hopes an adamantine wall,
And the base pageant last upon the scene,
Are grown the pretext for the eternal thrall
Which nips life's tree, and dooms man's worst –
    his second fall.

        Childe Harold's Pilgrimage, Canto IV, XCVII

Both Byron and Shelley call on Prometheus and his commitment to Man's future to help them weather what Shelley calls in his Preface to *The Revolt of Islam* 'the age of despair' that, for intellectuals like him, followed on what he had to call, in the lines above, the 'strife, deceit and fear' of the French Revolution. What is needed for the creation of a just, independent society after this setback, writes Shelley, is 'resolute perseverance and indefatigable hope, and long-suffering and long-believing courage'. Such perseverance and indefatigable hope are symbolically pre-eminent in the apparently hopelessly chained Prometheus. In the Preface to *The Revolt of Islam* (1818) Shelley writes:

> The revulsion occasioned by the atrocities of the
> demagogues, and the re-establishment of successive
> tyrannies in France, was terrible, and felt in the remotest
> corner of the civilised world. . . . This influence has
> tainted the literature of the age with the hopelessness
> of the minds from which it flows. Metaphysics, and
> inquiries into moral and political science, have become
> little else than vain attempts to revive exploded
> superstitions, or sophisms like those of Mr Malthus,
> calculated to lull the oppressors of mankind into a
> security of everlasting triumph.

The 'oppressors of Mankind' are gathered together as 'the Oppressor of Mankind', as Shelley called Zeus/Jove when, in the same spirit as *The Revolt of Islam,* he wrote *Prometheus Unbound* in the following year.

III

Shelley considered *Prometheus Unbound* his finest piece of work. It sold less than a score of copies, and is still never given a theatrical presentation or even thought of as a play. H. S. Mitford's is a typical attitude. He edited *The Oxford Book of English Romantic Verse 1798–1837* (1935), and like so many editors of dreary anthologies excluded the poetry from dramatic works, giving a very narrowed view of the range of verse. Songs from plays were admitted as they fitted the lyrical cliché. And he also made an exception of a passage from Shelley's *Prometheus Unbound* on the grounds that 'no one would call that a play'. Shelley's *play* (and indeed most of the dramatic efforts of the Romantic poets) is considered untheatrical and unplayable, and judged by the theatrical clichés of today it may seem irredeemable as a dramatic text. But George Bernard Shaw had the musical and Wagnerian insight to see in Shelley's *Prometheus Unbound* 'an English attempt at a Ring', and Wagner's ideas were deeply inspired by Aeschylus. Later critics, like Timothy Webb (1986), have also sought to justify and incorporate Shelley's attempts into the theatrical canon by stressing operatic models: '*Prometheus Unbound* in particular seems to owe a considerable debt to operatic models as well as to masque and, more obviously, to its Aeschylean prototype. Its exploration of musical analogies and its use of strategies and structures from opera and ballet extend the boundaries of dramatic form.' Isabel Quigly makes similar operatic parallels in her introduction to Shelley's selected poetry in the Penguin Poetry Library:

. . . *Prometheus Unbound*, a drama on so heroic a scale that his lack of dramatic competence does not matter, for this is not theatre but huge/metaphysical grand-opera, where the scenery can creak if the singing is good enough.

The preponderant cliché of naturalism in contemporary British theatre makes anything even a little different unwelcome, but there are salutory reminders from an Indian scholar whose traditions of non-European drama give him a sympathy for Shelley's play greater than any expressed in Shelley's native land:

It clearly represents a rejection of the literary theatre as known to the Western World. But all theatre is not the property of the relatively small continent of Europe. Shelley's thought and art in his singular iridescent poem seem in luminous fashion to look beyond the confines of Western usage and tradition to the more imaginative dramas of other civilisations, to the theatre of the dance, with its accompanying music, or to the theatre of the dancing shadow puppets of the Far East. His imagination deliberately and resoundingly defies our more temporal stages as developed for our human actors in flesh and blood. Curiously enough, on the contrary, it even invites Indian play of shadows, or puppet shows based on the epics.

And H. H. Anniah Gowda, the Professor of English at the University of Mysore, goes on to say something that confirms my despair of most contemporary theatre and that gave me, in what I've italicised, a nudge in the direction of my own *Prometheus*:

It is easy to conceive Shelley's infinite choreographic work as a chant for a dance not as yet created, a libretto for a musical drama not as yet composed, a poetic companion to some *future revelation in the*

imaginative film . . . Prometheus Unbound can be a
dramatic reality only when the theatre itself is unbound
from innumerable restrictions now confining it so
firmly that this liberation remains for the less daring
and imaginative minds an unthinkable change . . . The
student of practicable drama at the present does ill to
overlook even so apparently anti-theatrical a text as
Shelley's drama-poem. In such unlikely sources may lie
concealed the seeds of a future burgeoning. Now that
the winter has come to the theatre, even a new
Prometheus Unbound may not be far behind.

Dramatic Poetry from Medieval to Modern Times,
(Madras, 1972)

I have always thought that Shelley's *Prometheus Unbound*
had 'seeds of a future burgeoning', though the snow still
lies deep on most of our stages and the footsteps poets
have made on them have disappeared under new chill
flurries. I can only echo Ibsen when, in the face of hostility
to his *Peer Gynt*, he asserted that 'My book *is* poetry; and
if it isn't, it will become such.' Shelley's play, unfortu-
nately, is still in the process of becoming. And I have to say
that my *Prometheus is* a film; and if it isn't, it will become
such!

IV

Shelley's reaction to the idea of writing a parallel trilogy to
that of Aeschylus, with détente finally achieved between
the punisher and the punished, was that he wanted
absolutely no reconciliation. 'I was averse,' Shelley writes
in his Preface to *Prometheus Unbound*, 'from a catas-
trophe so feeble as that of reconciling the Champion with
the Oppressor of mankind.' No détente. As we do not
possess the other two plays of the *Prometheia*, Aeschylus'

Promethean trilogy, then we are left with undiluted defiance and enduring tyranny.

Karl Marx is said to have observed that he regretted that Shelley died at the age of twenty-nine, 'for Shelley was a thorough revolutionary and would have remained in the van of socialism all his life'. Marx's disputed remark was at the expense of Byron, who Marx is said to have prophesied would have become a 'reactionary bourgeois'. Paul Foot takes up this speculation in his *Red Shelley* (1984) and imagines Byron supporting the Reform Bill of 1832, which enfranchised only property owners, and Shelley supporting the extension of the Bill and the Chartist movement. These speculations are, according to the former leader of the Labour Party, Michael Foot, extremely unfair on Byron (*The Politics of Paradise: a Vindication of Byron*, 1988). After Byron's death in Greece, Michael Foot points out that Heinrich Heine (1797–1856) actually identifies Byron with Prometheus himself: 'He defied miserable men and still more miserable gods like Prometheus.' And the same identification was made all over Europe. Adam Mickiewicz (1798–1855), Poland's national bard, wrote that Byron 'had cursed and fumed like Prometheus, the Titan, whose shade he loved to evoke so often'. And in Italy, Mazzini (1805–72), the great soul of the Risorgimento, honoured the dead poet in these words: 'never did the "eternal spirit of the chainless mind" make a brighter apparition amongst us. He seems at times a transformation of that immortal Prometheus, of whom he has written so nobly, whose cry of agony, yet of futurity, sounded above the cradle of the European world.'

After Shelley and Byron, Prometheus' 'cry of agony yet futurity' gradually began to be identified with the struggle for socialism. Eight years after the death of Byron, Thomas Kibble Hervey (1799–1859) published an 83-line poem *Prometheus* (1832) which places the chained Titan, with contemporary geographical accuracy, in the frozen plains of Russia, with its oppressed serfs taking inspiration from their manacled champion:

> Amid this land of frozen plains and souls
> Are beating hearts that wake long weary nights,
> Unseen, to listen to thy far-off sigh;
> And stealthily the serf, amid his toils,
> Looks up to see thy form against the sky.

He writes of kings as 'the petty Joves of earth' and has a vision of freedom and deliverance with the masses, inspired by the American example of monarchless democracy, coming to liberate Prometheus:

> And thou shalt rise – the vulture and the chain
> Shall both be conquered by thine own stern will!
> Hark! o'er the far Atlantic comes a sound
> Of falling fetters, and a wild, glad cry
> Of myriad voices in a hymn to thee!
> Hail to that music! To its tune sublime
> Shall march the legions of the world of mind,
> On to thy rescue, o'er each land and sea.

John Goodwyn Barmby (1820–81), a Christian Socialist who is credited with the invention of the word 'communism', published a monthly magazine in the 1840s called THE PROMETHEAN or *Communist Apostle*. The second step towards Prometheus becoming a patron saint of socialism was probably the association of the Titan Fire-Giver with the heavy industries and technologies dependent on fire in one form or another. 'Thanks to fire . . . man has attained domination over the world,' writes Paul Ginestier in *The Poet and the Machine* (1961). In the heartland of German industry in the nineteenth century, the title of the magazine that kept its readers abreast with new industrial technology seemed almost inevitable: *Prometheus: Illustrierte Wochenschrift über die Fortschritte in Gewerbe, Industrie und Wissenschaft* (*Illustrated Weekly on Developments in*

Trade, Industry and Science, Leipzig, 1899–1921). Prometheus becomes the patron of technology and the smokestacks of the industry of the Rhine, the Ruhr, and the North of England where I myself grew up, inhaling the sulphurous fumes of the Promethean gift: 'The Iron Kingdom where his Majesty Fire reigns', as Guy de Maupassant puts it. This identification with industry transformed Prometheus from being, in the words of Timothy Richard Wutrich, in his study on *Prometheus and Faust* (1995), the 'primordial figure in the history of the concept of hope', to being what the Marxist classical scholar George Thomson, making the concept of hope more specifically political, calls Prometheus in *Aeschylus and Athens* (1941): 'the patron saint of the proletariat'. Karl Marx himself, who referred to Prometheus as 'the first saint and martyr of the philosopher's calendar', was, during his editorship of the *Rhineland Gazette*, depicted in cartoons as Prometheus bound to a printing press with the Prussian eagle gnawing his liver. At his feet, like the chorus of the Oceanides, the Daughters of Ocean represented the cities of the Rhineland pleading for freedom.

When the English poet and magazine editor John Lehmann wrote a book on the Caucasus in 1937 he called it *Prometheus and the Bolsheviks* – 'because Prometheus is the oldest symbol of the Caucasus, and can at the same time be considered as the oldest symbol of what the Bolsheviks have had as their aim: the deliverance of man from tyranny and barbarism by the seizure of material power.' On a *Sovtorgflot* boat on the Black Sea, heading for Sukhum in Georgia, Lehmann has a dream of meeting Prometheus, who says to him: 'I find myself passionately on the side of the Bolsheviks when I hear accounts of the Civil War struggles. *It reminds me of my own struggles with Jove over the fire business* [my italics].' Prometheus then announces that he has made a momentous decision: 'I have decided,' says Prometheus, 'to join the Party!' Then

Lehmann wakes from his dream, and the boat docks in Sukhum.

But as Prometheus gathers his supporters, so does the tyrant Zeus, whose parallel manifestations take on historically terrifying forms. As Shelley wrote, Humanity is 'heaven-oppressed' (*Prometheus Unbound*, 1.674). The ministers of Jupiter trample down the 'beloved race' of Prometheus. These ministers are 'thought-executing'. The brain of Jove is 'all-miscreative' (1.448). All monolithic ideologies, religious and political, are 'miscreative'. Zeus (or Jupiter, or Jove) is the image of recurrent tyranny and he wants to destroy Mankind through human agents like Hitler and Stalin; and, though Prometheus foiled his destruction of Mankind once by stealing fire, perhaps he now plays into the tyrant's hands by giving men the freedom to use fire as they will. And because Prometheus, in his socialist avatar, is the champion of the industrial worker, the miner, the steel-worker, Zeus particularly glories in fiery destruction and smoky pollution, and Mankind's slower death by poisoning the earth with factories fuelled by Promethean power.

The hasty and massive industrialisation of the socialist countries in the 1950s took little heed of the ecological consequences, and guide books to places like Romania glorified the industrial sites in a way that suggests that they were conducting Prometheans around the sacred temples of their Titanic champion. 'The town of Bicaz is already an important tourist centre,' we read in *Romania: a Guide Book* (Bucharest, 1967). And why? 'In this region beside the hydro-power station of Stejarul we find . . . the new mines of non-ferrous metals at Lesul Ursului and of barites at Obcina Voronetului, the cement mill at Bicaz, the timber-processing factory at Vaduri, the refinery at Darmesti – all of them industrial units built by socialism in its forward march.' The prose is straining to become a Promethean poetry, and the cumulative roll-call with its chemical and geographical names could in the hands of an Aeschylus or a Milton have epic scale. The writer is always relieved to leave natural scenic surroundings for the lyrical nomenclature of the chemical industries:

> Presently, however, this charming natural scenery will have to give way to a monumental achievement of man's hand. We are nearing the big industrial aggregate of Gheorghiu Georghiu-Dej Town [with its] huge tanks, cylindrical towers, silvery pipes, black pipes, white pipes curling gracefully . . . It supplies coke for electrodes, propane propylene for phenol, and butane-butylene for synthetic rubber.

Copşa Mică, once the most polluted town in Romania and maybe the world, whose carbon-black factory that blackened everything around it – houses, hills, people, sheep – and which is now derelict and its workers jobless and hopeless, gets this Promethean puff:

> We continue to travel along the Tirnava Valley and after ten km we reach Copşa Mică, one of the important centres of the Romanian chemical industry, nicknamed the 'retort' town. We shall be struck by the bizarre outline of the carbon-black works looking like a dark castle – and our attention will be arrested by the installations of the sulphuric acid works and of the first Romanian works for polyvinyl chloride . . .

In my film Hermes takes the golden statue of Prometheus to have it daubed and desecrated with carbon black thrown by the redundant workers of Copşa Mică. It took the whole crew days to get clean, and for weeks carbon black soiled everything we had. When we crossed the border into Bulgaria, the border guards asked our inter-preter if British people were always so dirty.

The pattern of rapid Promethean industrialisation was replicated all over the former socialist world. The steel works of Nowa Huta, where I also filmed, were hurriedly constructed on a site where there was neither iron ore nor coal to create a proletarian work force ten kilometres east of the ancient university town of Krakow, with its long-standing traditions of culture and religion. The idea of a bright future based on industrialisation and five-year plans created vast, technically out-of-date temples to Prometheus which are now, since 1989, rapidly becoming derelict 'rustbelts' with thousands out of work. The same fate has happened to the most 'Promethean' industries in Great Britain, coal and steel. Nick Danziger in *Danziger's Britain* uses the expression 'industrial genocide' to describe this end to heroic industry, and paints a frightening picture of its aftermath of unemployment, vandalised inner cities, children without hope turning to drugs and then to crime to maintain their habit.

One of the visions sent to torment Shelley's chained Prometheus is the beginning of the Industrial Revolution and urban industrialisation:

> Look! where round the wide horizon
> Many a million-peopled city
> Vomits smoke in the bright air.
> Hark the outcry of despair!

The Prometheus of a hundred and eighty years later has to harken to cries of despair from the now smokeless dereliction.

V

'No doubt it has often been stated that the conquest of fire definitely separated man from the animal,' writes Gaston Bachelard in *La Psychoanalyse du Feu* (1938), 'but perhaps it has not been noticed that the mind in its primitive state, together with its poetry and knowledge, had been developed in meditation before a fire . . . the *dreaming man* seated before his fireplace is the man concerned with inner depths, a man in the process of development.' And Dennis Donoghue equates the theft of fire with 'the origin of consciousness':

> Fire enabled them to move from nature to culture, but it made culture a dangerous possession: *it made tragedy possible* . . . We have found the stolen fire identified with reason and knowledge, but it is probably better to identify it with the symbolic imagination . . . Above all, Prometheus made possible the imaginative enhancement of experience, the metaphorical distinction between what happens to us and what we make of the happening. That is to say, Prometheus provided men with consciousness and the transformational grammar of experience.

The fire that primitive man gazes into and that prompts him, in his flame-lit reverie, to become a poet is one thing; the fire we are forced to gaze into as we cross millennia at the end of the twentieth century is another. The poetry from this fire-gazing is hard though essential to achieve, and is almost the artist's greatest challenge. The fire we must gaze into burns in Dresden, Hamburg, in the ovens of Auschwitz, in Hiroshima, Nagasaki, in all those places where non-combatants were burned to death; in the looted and destroyed villages of the Balkans; in the millions of Greek manuscripts and books burned in the library of Alexandria by Moslem fanatics, in Jewish and so-called 'decadent' books in Germany burned by Nazi fanatics; in the bonfire of the books of dissidents, including the poetry of Yannis Ritsos, in front of the Temple of Zeus in Athens under the Metaxas dictatorship; in Moslem books in the Institute for Oriental Studies of Sarajevo destroyed by rockets on 17 May 1992, with the incineration of the entire library of documents and manuscripts of Ottoman

Bosnia; in Salman Rushdie's *Satanic Verses* burned by affronted Moslems in Yorkshire, England. The fire in which Man discovered his poetry is used to destroy poetic endeavour. Poetry will either be tempered in that burning history or disappear. The meditative hearth now contains the Holocaust and the H-bomb. 'The atom smashers may be regarded as the most Promethean of the Prometheans. By releasing the power latent in the nucleus of the atom they made the theft of Prometheus a very minor piece of effrontery' (Robert S. De Ropp, *The New Prometheans: Creative and Destructive Forces in Modern Science*, London, 1972).

The flames that created reverie create nightmares. The flames that once created man's capacity for dreaming are now fuelled by tragedies, and the expression we seek from their contemplation has to imagine those worst things in the dancing fires that cast our shadows into the next millennium. And if I say that the fire offered by the Prometheus of Aeschylus had not yet acquired the accretions of our bestial and barbaric human history, I would have to add that I think that Aeschylus gazed into what, for him in the fifth century BC, was an equivalent historical destruction, the eradication of an entire civilisation in the razing of the city of Troy. The beacons that brought the news of the fall of Troy after ten years to Argos and the torches that accompanied the procession that honours the Furies at the end of the *Oresteia* were lit from the annihilation of Troy. The gift of fire was already ambiguous to Aeschylus. The destructive had to give birth to the celebratory fire, and the celebratory fire, like our own VJ street bonfires in 1945, can never be a different element from the destructive flame. The images of torches in procession, the destructive element as a redemptive symbol, is paralleled in the way Jewish pilgrims to Auschwitz place *Yohrzeit* (Remembrance) candles in the ovens where over a million were cremated, a candle into the heart of dark, destroying flame.

VI

The *Prometheus Bound* of Aeschylus ends with a great cry
to the light that is common to all and that unites the
audience with the surrounding universe and their suffering
champion:

ὦ πάντων
αἰθὴρ κοινὸν φάος εἱλίσσων,
ἐσορᾷς μ' ὡς ἔκδικα πάσχω.

This common light is at the heart of the experience of
Greek tragedy, as I have written in my introduction to my
play *The Trackers of Oxyrhynchus* (Faber, 1990). Why,
you might ask, should I – who have often claimed that we
cannot understand the essence of ancient tragedy unless we
remember that the common light united audience and per-
former, and have refused all offers to have my theatrical
presentations filmed – use the cinema for my *Prometheus*?

In fact, many years ago, I had wanted to stage the
original play of Aeschylus in Yorkshire, as one of what
have been called my *kamikaze* performances, on a
Caucasus of coalslack on some colliery spoil heap close to
a power station. It became a cinema venture because of a
feeling I had that my poetic reveries in front of our living-
room coal fire and my earliest experiences of films were
connected. Wolfgang Schivelbusch, a German historian of
the industrialisation of light in the nineteenth century,
articulates a parallel that I had always felt – between
gazing into fire where our poetry began, and looking at
images in the cinema, which needs the surrounding dark-
ness:

In light-based media, light does not simply illuminate
existing scenes, it creates them. The world of the

diorama and the cinema is an illusory dream world
that light opens up to the viewer. . . He can lose
himself in it in the same way that he can submerge
himself in contemplating the campfire or a candle. In
this respect the film is closer to the fire than the theatre.
An open-air performance in bright daylight is quite
feasible, while a camp-fire in the light of day is as
senseless, even invisible, as a film projected in daylight.
The power of artificial light to create its own reality
only reveals itself in darkness. In the dark, light is life.

The connection between my obsession with fire and my
obsession with movies led me to make a film about fire
and poetry. The other factor which led me to the cinema
is the way the size of the cinema screen can give heroic
stature to the most humble of faces, and this became an
essential requirement in a film where the most unlikely
wheezing ex-miner is slowly made to represent Prometheus
himself. Men projected onto large screens could become
Titans or gods.

In 1978 I worked at the Metropolitan Opera in New
York with John Dexter, doing a new English libretto for
Smetana's opera *Prodana Nevesta* (*The Bartered Bride*).
The designer was the great Czech scenographer Josef
Svoboda, with whom I spent time in Prague as I was
researching my scenario in Bohemia. He gave me a book
on his work by Jarka Burian, *The Scenography of Josef
Svoboda* (Wesleyan University Press, 1971). I had lived
and worked in Prague in the sixties and had seen many of
his truly innovative designs in the theatres there and his
thrilling combinations of film and stage at the *Laterna
Magika*, so I was very glad to have a book which
documented these productions and gave me detailed
information on those I hadn't seen. One in particular
stayed in my mind: the Staatsoper Munich production
by Everding of Carl Orff's opera *Prometheus* in 1968.

Svoboda tried to solve the problem of a man portraying a Titan by using simultaneous video to literally *project* the singing Prometheus onto the rock where he was bound so that the tenor sang from between his own projected Titan's eyes. Svoboda described his ingenious solution thus:

> . . . The main device was the use of live television to project an enlarged image of Prometheus' face onto the very surface of the rock to which he was nailed, in other words, we saw Prometheus 'in' the image of his face, thereby providing tremendous emphasis to his torment. We used the technique at special moments only, for maximum impact. The ending, during which I used dozens of low-voltage units, had its own special effectiveness. I had the entire frame of the proscenium lined with low-voltage units aimed at the rock and Prometheus. During the ending of the opera, the intensity of these units was gradually increased at the same time that the rock was gradually being withdrawn. The intensity of the special lights increased to a painful, blinding glare in which the TV image faded and the rock began to function as a mirror. The audience was blinded for nearly a full minute, in the meantime the whole setting – the rock and the stairs – disappeared, leaving only a blank space. Prometheus was consumed in the fire of light.

VII

What remained to do was to put the poetry I had nurtured in the flames of the family hearth into the cinema. I happen to believe that film and poetry have a great deal in common. One of the first things I learned from the ten film/poems I have made was that poetry could enter the inner world of people in documentary situations. Auden, probably the first poet to write verse specifically for a screen documentary, *Nightmail* (1936), is reported to have said in a lecture on 'Poetry and Film': 'Poetry can also be used to express the thoughts of characters, in rather the same way as Eugene O'Neill introduces "the interior voice" in *Strange Interlude*.' (Auden's lecture in 1936 to the North London Film Society is included in the form of an authorised report as an appendix in Edward Mendelson's edition of Auden's *Plays and Other Dramatic Writings*, Faber, 1989.)

I disagree wholeheartedly with Auden's opinion that 'The generally accepted metrical forms cannot be used in films, owing to the difficulty of cutting the film exactly according to the beat without distorting the visual content.' In my own film/poems I have used the quatrain of Gray's *Elegy* and the quatrain of Fitzgerald's *Rubaiyat of Omar Khayyam*, as well as octosyllabic couplets. Auden's remark, of course, only applies to the kind of task Auden was set – that is, to compose verse to an already edited picture, as a film composer usually produces his score. Although I sometimes work in this way, when the editor has come up with an exciting sequence, I usually begin drafting even before the editor has done his first rough assembly. In fact, when I wasn't on the shoot itself (and after my first collaboration with the BBC director Peter Symes, I always was present and sometimes composing on the spot), I would see all the rushes and begin sketching lines and sequences.

The person who wrote notes on Auden's lecture observes that 'Mr Auden even found it necessary to time his spoken verse with a stop-watch in order to fit it exactly to the shot on which it commented.' Auden was working before the video machine made it possible to have frame-accurate time code and easily replayed sequences. And perhaps the new digital editing has made it possible to experiment much more with the relations between poetry and film. Whereas manual editing on the Steenbeck gives a run-up, albeit in fast forward, to the sequence being worked on, and therefore a quick reprise of the wider context, digital editing with its speed can allow you to try many different variations in much shorter time. It also allows the editor to call up clusters of related imagery from any part of the logged and telecined rushes. This can be the visual equivalent of laterally garnered clusters of poetic imagery, and my deep-rooted way of letting disparate images grow together has been fed by the *Avid* or *Lightworks* editing programmes.

Auden clearly wanted to learn more about the technicalities of film-making in the thirties and to explore the possibilities of what he could do, not after the film was edited, but before and even during the shooting. He was to have been co-director on Grierson's planned sequel to *Nightmail*, to be called *Air Mail to Australia*. The endeavour was abandoned, but it shows that Auden was keen to extend his relationship with film. In 1935 Auden served as production manager and assistant director on another GPO Film Unit production, *Calendar of the Year*, in which he also played a small role as Father Christmas! Auden clearly saw the possibilities of film and poetry, and seems to have been willing to apprentice himself to all the processes, with a view to doing what I, in fact, have ended up doing in my own film/poems – being there as a constant presence during the shoot with a very sympathetic colleague like Peter Symes, and then, following the logic of the organic process developed during our collaborations, directing the films myself.

Another great figure in British cinema, the documentary film maker Humphrey Jennings, was also a poet both on the page and in his cinematic practice, and the perception of the affinity could also be found at the same time in the Soviet Union. Sergei Eisenstein began work on *Alexander Nevsky* in 1937, the year of my birth. When he began his shooting script he was inspired by Milton's *Paradise Lost*. Thus, 'Milton's imagery of the Battle of Heaven became the battle on the ice in *Alexander Nevsky*,' writes Marie Seaton (1978), Eisenstein's biographer. He broke lines of Milton down into scenes 'to illustrate how *cinematic construction could be found in poetry*.'

Pier Paolo Pasolini was a poet before he was a film director. Even towards the end of his career a film like *Teorema* (1968) began life in the form of a verse tragedy, and Pasolini used his own verse, as Eisenstein used Milton's, as a template for cinematic construction. Victor Erice, the Spanish director of *The Spirit of the Beehive* and *The Quince Tree Sun*, said, in an interview in the *Guardian* on 1 April 1993:

> As Pasolini used to say, there is the cinema of prose and the cinema of poetry, and I try for the latter kind . . . Nowadays, prose is triumphant. We are very frightened of poetry. Hollywood deals with prose and it is as powerful in Spain as everywhere else. I can't compete with it, still less beat it. All I would say is that there is another cinema and surely it should be allowed to exist.

There were earlier attempts before Pasolini to distinguish the cinema of prose from the cinema of poetry, and probably the first was by the Russian Victor Shklovsky, whose 'Poetry and Prose in the Cinema' was published in 1927. Maya Turovskaya, in her study of Tarkovsky, quotes Shklovsky's distinction:

> There is a cinema of prose and a cinema of poetry, two different genres; they differ not in their rhythm – or rather not only in their rhythm – but in the fact that in the cinema of poetry elements of form prevail over elements of meaning and it is they, rather than the meaning, which determine the composition.

She then goes on to ask a very important question: 'Why is it that at some moments in history the cinema feels the need for a poetic treatment of its raw material?' She answers her question by saying that this need 'is particularly sharply felt during periods of historical change, when our "normal", accepted notions and perceptions become inadequate in the face of changing realities, and new perceptions have to be developed.' And in these changing realities the often forgotten captive champion, Prometheus, tends to be remembered. Of course, she includes the films of Tarkovsky as 'poetic', and though Tarkovsky himself grew irritated with the label, he admires and quotes his father's poetry in his films and in his 'Reflections on Cinema', *Sculpting in Time*, and himself applies the adjective to the cinema of Kurosawa. Tarkovsky, who confesses that his favourite art form is the three-line Japanese *haiku,* writes: 'I find poetic links, the logic of poetry in cinema, extraordinarily pleasing.' And among those he designates as creating 'great spiritual treasures and that special beauty which is subject only to poetry' he includes not only poets in the literary sense – Pushkin, Mandelstam and Pasternak – but also film makers: Chaplin, the Russian Dovzhenko and the Japanese director Mizoguchi.

Pasolini also includes Chaplin and Mizoguchi, along with Bergman, as producers of 'great cinematic poems', but goes on to say that their films were not constructed according to the laws of what he calls 'the language of the cinema of poetry': 'This means that these films were not poetry, but narratives. Classic cinema was and is narrative, its language is that of prose. Its poetry is an inner poetry, as, for example, in the narratives of Chekhov or Melville.' For Pasolini the cinema of poetry means, among other things, making the spectator aware of the camera's presence, and 'a primarily formalist world-view of the author'. He speaks (in an article which, considering it is by a poet, is surprisingly bogged down with semiotic jargon) of an emergent 'prosody'.

Though much of this thinking comes from directors who are either poets themselves or have a close affinity with poetry, they are usually referring to a kind of cinema in which, as Pasolini defines it, we are aware of the camera and its movement and what he calls a 'free indirect subjective'. We are not talking about the actual use of verse, though again Tarkovsky uses his father's poetry to wonderful effect in *Mirror*. Nor are they talking about films which are cinematic versions of theatre – Shakespeare, say, or Rostand's *Cyrano* with Gerard Depardieu. My own *Prometheus* brings my experience of film verse and theatre verse together.

There is an underlying connection between verse, metrical poetry and film which my colleague Peter Symes draws attention to in his introduction to a volume of my film/poems, *The Shadow of Hiroshima* (Faber, 1995). The 24 (or 25) frames per second have what can be called a prosodic motion. In my first experiences of the cutting room of Jess Palmer at the BBC in 1981 I realised that my own rhythmic preoccupations had a parallel in what I now think of as the scansions of edited sequences. It is not merely the 24 frames per second, nor the metrical beats in a verse line, but how they succeed one another and build into gratifications or disappointments of expectation. Maya Turovskaya describes a similar recognition with regard to Tarkovsky: 'Feeling the rhythmicity of a shot is rather like feeling a truthful word in literature.' In poetry, of course, the truthful word is also the right metrical word, the word with its truth and its sound placed on the most telling grid of the metric. The cinematic construction in poetry that Eisenstein found in Milton is paralleled by the poetic construction of cinema. And, I have always thought, the two prosodies can be plaited, metrical beat and cinematic scansion.

VIII

At the very end of the film, when there is a kind of *Götter-dämmerung* caused by the Old Man's flung cigarette, intended to destroy Hermes, the golden statue of Prometheus is consumed 'in his own concoction bloody flames'. We see real red and yellow flames consuming the black-and-white projected flames on the Palace Cinema screen, as the whole collected cast of statues melt and scream like humans in a conflagration. We only had one chance to film it, and although the charred limbs fell apart and tumbled down the rocks in a quarry belonging to Titan Cement, Elefsina, nonetheless what remained was the chained but still defiantly clenched fist of the champion of Mankind, burned off at the shoulder. And what remained of the silver statue of Hermes was a fist still grasping his *caduceus*, the symbol of his office. No détente!

There are times in all art when you accept what you are given, and this was one. However, as I often do, when everyone else had left for England I went back and looked round the quarry. At the foot of the towering rock was the charred head of Prometheus, matted blackened fibreglass still with the Titan's features, looking uncannily like the photograph of the Iraqi soldier burned in his truck on the road to Basra during the Gulf War, about whom I had written my poem 'A Cold Coming'. What was remarkable about this incinerated head was that in its eyes it retained the gold leaf it had been painstakingly gilded with. So that for all its having passed through holocaust it retained its golden visions. The vision seen by the golden eyes in the carbonised profile isn't diminished. They take their sheen and glitter from 'the fire of light', from the future, from the flicker of the screen whenever their journey is projected, and witnessed by new eyes. As I held the head I remembered that wonderful poem of Yannis Ritsos on the

Bulgarian poet Geo Melev (1895–1925), who had a glass
eye, and when he was arrested and burned alive by the
police, all that was left of him in the crematorium was the
blue glass eye:

> His eye is being kept in the Museum of Revolution
> like a seeing stone of the struggle. I saw his eye.
> In his pupil there was the full story of the Revolution,
> blue scenes of blood-stained years
> blue scenes with red flags
> with dead who carry in their raised hands a blue day.
> His eye never closes,
> this eye keeps vigil over Sofia.
> This eye is a blue star in all the nights.
> This eye sees and illuminates and judges.
> Whoever looks at this eye wins back his eyes.
> Whoever looks at this eye sees the world.
>
> (trans. Ninetta Makrinikola)

Poetry rises out of its own ashes and continues its ancient
dream in front of fire. Not only the animated flame but
also smoking ash and cinders with their bits of bone,
rings, a blue glass eye, the golden pupils of the first
champion of Mankind, strike the aboriginal poetic spark.
Whoever looks into the golden eyes of Prometheus set in
the cremated sockets sees the early hope of the world
and knows its late despair.

Tony Harrison
Terme di Caracalla, Rome
Delphi, Greece
1998

Prometheus was a Channel 4 Film, in association with the Arts Council of England.

Hermes Michael Feast
Old Man/Grandad Walter Sparrow
Mam (Io) Fern Smith
Boy Jonathan Waistnidge
Dad Steve Huison
Grandma Audrey Haggerty

Miners Dave Hill, Tim Hall, Roger Gren, Ian Clayton, Paul Knaggs, James Banks, Dave Parker, Alan Hobson, Stewart Merrill

Daughters of Ocean Catherine Pidd, Maureen Craven, Beverley Ashby, Sue Barker, Sandra Hookham, Clare Hookham, Jane Riley, Lesley Pickersgill, Beverley Brighton, Vicky McCallister, Linda Callear, Jean McCauley

Written and directed by Tony Harrison
Director of Photography Alistair Cameron
Production Designer Jocelyn Herbert
Editor Luke Dunkley
Composer Richard Blackford
Production Manager Peter Flynn
Location Manager Joel Holmes
Executive Producer Michael Kustow
Producer Andrew Holmes

1. EXT. COOLING TOWERS, YORKSHIRE, DAWN

The sun rises between steaming cooling towers in Yorkshire.

2. EXT. KRATOS AND BIA HEADQUARTERS, COOLING TOWER, DAY

Close-up of flame logo (derived from the Greek forest fire-hazard warning sign) on brilliant white door. The logo is a combination of notices forbidding activities, like NO SMOKING, *but also in its black, white and red rather reminiscent of Nazi insignia.*

Pull back to show that the logo is on a white door at the top of staircase, with red iron railings, leading from the large cooling tower of a power station.

3. INT. CAB OF CATTLE-TRUCK, DAY

Close-up of black rubber glove violently hitting the horn on the steering wheel of a truck.

Pull back to reveal: Bia (Violence) in white overalls, black chemical exposure mask and red hard hat, sounding the horn of a cattle-truck.

4. INT. COOLING TOWER, DAY

With the sound still blaring, cut to interior of the cooling tower. In the centre of a white circular platform with a central white and red walkway stands Kratos (Force), his head raised towards the open circle of the top of the tower as if receiving his morning briefing from Zeus.

287

There is steam seeping through the slats on either side.

The 'briefing' comes from the disembodied voice of Hermes reverberating through the cooling tower.

VOICE OF HERMES

Zeus commands you don the gear
of Kratos (Force) and Violence (Bia)
and, in this guise, you give some grief
to those who love the fire-thief.

The blaring of the truck horn is echoed and reverberated inside the vast cooling tower.

Kratos begins to walk forward towards the door of the cooling tower.

Kratos (Force) has the same white overalls, black chemical exposure mask and red hard hat as Bia (Violence).

The echoing klaxon continues abrasively and more insistently.

5. EXT. KRATOS AND BIA HEADQUARTERS, DAY

Kratos (Force) walks down the steps of the cooling tower, opens the truck door, and his black-gloved hand grasps the wrist of Bia (Violence) and stops the strident klaxon fanfare.

6. INT. KRATOS AND BIA CATTLE-TRUCK, DAY

A rubber-gloved hand thrusts a tape into the cab tape deck.

String quartet music issues from cab. It is music designed to keep Bia (Violence) tranquilised during his journey.

Bia (Violence) gives a final defiant blast of the horn.

Yesterday's copy of the Doncaster Star *rests on the dashboard. It reads: 'Last Yorkshire Pit to Close Tomorrow.'*

7. EXT. COOLING TOWERS, DAY

Cattle-truck pulls away from the steaming cooling tower, which wheezes like a giant version of a smoker's lungs, the lungs of the Old Man.

8. INT. OLD MAN'S HOUSE, DAWN

Old Man, up early with his cough, sees a strange truck pass through a deserted street. It is the cattle-truck driven by Force and Violence.

Old Man sits down. He picks up a paper, the same Doncaster Star *that we saw in the passing cattle-truck and which we will see the Boy using to make 'chips' to light a fire. The paper announces the closure of the last pit in Yorkshire, with a picture of Michael Heseltine, in an article reviewing the whole struggle over pit closures from the Miners' Strike of 1984 to the present.*

Old Man gobs at the picture of Heseltine and the coaly green phlegm runs down the picture.

OLD MAN
(looking at paper)

Bastard Heseltine!

He screws up the paper with the phlegm and throws it into the dead coal-fire grate behind the one-bar electric fire.

OLD MAN

Bastard coal!

Old Man stares at his carving of STRIKING MINER, *1984 in the Promethean pose. It is a carving in coal*

289

of a miner with a defiantly raised right fist.
Cattle-truck string-quartet music leading to:

9. INT. PARENTS' BEDROOM, BOY'S HOUSE, DAWN

Dad is up and draws the curtains and sees the
cattle-truck pass. He sees the Zeus painted on the roof.

The cattle-truck's horn is sounded violently.

Mam seems to be waking from a violent nightmare.

Dad opens bedroom door, shouting to Boy, banging on
his bedroom door.

DAD
Come on, lad, look sharp. Get t'fire going.

BOY
(*from inside his room*)
It's too hot for a fire!

DAD
(*going into bathroom*)
I want a *coal* fire burning in this house today of all days.
And use paper not wood. And tha can stick that kettle
on, while tha's at it.

Boy emerges from bedroom, putting on a red Barnsley
FC jersey. He goes downstairs.

10. EXT. KIRKBY MAIN COLLIERY, SPOIL HEAP

Cattle-truck stops outside the colliery, gleaming white on
the top of a black spoil heap of slack.

Kratos and Bia have a view of the colliery's winding
gear. They are waiting for something to happen.

11. INT. CAB OF CATTLE-TRUCK, DAY

Kratos (Force) opens the newspaper with the headline

reading: 'Last Yorkshire Pit to Close Tomorrow'.
Sub-headline: 'Arthur's Nightmare Prophecy Fulfilled'.

The cab of the truck has, hanging from the roof, like a
typical truckdriver's talisman, a little miniature
Prometheus, swinging and dangling from a little chain.
We see Prometheus swaying from Force and Violence's
point of view as the truck comes to a halt on top of the
spoil heap of slack.

Kratos (Force) opens the paper, which fills the whole
frame. Then he folds it up and puts it down on the ledge
above the dashboard.

Paper becomes the paper in the Boy's hand.

12. INT. FRONT ROOM OF HOUSE NEAR COLLIERY,
DAY/DAWN

Close-up on front page of newspaper announcing pit
closures, the same front page we have already seen. The
sound of paper being rolled, then a pair of hands rolling
the page into a tube which is then flattened. Boy is
lighting the household fire by first plaiting pages from
the newspapers into 'chips'. As he plaits, the Boy is
heard reciting the homework he has to learn for class
today:

BOY

'Men had eyes but didn't see.
The sight they now have came from me.
They had ears, but never heard
the beauty of a sound or word,
so that Man's earthly life did seem,
until my deed, a cloudy dream,
until I opened ears and eyes
to all the life of earth and skies.
Before I came men would be found

in sunless dwellings underground.
They saw no difference between
the winter and the springtime scene.
Without me Man would not now know
the earth and all that lies below,
underground treasures for his use
to free him from the grip of Zeus.
With Prometheus life began
to flourish for benighted Man.
My gift of fire made Mankind free
but I stay in captivity.'

> *The Boy plaits more pages, from what is in fact his*
> *Dad's archive on the pit closures, with prominent front*
> *pages from:* Doncaster Star, *Tuesday, 13 October 1992;*
> Yorkshire Post, *Wednesday, 14 October 1992; and*
> *various other papers saved over the years for the*
> *scrapbook of the miners' struggle and successive pit*
> *closures.*

> *He puts the 'chips' on top of some screwed-up*
> *newspaper in the fire grate.*

13. EXT. STREET OUTSIDE BOY'S HOUSE, DAY

Long street with Colliery Band, a straggling remnant of
a once great tradition, promenading and playing out the
last shift of the closing colliery. Miner comes out of
house and joins the straggling march. We pick them up
from the front in wide and cut back to:

14. INT. BOY'S HOUSE, DAY

Boy puts first lumps of coal on top of his plaited paper
chips and the scrumpled paper.

Extra close-up of match flame. Hold on flame. Boy looks
at the match flame, totally fascinated by it, until his

fingers are burnt and he throws away the match, then he lights another and applies the flame to the paper quickly and throws the match into the grate.

The fire begins in the papers and builds. To help it along the Boy puts a shovel over the grate and then a newspaper. The fire roars behind headlines of Heseltine's closures of the pit.

Extra close-up of photo of a group of Miners (the twelve whose fate we will follow) has flames dancing and roaring behind it as the fire draws, then it browns, then bursts into flame.

The Boy, used to the routine, scrumples up the burning paper and extinguishes the flames and throws the ball of paper into the fire. He burns his hand a little as he does so, and blows on the burn to cool it.

Close-up of fire now burning brightly. Sound of Boy blowing on burned hand blends with Colliery Band music outside in the street coming nearer.

16. EXT. STREET, DAY

Kirkby Main Colliery Band marches down the street, collecting Miners on the last shift of the last Yorkshire pit to march to the colliery.

17. EXT. STREET, DAY

Colliery Band still promenading down the street, playing the Miners out of their houses.

Colliery Band passes Women waiting for works bus, 'Oceanus', to collect them for work. Badinage between the two groups.

Oceanus bus picks up Women.

18. INT. OCEANUS BUS, DAY

Badinage with driver, group badinage.

As Oceanus bus overtakes the Band, Women rush to back seat of bus, and as the Band plays a crescendo they all hit the same high note in unison.

19. EXT. STREET, DAY

We see the Women in the back window of the bus, all with mouths open, singing to a crescendo note from the Colliery Band.

Mix through to illustration in Boy's book. It shows Prometheus as a golden statue with his right fist raised in defiance and flame in a rod of fennel-stalk in his left.

20. INT. BOY'S HOUSE, DAY

Boy is still reading his Prometheus book by the fire, at a different page.

BOY

'My gift of fire made Mankind free
but I stay in captivity.'

He turns his head at the sound of the door opening. His point of view of his Dad, entering ready for the pit's last shift. Dad gives a small nod and smiles, but grimly. He's preoccupied with this being his last day of work.

Boy desperately still trying to commit to memory the passage from Prometheus.

DAD

I don't know, lad, all that there bleeding sitting on thi backside, bloody reading.

BOY

'ave gotta learn it for us 'omework,
'ave *gotta* learn it!

DAD

God knows why they feed yer all that crap.

BOY

Ah've gotta learn this speech for t'class today.
Bloody great chunk to learn by heart.

*Dad takes the book to have a look at it. Flicks
through the pages.*

DAD
(*looking at cover of book*)

So who's Pro-me-the-us when he's at home.

BOY

It's pronounced Pro-me-theus.
PRO-ME-THEUS . . . USE . . . USE.

DAD

So what bloody *use* wor 'e, then?

BOY

Well, for a start your job'd never've existed.

DAD
(*gazing into the coal fire*)

It dun't no more!

BOY

He stole fire from t'gods and gave it to men down here.
So now there's coal and all that. He ended up chained to
a rock for thirty thousand years, and a bloody great
eagle came and ate his liver every day, as a punishment
for stealing fire.

DAD

Serves him bloody reet for thieving. And he shouldn't
have bloody bothered, if pits was his idea!

*Dad notices that the papers he was saving have been
burned.*

DAD

Hey, have you burned t'papers from that lot? Ah'll clip
thi lug if tha's used them papers that were there to make
chips. They went reet back to '84, before tha were even
born, them did, and tha's bloody burned 'em. There were
photos of all t'lads in it. Me an' all. Ah don't supposed
that bothered thee a bit. Didn't you ever stop to think? I
wor off to mek a scrapbook, scrap-heap book more like!
It's bad enough being jobless wi'out being chucked on
t'fire by thee!

*Dad picks up the Old Man's carving in coal and flings
that in the fire. The carving is of a miner in pit gear in
the Promethean pose and has an etched brass caption
reading* STRIKING MINER, 1984.

Yer might as well burn your grandad's carving. It's only
bloody coal.

*The carving begins to burn in the fire. The brass
plaque saying* STRIKING MINER, 1984 *melts in the
flame. Dad grabs the book the Boy is reading.*

I'll chuck this bloody book of thine in t'fire! Your bloody
what's his bloody name 's off into his own concoction,
bloody flames. Serves 'im reet for thieving, and serves
thee reet for taking no bloody notice.

BOY
(*struggling to retrieve his book*)
It belongs to t'school. They'll mek us pay.
And after today there won't be that much brass.

DAD

I'll give thi bloody brass.
I'll show bloody Goldenballs what for!

*Dad snatches book. He rips pages out of it and flings
them into the fire.*

DAD

Yer bloody fire-giver's gone up t'flue.

Dad storms out of the room back into the kitchen, slamming the door.

Boy manages to retrieve a page of the book with the charred fragment of the golden Statue of Prometheus on it. He clenches it in his fist, still smoking, and shouts angrily at the kitchen door.

BOY

Burning books 's what Nazis do.

Dad comes racing back out of the kitchen and clips the Boy round the head. The Boy runs out of the house. His foot kicks a toy fire engine as he runs.

20. EXT. SAME HOUSE, DAY

Boy opens the door and runs out, holding his head and sobbing, just as the Colliery Band come to play his Dad out. When the Boy sees his Dad he begins to run away down the street, and camera moves in to close-up of Dad looking hurt and puzzled and up then to show Mam (Io) leaning out of the bedroom window.

MAM

Jack, come back. He didn't mean it. He's upset, your dad.

21. EXT. STREET, DAY

Cut to Boy running with Colliery Band in background behind.

BOY

Nazi get!

22. EXT. BOY'S HOUSE, DAY

Mam's face registers that she's had no response. She leans further out of the window and then with a sigh retreats. As she pulls back into the room, and her eyes make an upward movement of despair and resignation, camera follows the eye-movement and cranes up beyond her to the smoking chimney of the house and following the direction of the smoke reveals the steaming cooling towers of the power station.

Cut to:

23. EXT. COOLING TOWERS, DAY

Close-up of shadows of steam crossing the bodies of the cooling towers left to right.

24. EXT. KIRKBY MAIN COLLIERY, SPOIL HEAP, DAY

Cooling towers in background. Boy runs over the pit-hill en route to the wrecked bus yard.

25. EXT. STREET, DAY

Mam hurries down street after the runaway Boy. She passes Colliery Band, who have just played her husband out of his house.

26. INT. OLD MAN'S HOUSE, DAY

Close-up of the glowing single element in a one-bar electric fire. In the curved silver surface divided by the element is the reflection of the Old Man. He is wheezing heavily.

On his mantelpiece are carvings of miners done in coal. There is one identical to the STRIKING MINER, 1984 *in the Promethean pose that Dad threw in the fire.*

Old Man tears a strip of paper from same Doncaster
Star *we saw the Boy use to light the fire. He twists the
paper and lights it at the electric element, then lights a
cigarette.*

*Close-up of Old Man's reflection in electric fire as he
lights his fag.*

*The first drag gives him a terrible coughing fit. He drops
the lighted spill onto the carpet and stamps out the fire
with his slipper. Frantically tries to sweep up the
blackened paper and clean the black mark on the carpet.*

27. INT. UPSTAIRS, OLD MAN'S HOUSE, DAY

*Grandma, the wife of the Old Man, is looking through
the bedroom net curtains at the marching Band. She's in
her nightie and there are tears flowing down her cheeks.*

*She sniffs the air, smells the Old Man's cigarette smoke
and hears the coughing fit. She turns and shouts:*

GRANDMA
Are you lighting up again, you barmy beggar? You'll be
underground again sooner than you think. And if you're
going to be carving damned coal all day put some papers
down.

28. INT. OLD MAN'S HOUSE, DOWNSTAIRS, DAY

*Old Man makes a 'stop nagging' face. Then is racked by
coughing.*

*Close-up on coughing mouth, then cut to Colliery Band,
which seems to 'translate' the coughing into staccato
brass.*

*Old Man puts on his overcoat and leaves the house by
the back door.*

29. EXT. OLD MAN'S HOUSE, DAY

Old Man comes out of the back door beneath the cooling tower.

30. EXT. OLD MAN'S HOUSE, DAY

Grandma watches the Band and Miners passing her house from the bedroom window.

31. EXT. STREET, DAY

Colliery Band is marching and playing at the end of the road.

Old Man tries to catch up with the Colliery Band. He coughs. He makes another step forward.

Cooling towers appear at the end of the road. They wheeze like a smoker's lungs.

32. EXT. KIRKBY MAIN COLLIERY, SPOIL HEAP, DAY

A silver Statue of Hermes pointing his caduceus (a rod with an emblem at the end depicting the same 'fire forbidden' sign we saw on the cattle-truck).

Hermes is pointing at Boy running across the vast black spoil heap in his red Barnsley FC football jersey.

Back to Hermes pointing from a colliery gantry at Boy running on the vast colliery spoil heap, a Caucasus of coal-slack alongside a conveyor pouring out coal. Pan from Boy to pouring conveyor, then to:

33. EXT. CANAL, DAY

Close-up of coal pouring into a coal barge.

Barge moves on canal towards cooling towers.

Heavy traffic hurtles across the A1 road-bridge over the canal.

34. EXT. PEDESTRIAN CANAL BRIDGE, DAY

Old Man walks over the canal bridge dominated by the cooling towers. He leans on the parapet and coughs. In spite of the coughing fit he takes another deep drag on his fag. He smokes. He sees:

35. EXT. CANAL PATH AND CANAL, COOLING TOWERS, DAY

Mam runs on the canal path in the direction of the cooling towers.

The barge we've seen filled with newly hewn coal moves, low in the water, laden with coal, towards the cooling towers of the power station.

Traffic hurtles by on the bridge above.

                    VOICE OF OLD MAN
I know where he'll be.

36. EXT. COOLING TOWERS, DAY

Close-up on shadows of steam crossing the barrel chambers of the towers.

37. EXT. BUS-WRECKING YARD BENEATH COOLING TOWERS, DAY

Pan down from cooling towers to discover Boy entering bus-wrecking yard. Track with Boy along the rusty hubs, broken windows, and doors of various buses.

Boy wanders round wrecked buses, into the cabs, trying seats, upstairs and downstairs. Details of dereliction. He climbs the stairs of one bus and sits down on a seat.

Boy looks at the charred fragment of the burned book, the golden head of Prometheus haloed in black fire-charred edges.

As he looks at the picture we hear the Colliery Band playing a mournful elegiac tune for the last shift of the last Yorkshire pit.

38. EXT. KIRKBY MAIN COLLIERY ENTRANCE, DAY

The Colliery Band plays the last shift into the colliery gate. Their feet crunch on the coal slack as they file in.

39. INT. COLLIERY ENTRANCE, DAY

Close-up on man's hand counting out twelve piles of two brass tallies given to each Miner as he clocks on.

40. INT. OCEANUS BUS, DAY

Women fish factory workers chat on their bus, as the Oceanus bus passes the cooling towers.

41. EXT. KIRKBY MAIN COLLIERY ENTRANCE, DAY

The feet of the last shift Miners crunch on the coal slack as they enter to the music of the Colliery Band.

42. EXT. KIRKBY MAIN SPOIL HEAP, DAY

Mam runs anxiously on top of the spoil heap with cooling towers breathing steam behind her.

43. EXT. KIRKBY MAIN COLLIERY, DAY

The Band continues to play its 'threnody'. The colliery sign is reflected in the tuba bell.

Close-ups of various instrumentalists.

44. EXT. OCEANUS FISH FACTORY, DAY

Oceanus bus arrives at the factory.

45. EXT. BUS-WRECKING YARD, DAY

Boy leaves the upstairs of one wrecked bus past a mirror and a NO SMOKING *sign.*

46. INT. KIRKBY MAIN COLLIERY ENTRANCE, DAY

Man's hand continues to sort the brass tallies into pairs. Miners clock on and take brass tallies.

47. EXT. OCEANUS FISH FACTORY, DAY

Women enter the Oceanus fish factory.

48. INT. KIRKBY MAIN COLLIERY, DAY

Miners clock on and take a pair of brass tallies from the office counter ledge.

49. EXT. NEAR CANAL, DAY

Old Man walks and wheezes past a wrecked barge dominated by cooling towers.

50. EXT. BUS-WRECKING YARD, DAY

Boy enters the cab of another wrecked bus and starts to 'drive' it.

51. INT. OCEANUS FISH FACTORY, DAY

Oceanus Women, now in their fish-factory overalls and caps, pass through a hanging blue plastic curtain, followed by Hermes in the guise of an Oceanus foreman. He looks at them ominously.

52. INT. CHANGING ROOMS, KIRKBY MAIN COLLIERY, DAY

Miners, now in their, pit gear, pass chatting through a grimy plastic curtain.

53. INT. CORRIDOR, KIRKBY MAIN COLLIERY, DAY

The last shift passes windows in silhouette. One of the windows is broken, showing a green tree outside. The miners' boots clatter and echo.

54. EXT. BUS-WRECKING YARD, DAY

Old Man enters the bus-wrecking yard. He appears at the entrance of the bus the Boy is 'driving'.

OLD MAN
Thi mam's after thee!

BOY
That's just too bad.
'Cos I'm off. I got clouted by mi dad.

OLD MAN
What for? How did yer earn yer clout?

BOY
Burnt papers he were saving to cut out.

OLD MAN
What papers?

BOY
All t'*Posts* and *Stars* wi' bits
about 'em closing down all t'bloody pits.

OLD MAN
He'd not usually clout thee, would thi dad.
He's laid off after today and he feels bad.

BOY

He chucked my schoolbook into t'fire an all!

OLD MAN

He's lost his job, love! He feels small.

Boy and Old Man fall silent.

55. INT. MIRROR ROOM, KIRKBY MAIN COLLIERY, DAY

Dad looks at himself in a mirror which has on it THIS MAN IS RESPONSIBLE FOR YOUR SAFETY. *He greets his reflection with a wry smile, which fades rapidly.*

56. EXT. LIMITS OF 'CONTRABAND ZONE', COLLIERY, DAY

Miners are taking their last drags on their cigarettes. The wall behind them is painted in red-and-white warning stripes over which is printed in large black capitals: CONTRABAND ZONE.

A pit-boot grinds out the last cigarette.

The word CONTRABAND *is left as a Miner leaves the frame.*

57. INT. ENTRANCE TO PIT-CAGE, DAY

Hermes, this time in the gear of a colliery Tallyman awaits the arrival of the last shift. There is a contemptuous anticipation on his face as we hear the Miners approaching.

The Miners give the Tallyman one of their tallies. As each does this he whispers under his breath: 'Cunt!'

Miners enter the cage. Hermes (Tallyman) lets down the metal screen over the cage and the cage door closes. As the cage descends all the Miners shout together: 'Cunt!'

Hermes looks down the shaft with great contempt and speaks in ancient Greek the following lines from Aeschylus, Prometheus Bound, *944–6:*

HERMES

σὲ τὸν σοφιστήν, τὸν πικρῶς ὑπέρπικρον,
τὸν ἐξαμαρτόντ' εἰς θεοὺς ἐφημέροις
πορόντα τιμάς, τὸν πυρὸς κλέπτην λέγω.

*Hermes chinks the twelve tallies in his hand as he
walks away.*

58. INT. MIRROR ROOM, DAY

*Hermes regards himself in the mirror over which is
written:* THIS MAN IS RESPONSIBLE FOR YOUR SAFETY.

HERMES

You never expected I could speak
so fluently in ancient Greek.
Well, the truth is that I can
because I'm a god, and not a man.

*Hermes throws the twelve Miners' tallies to the
ground. He appears as a naked silver statue in the
mirror, and then in human form in a silver suit with
his caduceus in his hand.*

HERMES

And why, you might ask, should gods come
into this world of 'Ee-by-gum'?
Those dropped aitches help disguise
the fact I've flown down from the skies.
Just as steel-capped boots conceal
the wings that sprout out of each heel.
I hid the fact, by talking broad,
that I'm a posh Olympian lord.
It took just a few 'by 'eckers like's
and 'ecky thumps' to con these Tykes
into believing that this god
was just a fellow Northern sod,
playing darts and dominoes

and, Zeus help me, speaking *prose*!
I mean an immortal, Hermes, me,
not spouting proper poetry!

59. INT. CONTRABAND SIGN, MIRROR ROOM,
COLLIERY, DAY

*The shadow of the caduceus of Hermes passes across a
white sign with red letters reading:*

NATIONAL COAL BOARD
NORTH EASTERN DIVISION
NO. 2 (DONCASTER) AREA
CONTRABAND

ANY PERSON WHO TAKES CONTRABAND BELOW
GROUND AT THIS MINE, OR IS IN POSSESSION
OF CONTRABAND BELOW GROUND, OR IS FOUND
IN POSSESSION OF CONTRABAND ON BEING
SEARCHED WHEN ABOUT TO GO BELOW GROUND
IS LIABLE TO BE SUMMARILY DISMISSED
FROM HIS EMPLOYMENT AND DEBARRED FROM
SUBSEQUENT EMPLOYMENT IN THE INDUSTRY.

SUCH PERSONS MAY ALSO BE PROSECUTED
UNDER THE MINES AND QUARRIES ACT.

CONTRABAND INCLUDES ANY CIGAR OR CIGARETTE,
ANY PIPE OR OTHER CONTRIVANCE FOR SMOKING,
OR ANY MATCH OR MECHANICAL LIGHTER.

60. EXT. PIT WINDING GEAR, DAY

*The wheels of the pit winding gear spin and groan to a
creaky halt.*

61. EXT. SPOIL HEAPS, COLLIERY, DAY

Hermes walks on the colliery spoil heaps, speaking:

HERMES

This is the *terminus ad quem*
for bolshy bastards such as them.
Terminus ad quem and that in
local lingo, not in Latin,
the language into which one slips
when one's a god, means "ad their chips!'
In local lingo, note, gods rhyme
effortlessly all the time.
Poetry of this posh sort'll
never come from a mere mortal.
It's quite beyond mere mortal reach,
this pure Olympian form of speech.
It's a pure Olympian privilege
forbidden folk from Ferrybridge.
Olympians who serve Zeus speak
(apart from fluent ancient Greek)
such local lingos as one needs
when slumming it in Hull or Leeds.
And local lingos gods transform
by giving them poetic form.

*Hermes walks up a sloping stretch of the spoil heap. The
sound of a groaning dumper truck.*

62. EXT. COLLIERY, RAILWAY LOADING BAY, DAY

*A dumper truck tips a load of coal into a rail container
linked to others in a seemingly endless line. In the right
foreground is a red metal box reading:* FIRE HOSE.

The sound of a match being struck.

63. INT. WRECKED BUS, DAY

*The sound of the striking match came from the Old Man
lighting up a cigarette. He leans back exhaling smoke,
ready for the 'journey'.*

BOY

But I have to tell yer even an old bloke,
has to go upstairs if he wants to smoke.

OLD MAN

Them stairs 'll bloody kill me with my cough.

BOY
(*becoming 'official'*)
You must either smoke upstairs, sir, or get off.

64. EXT. WRECKING YARD, DAY

Old Man gets off, coughing.

OLD MAN

What are you talking like that for?

BOY

Like what?

OLD MAN

Like a bloody panto!

BOY
No, I'm not!

OLD MAN

You are! You're rhyming like that geezer
in *Aladdin*, Uncle Ebeneezer!

BOY

Abanazar! *Abanazar*! Ebeneezer's *Scrooge*.

OLD MAN

We sound like t'comic and his stooge.

*Old Man drags on his cigarette and contemplates the
shadows of steam drifting across the cooling towers.
His boots rest on an old chain.*

OLD MAN

I suppose it suits the bloody time
when Britain's one long pantomime,
where t'workers have been bloody conned
and someone waves a sodding wand
and down comes all the winding gear
that's stood in place a hundred year.
Them Tories twisting and two-timing . . .
Tha's got me at it, bloody rhyming.
Stop it!

BOY

Can't help it!

OLD MAN

Bloody try!

BOY

You mean try talking normal.

OLD MAN

Ay!

BOY

It's thee an' all. You spoiled it then
by saying Ay.

OLD MAN

Well, I won't again.

*They look at each other, aware that they are still
rhyming.*

OLD MAN

Gi' us a lift to t'pictures then. I'll pay.
Ah bet fare's rocketed since my day.
It cost a penny then from here to there.

BOY

A penny? It's 20p now, t'single fare.

OLD MAN

Ah've got us bus pass. Ah don't 'ave to pay.

BOY

Show us it!

Old Man fishes out bus pass.

BOY

Sit down, then, OK!

Boy begins to 'drive' bus.

BOY

Brrrm-brrrm-brrrm . . .

VOICE OF HERMES

Constant theft! First fire, now this –
pinching poetic artifice!
How can Olympus stay intact
if *poetry* comes to *Pontefract*?

BOY

Brrrm! Brrrm! Brrrm!

OLD MAN

By 'eck, lad, this bus is bloody slow.
At this rate I'll be missing t'picture show.
I'll walk there under mi own steam.
Stay in your broken bus and dream.

BOY

Tha can talk, Grandad. Tha's never seen
a single picture on that Palace screen.
It closed down forty year ago.

OLD MAN

I'm off, or else I'll miss mi show.
Don't tell thi grandma where I am.
And I'll not tell on thee. She's mad, thi mam.
I'll not let on that tha's been skiving.
Or that tha's got no licence and tha's driving.

Boy and Old Man make a silent agreement to connive.

Old Man stares at the shadows of steam across the barrel of the cooling towers above them as if looking for inspiration there.

Then out to Boy, cheerfully back in his dream of the 'pictures'.

OLD MAN

I'll get missen some humbugs or a piece
of liquorice.

BOY

And, me, I'm off to Greece.

OLD MAN

Send us a postcard.

BOY

Ay, and you enjoy
your Ginger Rogers and her brother Roy!
(*To himself.*) Barmy!

OLD MAN

(*overhearing as he walks away*)
If I'm barmy so are thee.
Birds of a barmy feather, thee and me.

Old Man looks at the shadows on the cooling tower. He lights up a cigarette and walks out of the wrecked bus yard, dominated by the cooling towers. He coughs.

Boy drives bus.

65. EXT. AERIAL SHOT, COOLING TOWERS, DAY

VOICE OF HERMES

What my boss Zeus longed to do
was melt Man down and mould a new,

smelt the old stock and recast
a better Mankind from the last.

66. EXT. CHURCHYARD, DAY

Old Man continues his walk through a graveyard
dominated by the power station cooling towers. Breathless
and coughing, he leans on a stone cross. In the distance
behind him is the winding gear of the colliery.

                    VOICE OF HERMES
And 'better' was his way of saying
Man with a bent for more obeying.
Zeus would have fulfilled his dreams
but for Prometheus and his schemes,
whose theft of fire first blurred the line
dividing Mankind and divine,
letting lower challenge higher
by giving mere men Zeus's fire.

67. EXT. WRECKING YARD, DAY

The Boy 'drives' his bus. Then he leaves the bus and
enters a fire engine. He is deep in thought about his
burnt book and the row with his Dad. Shadows of steam
on cooling towers. Then he breaks his mood and
imitates the fire-engine siren, 'driving' it at breakneck
speed. He pulls the lever of the cracked bell on the roof
of the wrecked fire engine.

The cracked bell keeps tolling.

68. EXT. STREET, PALACE CINEMA, KNOTTINGLEY, DAY

Old Man takes his walk to the Palace Cinema past
various locations dominated by the cooling towers until,
with the cooling towers behind him, we see him coming
up the street towards the cinema.

He has a secret entrance into the derelict cinema. He looks round, stubs out a cigarette, and enters.

69. INT. PALACE CINEMA, DAY

There are one or two scattered stall seats left in the ruin, one of which is the Old Man's favourite.

We see his face look at the screen, lighten up when he sees that there is an image, then darken when he sees that it is Hermes entering the boot room of Kirkby Main Colliery.

He sits in his seat and lights up.

Cut to:

70. INT. COLLIERY, BOOT MACHINE CORRIDOR, DAY

Hermes goes into his fire-precaution routine and addresses the audience to this film and the solitary figure of the Old Man in the derelict Palace Cinema.

HERMES
Though fire, we don't have any doubt,
has little chance of breaking out,
nonetheless the laws require
your cinema to plan for fire,
so before this film proceeds too far
please check *now* where the exits are.
Since fire's what this film's about,
you ought to know a quick way out!
Turn your eyes left, turn your eyes right
and note the nearest exit light,
on either side in red or green.

Audiences in cinema hopefully go through the cautionary procedure.

How obedient you've been!

71. INT. PALACE CINEMA, DAY

The Old Man is the one spectator, sitting on one of the few seats left, chain-smoking.

OLD MAN

Bollocks! I've known where
t'exits are for fifty year!

HERMES
(*on the tattered screen in black and white*)
But even a venerable sire
of seventy years must watch for fire.

Hermes turns politely but icily stern with the Old Man, who is dragging deeply on his cigarette.

HERMES

And may we remind our clientele
they may not smoke.

OLD MAN
(*puffing away*)
Like bloody 'ell!

He takes another ostentatious puff.

That's when I stopped bloody going
no matter what great flick were showing.
If it were a Cagney or a Bogart on
even then I wouldn't'a gone.
No, when fags were finally forbidden
in this rat-infested and flea-ridden
bug'utch, bugger it, I thought,
I'll bloody smoke and not get caught.
I smoked, got caught, and allus chucked
out on mi lug'ole. Films were fucked.
I just stopped seeing picture shows.
T'whole bloody place all full of *nos*:
no bloody smoking, spitting, booze,

no even lighting up in t'loos.
Ay, I bloody tried that too,
having a quiet drag in t'loo.
But t'old maid wi' her ice-cream tray
saw t'smoke and gave the game away.
I smoked that fast it made a fug
and got me chucked out on mi lug.
Then I said, 'Sod it! That's me done!'
Forbidding fags spoiled all my fun.

In t'pit and t'flea-pit cigarettes
were contraband to these tight gets.
Underground makes sense. But bloody 'ell,
banning fags in t'flicks as well!
Sometimes I think t'whole bloody land
's made bloody baccy contraband.

When Bogey lit up so did I,
smoke curling past my one closed eye.
Bogey gets best smoker's prize,
cig-smoke crinkling up his eyes.

  Old Man demonstrates.

All t'gangsters had a swirling cloak
cast all around 'em in thick smoke.
When they inhaled their smoke I did
and so did every other kid,
when they exhaled so did a crowd
of kids, synchronised in one huge cloud.
So it were no fun if I weren't free
to light my fag with Edward G.
And summat these days tha don't get 's
heroes smoking cigarettes.
I'd love to rerun every bit
of bloody film where fags get lit.
I'd like to watch a thousand clips
of ciggies dangling from wet lips,

the mean lips of Chicago hoods
on corners in bleak neighbourhoods,
loitering in dark parts of town
to gun some other gangster down,
them painted scarlet lips that pout
to blow some perfect smoke-rings out,
what I now know as prostitutes
with six-inch heels who smoked cheroots.
Brilliant the way pairs broke
the ice between 'em with a smoke!

Who smokes now? Them were the days
when women smoked in negligées.
Those elegant and high-heeled dames
leaning into men's match-flames,
too close for comfort, with their eyes
locked rock-steady on the guy's,
then that first stream of exhaled smoke
blown straight into the gob-smacked bloke.
I learned cig-skills from what I'd seen
sexy smokers do on t'screen.

*Hermes looks contemptuously from the black-and-
white screen.*

I were convinced that good cig-suction
were t'secret weapon of seduction.
It seemed that shared cigs allus led
them passionate puffers off to bed.
And when you knew they'd had their shag
first thing both did were light a fag!

And have a fag 's what I do here
in memory of yesteryear.
'Cos now this place is derelict
I can't get chucked out, nabbed or nicked
for smoking all them fags their law
wouldn't let me smoke afore.

I come here now to treat missen
to all them fags not dragged on then.

> *Old Man looks down at his feet: close-up of hundreds
> of fag-ends. The memory of forbidden fags makes him
> defiant.*

> *Old Man rises from his seat into the pose of
> Prometheus, the fist in defiance of the image of
> Hermes in black and white on the tattered screen.*

Smokers of the world unite!

> *He speaks to the audiences at whatever cinemas*
> Prometheus *is shown.*

On t'count o' three, all light up, right?
One . . . two . . . three . . .

> *He's disappointed.*

                  You've all been cowed.
I've changed the law and it's allowed.
Try again then. one . . . two . . . three . . .
all light your fags now, after me.

> *Old Man lights his cigarette, inhales deeply with
> defiant satisfaction, then collapses coughing into his
> seat. It takes him some time to recover.*

72. INT. COLLIERY, BOOT-CLEANING MACHINE, DAY

HERMES

Before that clapped-out cloth-capped sod
dared interrupt this ancient god,
I was explaining Zeus's plan
to finish off the world of Man
was foiled by the Promethean theft
for men like him with one lung left
who flaunt the filched fire day and night

by keeping cigarettes alight.
This angers Zeus, but all that smoke
'll make that cancerous codger croak,
so Zeus is gratified how fire that first
made Man euphoric's now reversed,
watching this fire-thief supporter
's breath get short and ever shorter,
not Armageddon but still fun
to watch men dying one by one,
especially from ills Man gets
from coal-face work or cigarettes!
The day Zeus tires of the joke
he'll wipe the lot out at one stroke.
Smog, pollution, smoker's cough
might do as well to bring that off.
So Armageddon's put on hold
till Zeus is bored or Man too bold.
Zeus loves the ozone layer in shreds
and slumming it in human beds!

*Hermes looks down at his elegant silver boots, which
are smirched by his walk on the spoil heap.*

This filthy slag-shit scarcely suits
one's svelte gods-wear silver boots.
After my god's toe this machine
'll brush no more men's pit-boots clean.

73. EXT. COLLIERY WINDING GEAR, DAY

Still winding gear creaks into life. Cut to:

74. INT. PIT CAGE, DAY

*Pit cage ascending and gates opening. Twelve Miners
stand stunned by what they see. It is as if they have been
underground for years. The mine is deserted and in
ruins.*

319

75. EXT. DERELICT COLLIERY, DAY

The pit is deserted, and totally derelict. Doors fallen down. The mirror with the THIS MAN IS RESPONSIBLE FOR YOUR SAFETY *inscription: a Miner stares at it in reflection, then a chunk of falling rubble shatters it.*

A fire bucket, still full of water, falls, settles and rocks, slopping its water.

The red and white bricks that made the wall announcing the CONTRABAND ZONE: *a partial section of the wall reads* CON. *Half a headgear wheel falls.*

As the Miners walk forward, astonished, plaster falls from the roof. It seems that the place is about to fall down. The cage door falls and breaks a pillar. The Miners run down a corridor of rubble and tangled machinery and straight into a cattle-truck.

The Silver Statue of Hermes points his caduceus.

76. EXT. CATTLE-TRUCK, DAY

The back of the cattle-truck of Kratos and Bia is slammed shut and bolted by a hand in black rubber gloves.

77. INT. CATTLE-TRUCK, DAY

Through the slats of the cattle-truck the Miners see the cooling towers. The truck starts up, throwing some Miners onto the floor.

MINER 1

Hey, bloody hell fire!

MINER 2
What the fuck!

MINER 3
Where the 'ell 're we off to, take a look.

78. EXT. AT BRIDGE OVER CANAL, DAY

*The cattle-truck speeds over the bridge dominated by
cooling towers.*

> MINER 4
>
> Just crossing t'bridge that goes over t'canal.
> And there's barge with thi brother on it, Mal.
> Shove thi gob through here. Give him a yell.

79. EXT. CANAL NEAR BRIDGE, DAY

*A barge is about to pass under the bridge where the truck
is passing. Voice of Miner 5 shouting 'Brian! Brian!'*

80. INT. CATTLE-TRUCK, DAY

> MINER 5
>
> Brian! Brian!

> MINER 4
>
> Did he hear you?

> MINER 5
>
> Did 'e 'ell!

81. EXT. AI, NEAR POWER STATION, DAY

*The truck passes the cooling towers. Pan with truck as
it heads down motorway, and hold on sign reading:*
AI THE SOUTH.

82. EXT. CANAL, DAY

*Cut back to barge and close-up of wake of barge
churning water, which mixes into:*

83. INT. OCEANUS FISH FACTORY, DAY

*Close-up of fish in bubbling water. Pan up to fish
emerging from water on conveyor.*

Hermes in the overalls of an Oceanus foreman driving a fork-lift truck enters the tank room, glances at the struggling fish and drives on through a heavy blue plastic curtain.

HERMES
(*driving fork-lift*)
Zeus always wanted the entire
plays of Aeschylus destroyed by fire,
Aeschylus's . . .

Hermes realises that no one in the cinema audience has any idea who Aeschylus is.

OK! Stop!
You! With the popcorn and the pop!
who don't (perhaps!) already know it,
Aeschylus, the great Greek poet,
died (by one of Zeus's tricks!)
in the year four fifty-six,
that's BC, and he sang the praise
of bloody Prometheus in his plays.
Especially one that's still around
and famous as *Prometheus Bound*.
And that play with its rebel views in
needs spin-doctoring and defusing.
And that's where my slick skills come in.
I'm employed to give Zeus spin.
And making statues is the way
I've chosen to defuse that play.
For which I now create my cast
I swear to Zeus will be the last.

Hermes drives through another blue plastic curtain with some of the Oceanus Women standing on the pallet. Then another curtain and more women. The fork-lift emerges through the final hanging blue plastic curtain out to the loading bay. As they pass through

the curtain the Women all sing a high sustained note,
which is smothered as a cloth of blue silk falls over
them. Their shapes, heads and arms, struggle under
the cloth and then freeze.

Three heads covered with blue cloth fill the frame.
Then mix to:

84. EXT. HUMBER ESTUARY AND BRIDGE, DAY

The blue cloth begins to billow and flutter and we pull
back to reveal a drifting pontoon approaching the
Humber Bridge with shapes covered by the cloth.

The blue cloth blows into the air. The shapes are
revealed as the Daughters of Ocean.

Hermes is on a vantage point on the bridge watching
them approach slowly.

85. EXT. HUMBER ESTUARY AND BRIDGE, DAY

The Daughters of Ocean nearer the Bridge.

HERMES
This choir's just Zeus's little quirk.
They handled scales so well at work.
What sport to squeeze these lumpen proles
into the choral corset of posh roles,
to warble a mournful little number
as they start drifting down the Humber,
just as their menfolk start their route
to death down a scrap-metal chute,
and drift through Europe all the way
to Elefsina for my play,
bewailing the dire fate that falls
on Firegrabber, Goldenballs.
I promise you that we'll require
the sweetener service of a choir
when men go shrieking in the fire.

*The hand of Hermes with its nails painted silver
plucks a cable of the Humber Bridge and it gives out a
Humberside-wide bass note.*

86. INT. PALACE CINEMA, DAY

*Old Man is woken from a nap by the note of the
Humber Bridge.*

87. EXT. HUMBER BRIDGE, SPIDERMAN WALKWAY ACCESS GATE, DAY

*Hermes opens the gate to the curved spiderman walkway
to the tower of the Humber Bridge.*

> HERMES

When I'm not in human guise
this little lyre's about my size.
I'll walk up on my god-size lyre
that gives the note that starts my choir.
For ages now I've longed to strum
my Humber harp/harmonium.

> *Hermes closes the metal door of the walkway. It sends
> out a huge reverberant note, which is picked up by the
> Daughters of Ocean on the Humber. Hermes smiles
> with satisfaction.*

> *Hermes begins to climb the rest of the walkway. The
> 'strings' of the Humber Bridge lyre continue to
> reverberate as he climbs to the top.*

> *Cut to:*

88. EXT. TOWER WALKWAY, DAY

*As the cattle-truck moves towards the Humber Bridge,
Hermes is revealed in a central commanding position on
the tower walkway of the bridge.*

HERMES
(*on tower*)
Now let my god-size Yorkshire lyre
descant on all the doom of FIRE!

*Hermes 'conducts' with a slow, measured movement
of his caduceus. A vast, eery, reverberant hum comes
from the 'lyre' (Humber Bridge), and the Daughters of
Ocean harmonise around the hum.*

89. INT. CATTLE-TRUCK, DAY

*The reverberant hum of the Humber Bridge 'lyre' and
the voices of the Daughters of Ocean singing something
infinitely sad is heard by the Miners in the truck.*

MINER 5
That's a bloody creepy noise off t'sea.

MINER 3
Sounds like a funeral dirge to me.

*Close-ups of Miners' faces puzzled and rather frightened
by the singing. They fall silent as the dirge recedes.*

MINER 1
Have you noticed summat?

MINER 2
What?

MINER 1
Every time
we make a sentence it ends up wi' a rhyme!

MINER 3
I'm not joining in, I'm not, old son.

MINER 5
Except someone'll complete what you've begun!
Like I've just gone and done it now missen!

MINER 6

So what do you think 's happening to us then?

MINER 5

God knows, but t'bloody world goes speeding by.

MINER 6

Are we off south?

MINER 5
(*looking through slats*)
Looks like it. Ay!

MINER 1

An t'barmiest thing of all's like when
we talk in bloody rhyme like I did then.
I don't like it. It's more than bloody queer
spouting bloody poetry like King Lear.

MINER 3

It could well launch us on a new career.
Did you hear that? Did you hear me?
It just came out like that, rhyme number three.
Hey, now we're redundant, we could all go
to bloody Blackpool as a Pierrot show.

The Miners are unresponsive.

90. EXT. MOTORWAY, DUSK

The cattle-truck is seen from a motorway bridge among heavy traffic. It passes under the bridge.

91. INT. CATTLE-TRUCK, NIGHT

Miners' point of view from inside truck of receding gas station and laughing attendant.

92. EXT. CHANNEL FERRY HARBOUR, DAY

The cattle-truck approaches the open hatch of a ferry.

VOICE OF HERMES

And now they go across rough sea
into my scrap-heap *pot-pourri*,
the last ingredients for the pan
part scrap metal, part scrap man,
the fag-end of the Fire-thief's soul
stirred into my mixture whole.

Fag-end Prometheans cock no snook,
confined in their own piss and puke.
So, with your bowels and bladders full,
bid your fond farewells to ''ull'!

93. INT. CATTLE-TRUCK, FERRY, DAY

*Bars of light across the faces of Miners are extinguished
as the ferry hatch closes slowly. The fluorescent light in
the hold falls onto one Miner who is looking decidedly
queasy. Miner 2 notices that he looks seasick.*

MINER 1

Puke into your helmet, then we'll slop
t'whole lot out when t'buggers stop,
after we've landed, for a piss or drink.

MINER 2

It's already too much is this stink.
Some bugger I could bloody hit
's gone and done a secret shit.

> *The seasick Miner pukes, but onto the top of his
> helmet, not inside it.*

MINER 3
(*taking charge*)

Right! Anyone who has to go

has to use his helmet as a po.
Then shove it peak first through t'truck slat
and slop the contents out, like that.
Show some discipline. Then we'll dispose
on t'open road of all t'full pos.
Turds tha'll have to spike and flick
through t'slats, and if tha's sick
puke into t'helmet, chuck it, vomit
's got a bloody foul stink from it.

MINER 4
Making poetry out of stuff like this!
Tha's t'bloody Shakespeare of puke and piss.
I never thought I'd hear an ode
on DIYing a commode.

94. EXT. AUTOBAHN, GERMANY, DAY

The cattle-truck turns off a German autobahn.

95. INT. CATTLE-TRUCK, NIGHT

*Headlights of oncoming trucks and cars send bars of
light into the cattle-truck, revealing sickly-looking
captive passengers, all awake, staring. One steadies a
slopping helmet. As the truck stops at a service station
the helmet's contents slop over. The Miners leap to their
feet to avoid the spillage.*

96. INT. CATTLE-TRUCK, SERVICE STATION, BERLIN–
DRESDEN, NIGHT

MINER 4
(*sudden dark despair*)
I can't stand much more of this.

MINER 2
I smell pizza!

MINER 6
I smell piss.

MINER
(*listening at slats*)
Germany! I can just make out
that t'lingo that they're talking's Kraut.

97. EXT. FOUNDRY, NIGHT

The cattle-truck turns off the autobahn towards a vast industrial plant.

The cattle-truck tips the Miners onto a chute, which leads into a cauldron of molten metal.

98. INT. FOUNDRY CHUTE, NIGHT

Frightened screams.

Fingernails scraping rust off the chute as the Miners try to stop sliding.

Helmets and boots sink into the fiery porridge.

A helmet melts. Shrill, terrifying screaming, clouds of smoke.

Miner 4, the last to enter the fiery cauldron, slides towards the fire with a blood-curdling scream.

Then an almost peaceful 'liquid' music (Daughters of Ocean) as we cut to:

A trickle of gold running down a channel towards the mould which will create the Statue of Prometheus.

Someone in the same costume as Kratos and Bia scrapes away a little sand and reveals the golden fist of the Statue of Prometheus.

VOICE OF HERMES

Miners from that molten muck 'll
melt into each golden knuckle.
A fag-end Prometheus still exists
in their recycled strikers' fists.

99. EXT. FOUNDRY, DAWN

*A vast door like an aeroplane hangar with the fire-
forbidden logo.*

*The golden Statue of Prometheus made of melted-down
miners comes out of the foundry to a fanfare. The whole
statue is swathed in red-and-white hazard tape, as if
mummified. In the left hand is a blazing torch.*

*Hermes stops the truck, raising his caduceus like a
traffic cop. He gets Force and Violence to climb onto
the truck and tear the blazing torch from the left hand
of Prometheus.*

*A boot stamps on the burning end of the statue's fennel
stalk.*

100. INT. PALACE CINEMA, DAY

Old Man looks at his cigarette.

101. EXT. FOUNDRY, DAY

*The caduceus of Hermes indicates the direction of the
truck and statue.*

Cut to:

102. EXT. ROAD IN GERMANY, DAY

*The Statue of Prometheus travelling along a road in
Germany. As it moves, the hazard tape begins to unwrap
and flap and is gradually ripped off by the wind,*

revealing the golden statue. Hazard tape snags on trees and telegraph poles, etc.

Close-ups of flapping tape and bits of the radiant golden giant.

The Statue of Prometheus sheds its final length of hazard tape and is revealed in all its glory.

103. EXT. BERLIN–DRESDEN ROAD, DAY

A Dresden fire-fighter truck overtakes the statue of Prometheus with its lights flashing and its siren wailing.

The noise of the fire-truck siren becomes the noise made by the Boy driving his wrecked fire-truck in the Ferrybridge wrecking yard.

104. EXT. WRECKING YARD, DAY

                          BOY
Errr! Errr! Err!

> *We hear the Boy making his fire-engine sounds, then mix back to the sound of the Dresden fire-truck's siren as it overtakes the Statue of Prometheus on the road to Dresden.*

105. EXT. DRESDEN ROAD, DAY

Dresden fire-truck reveals sign saying DRESDEN. *Statue disappearing in distance.*

The caduceus taps the DRESDEN *sign. Pull back to reveal Hermes, sweeping his caduceus in the direction of the Statue of Prometheus heading for Dresden.*

                   VOICE OF HERMES
With the new millennium nigh
Zeus wants his forces standing by

331

to make one final all-out thrust
to grind Prometheus into dust.
And Dresden, city of destructive flame,
's the best for blackening his good name.
Those thirty-five thousand fire flayed
won't cheer Prometheus on parade.
Nor will their descendants cheer
when we take Prometheus here.

107. EXT. CAROLABRUCKE, DRESDEN, DAY

The Statue of Prometheus crosses the Carolabrucke from
the Albertplatz and Albertstrasse direction towards the
Albertinum.

VOICE OF HERMES

I'll make them so rue fire that men'll
want to fuck him with his fennel.
Thirty-five thousand in two days
perished in the Dresden blaze.
Even though the targets then
were blasphemous icons more than men –

108. INT. PALACE CINEMA, DAY

HERMES
(from the screen)

Promethean icons Zeus's ire
wanted blasting in the fire.

OLD MAN
(to Hermes on the screen)

I want to see t'newsreels that I saw
on Saturday mornings during t'war.
And show us what were justly done
by Bomber Harris to the Hun.
When Bomber Harris turned on t'heat
I cheered it from this very seat.

332

You should have heard t'whole Palace roar
to see the Jerries get what for.
T'whole Palace bug'utch cheered and clapped
when . . .

HERMES
(*completing his couplet on the tattered screen*)
. . . my master Zeus had Dresden zapped!

The Old Man stares at Hermes on the screen.

109. EXT. SEMPER OPER, DRESDEN, DAY

HERMES
Zeus gutted this. To know the cause,
come through the Semper Oper's doors
though I advise a moment's pause
to reflect on Zeus and let reflection
awe you into genuflection.

Hermes duly genuflects to the relief of Zeus.

110. INT. PALACE CINEMA, DAY

Old Man sits staring at the relief of Zeus.

OLD MAN
I'll tell thee summat. I'm not awed
by any bloody overlord.
In Yorkshire we've got us own sign
when we're saluting owt divine.

Old Man makes a V-sign and raspberry noise at Zeus.

On the screen the hand of Hermes with silver-painted fingernails strokes the eagle of Zeus on the same relief. As his hand strokes and moves down the body of the eagle the Old Man coughs, and the defiant V-sign crumples as he's wracked by coughing.

Hermes enters the Semper Oper.

333

III. INT. SEMPER OPER, DRESDEN, DAY

*Hermes shows us the painted lunette of Prometheus
chained to the rock.*

VOICE OF HERMES

Though now the damned thing's been redone
this was Zeus's target number one.

112. EXT. SEMPER OPER, SMOKE-BLACKENED STATUE
OF PROMETHEUS

VOICE OF HERMES
(continuing)

And target two, Prometheus, black
from the bomb-blitz blaze, but back
on the Opera as he was before
the Allies bombed him in the war,
reinstated where his gaze
once watched the whole of Dresden blaze.
(Here is Dresden's true destroyer
filthy from his own filched *Feuer*!)

113. EXT. ZWINGER PALACE, DRESDEN, RELIEF OF
PROMETHEUS FREED BY HERCULES

VOICE OF HERMES
(continuing)

And target three, much worse, this frieze:
Prometheus freed by Hercules,
who shot an arrow from his quiver
through the bird that gnawed the liver
of Prometheus, and now comes to rend
the lungs of our fag-flaunting friend.
Unlike the Titan's liver though
his lungs aren't likely to regrow.
This pitiful, pulmonary prole

334

carves scrap-heap miners out of coal,
conniving in that blasphemy
that it wasn't Zeus at all but he,
Prometheus, who formed man from clay,
target four, that, to this day
Dresden flaunts up here, restored,
provoking my Olympian Lord.

114. EXT. KUNSTSCHULE, DRESDEN, RELIEF OF AESCHYLUS

VOICE OF HERMES
(*continuing*)

And that same eagle also split
the skull of Aeschylus, the poet-shit,
and shattered the bald pate when it dropped
a tortoise from the sky, and stopped
the blasphemous poetic flow
some two millennia ago,
Aeschylus, pro-Promethean bard,
back up in Dresden, with beard charred,
and with a layer of firestorm soot
like a skinhead haircut on his nut.
If Zeus were with me, what he'd do
is give this poet a piss shampoo.
Zeus likes to pump his pungent pee
all over poets and poetry.
First burst to Aeschylus, then squirt a
shower on Shakespeare, Schiller, Goethe.
Poets have taught Mankind to breach
the boundaries Zeus put round speech,
and the fire Prometheus stole
created man's poetic soul.

115. EXT. RIVER NEAR AUGUSTUSBRUCKE, DRESDEN, DAY

The boy's Mam, who has run across Europe, collecting
wood and paper to make a fire under the bridge.

VOICE OF HERMES
(*continuing*)
The Yorkshire mam! She'll always hear
the boots of Kratos and of Bia.
Force and Violence get their fun
keeping the poor cow on the run.
This is the cow I've let them hound
like Io in *Prometheus Bound*.

Poor Kratos and his sidekick Bia
miss the swastikas of yesteryear.
They've come to Dresden and they've sighed
for the good old days of genocide.
How they've yearned to reinstate
the furnace as a people's fate.

Kratos and Bia's R&R's
more butch barbarity than bars,
and so to keep them entertained
until I get Prometheus chained,
I've let them have her as their toy
to drive demented then destroy.
To death, through Dresden from Doncaster
dogged and hounded, faster, faster,
she'll suffer, this fire-kindling *Frau*
(in the likeness of a Friesian cow),
the sort of fate that's been assigned
to those considered not one's kind,
those hate's gadflies force to flee,
schizophrenic, gypsy, refugee.
They'll turn the screw of paranoia
then, fun done, finish her in . . . *Feuer*.

She now thinks of *Feuer* as her friend
where thousands met a fiery end.

116. EXT. FOOTBALL STADIUM, DAY

*The Statue of Prometheus centred in the Dresden
football stadium. Hermes uses his caduceus to bring on
the great floodlights, which glare at the Statue like
interrogation lights.*

HERMES
Now to summon up the choir
of thousands perished in the fire.

> *With his caduceus Hermes summons up the ghosts of
> those who died in the Dresden fire-storm of 13–14
> February 1945. They rouse as drones from different
> stands in the stadium.*
>
> *Hermes first points the caduceus at the North Stand.
> From the dark, empty stand comes a drone composed
> of voices and RAF bombers carrying their loads to
> shed over Dresden.*
>
> *A whisper of the voices of the dead comes through the
> drone. They are whispering their names:*

NORTH CHOIR
Zeilig, Albin
Grafe, Bruno
Lachmann, Frida
Mehnert, Rolf
Kuhnscharf, Walter . . .

> *Hermes points his caduceus to the empty South Stand.
> The drone is heard in stereo as more names join those
> being whispered from the North Stand.*

SOUTH CHOIR
Dietz, Jurgen

Schroter, Hans
Hennig, Annerose
Mühler . . .

*Hermes points his caduceus at the West Stand and
more voices swell the growing counterpoint. Then he
points his caduceus at the East Stand and the drone
swells to a crescendo, which leads to the Chorus of
Ghosts, singing in unison the words of two witnesses
who, like many thousands, were burned or asphyxiated
in the cellars where they took refuge from the firestorm.*

CHORUS OF GHOSTS

Wir sassen im Keller
Wartend auf den Tod.
Das Haus brannte
in Keller lief Phosphor.

*Over the drone three Boys sing with the Choir of
Ghosts. Boys 1 and 3 carry charred, buckled old
Dresden street signs: one reads* HOLBEINSTRASSE, *the
other* GOETHESTRASSE.

BOY 1

Kreuzkirche, wo ich sange,
Zerstort.

BOY 2

Kreuzschule, wo ich studierte,
Zerstort.

BOY 3

Kreuzstrasse, wo ich spielte
Zerstort.

BOYS 1, 2, 3
(*overlapping*)

Kreuzkirche, Dornkirche, Frauenkirche,
Wo wir sangen,
Zerstort.

Kreuzschule, Hochschule, Oberschule,
Wo wir studierten,
Zerstort.

Kreuzstrasse, Dürerstrasse, Rosenstrasse,
Wo wir spielten,
Zerstort.

*The Chorus of Ghosts takes up the list of Dresden
streets gutted by the fire.*

CHORUS OF GHOSTS
Dürerstrasse, Cranachstrasse, Holbeinstrasse,
Goethestrasse, Webergasse, Albrechtstrasse,
Christianstrasse, Friedrichstrasse, Alter Markt,
Johannesstrasse, Mathildenstrasse, Marienstrasse,
Pragerstrasse, Munchenstrasse, Ziegelstrasse,
Zinzendorfstrasse, Pirnaischestrasse, Zirkusstrasse.

117. INT. PALACE CINEMA, DAY

*Archive film of the Dresden bombing is seen on the
tattered screen in the Palace Cinema, Knottingley, by the
Old Man, who coughs and laughs and makes triumphant
whoops as he watches the Allied damage of Dresden as
he might have done at the newsreel in that cinema fifty
years before.*

*Then the Old Man becomes silent, concentrating and
inhaling cigarette smoke deeply. A recognition of the fifty
intervening years sobers the Old Man's impersonation of
his younger self. He is overcome with sobbing. He
coughs. He lights another cigarette.*

*The image of the tattered screen becomes a still again,
displayed in the hands of one of the three Boys standing
beneath Prometheus, and we widen out back in the
stadium in Dresden, with Hermes conducting the
gathered ghosts with his caduceus.*

339

118. EXT. FOOTBALL STADIUM, DRESDEN, NIGHT

CHORUS OF GHOSTS

Kirchen und Kapellen,
Fünfundzwanzig zerstort.

Sehenwurdigkeiten,
Siebzehn zerstort.

Theater und Oper,
Alle fünf zerstort.

Waren und Kaufhauser,
Einunddreissig zerstort.

Hotels und Gastatten,
Siebenundfünfzig zerstort.

Bankhauser,
Vierundzwanzig zerstort.

Lichtspielhauser,
Neunzehn zerstort.

Total Gebaude,
Elftausendneunhundertundsechzehn zerstort.

Total Männer,
Frauen und Kinder, Fünfunddreissigtausend zerstort.

*Hermes acts as the conductor of the anti-Promethean
Chorus. As the Chorus reaches a climax a helicopter
shot reveals the Statue of Prometheus alone in the
stadium. The interrogation lights switch off.*

119. EXT. FOOTBALL STADIUM, DRESDEN, NIGHT

*The Zeus-eye (helicopter) shot of the 'trial' of
Prometheus. The golden statue becomes smaller and
smaller. Then the floodlights switch off. Black.*

120. EXT. GERMAN/CZECH BORDER, DAY

A Vietnamese sells garden gnomes at a border stop.
Prostitutes flag down cars and trucks.

HERMES

Kratos and Bia
like to cross the border here.
For fifty Marks they get a shag
or blow-job from some border slag,
and buy a dwarf from this collection,
preferably one with an erection.
A man drives from Dresden in his new
'free market' BMW,
finds a quiet place and parks
and gets sucked off for fifty marks.
Old East-bloc men can now afford a
quick blow-job across the border,
when Deutschmarks fell into their laps
at the Berlin Wall's collapse.
After blow-jobs they buy these
new deities from Vietnamese,
who buy these dwarves from Poles and sell
to New Europe's clientele.
Does Europe now say prayers at night
to a trouser-dropping troglodyte?
The new united Europe's dawn's
heralded by louche leprechauns.
The new rich fill their bijou homes
with prick-proud pixies and lewd gnomes.
These gods with red conks and cocks
replace a Pantheon more orthodox.

121. INT. CHURCH, MOST, CZECH REPUBLIC, DAY

VOICE OF HERMES

Europe's given far holier homes
to equally repulsive gnomes,

341

and used fire to frighten, with Hell's blaze
wrapping the damned in flame duvets.
And Zeus quite likes Mankind to dwell
on the fires of Holocaust and Hell.

> Io (Mam) hides in the Gothic Church in Most: calm,
> white and beautiful. The statues of angels and saints
> in gilded wood make wooing, welcoming gestures to
> the exhausted woman. One angel serenades her weary
> spirit with a harp, another with a cello. She feels the
> temptation of abandon.

> She sees the friezes of hellfire and its denizens. She
> gravitates to the candles underneath a crucified Christ.

VOICE OF HERMES

But candles in fire's gentler guise
makes Zeus throw lightning round the skies.
Kratos and Bia can cut up rough
when they find candlelight to snuff.
And when she closes her cow eyes
feeling safe – surprise! surprise!

> Io is almost asleep on her feet when she hears the
> sound of the heavy church door being opened and
> a pair of rubber boots running towards her. She
> hurriedly steals a candle and runs along a white
> colonnade and out of the church, protecting the
> candle flame with a cupped hand as she runs,
> desperate to keep it alight to give her the source of
> a fire in the nights she spends in the open.

> Io runs and jumps on a Litvinov tram as Kratos and
> Bia pursue her. The candle is still burning in her hand.

122. INT. TRAM, LITVINOV, CZECH REPUBLIC, DAY

Io leaps on the tram as it moves off and saves her from
her pursuers, but a Male Passenger turns on her as she

enters and shouts that she mustn't have a lighted candle
as the tram goes through potentially dangerous chemical
emissions. The whole length of the tramway has signs
that reinforce this message. The Male Passenger blows
out the lighted candle.

A Woman takes pity on her, realising that this dirty,
ragged woman has no ticket: she punches one of her
own tickets and gives it to Io. Io sits down and the wax
from her extinguished candle runs over her hands.

The tram passes the chemical works on the right, and on
the left Io sees the truck with the Statue of Prometheus.

123. EXT. TRAM TERMINUS, LITVINOV, CZECH
REPUBLIC, DAY

Io alights and runs with her extinguished candle through
a long subway. She runs away at great speed.

124. INT. PALACE CINEMA, KNOTTINGLEY, DAY

Hermes is pointing with his caduceus at signs saying, in
Czech, 'Switch off engines when red light is flashing' –
SVÍTÍ-LÍ ČERVENA – STOP – NÉKUŘTE VYPNĚTE MOTORY.

HERMES
Very inflammable. It could go off
at any moment. Litvinov.

Hermes reads the warning sign in Czech:

Svítí-lí červena . . . nékuřte!
You, you smoke-racked wreck,
Nékuřte means 'Don't Smoke' in Czech.
and you, with the popcorn and the pop,
do you know *'stop'* in Czech means 'stop'?
When the warning light here flashes red
tram-drivers brake and quake with dread.

With such combustible emissions
cars have to switch off their ignitions
or everything on track or road
'd automatically explode.
It's so volatile all it 'd need
's some wanker with his fennel weed,
old curdled crud-lung with his brand
of carcinogenous contraband,
to blow the whole caboodle through
all your screens and over you.
Well, let that smoke-racked scoffer scoff,
he'll croak soon from his smoker's cough
and that collected coal-dust clung
round the crumbling walls of his one lung.
All the smoke's come home to roost
from all the fires his coal produced.

> *The defiant Old Man raises his Promethean fist and
> stands.*

OLD MAN

And I were glad we could produce
fuel for fires that angered Zeus.
That bloody Zeus that you kowtow to
but a man like me will never bow to!
Power stations fuelled by t'pits
blow smoke at you immortal shits.

> *Old Man coughs with the effort of defiance. He
> collapses into his stalls seat.*

HERMES
(smiling at his predicament)
It's doomed, all that. You wasted time
grovelling underground in grime.
Those steaming fortresses you pray
'll last till your grandchildren's day
are doomed, *doomed*, on their way out,

destined (as you'd say) to be *nowt!*
Nowt! Nowt! Nowt! Nowt!

OLD MAN

They'll outlast me.

HERMES
Without a doubt!
Before this screen here reads THE END
you'll be dead, my croaking friend.

OLD MAN
Well, I'm not sorry that I'm ailing
seeing t'dream I worked for failing.

HERMES
History spat you out like phlegm,
shop steward of the NUM
expecting, of all things, to create
in class-torn Britain a fair state!
So I'd unclench your weedy fist
you smoke-demolished Socialist.

Old Man has a coughing fit.

125. EXT. WARNING SIGN, LITVINOV, CZECH
REPUBLIC, DAY

*Hermes sweeps his caduceus across the screen, which
recolours up.*

126. EXT. HERKULES COAL CO, MOST/LITVINOV,
CZECH REPUBLIC, DAY

Io runs up a path past a sign with the name HERKULES
written on it. Hold on sign.

The Statue of Prometheus continues its journey.

127. EXT. USTI NAD LABEM, MOST EDVARDA BENEŠE, DAY

The Statue of Prometheus passes over the Beneš Bridge, and at the same time the Daughters of Ocean pass singing beneath it. They look towards a derelict hotel on the wooded hillside.

In the derelict Palace Hotel is Io, watching.

128. EXT. DERELICT PALACE HOTEL, USTI NAD LABEM, DAY

Io runs along a hedge, sees the hotel and enters by the steps that lead into the totally derelict foyer.

129. INT. DERELICT PALACE HOTEL, USTI NAD LABEM, DAY

Io enters the derelict foyer. The roof of the floor above has collapsed into the foyer. On one wall are the remains of a painting of a girl in Czech costume holding a large glass of beer marked '12'. The inscription beneath the peasant girl is fragmentary but probably reads: PIVO DOBRE, DEVKY HEZKE/JSOU DARY ZEMĚ ČESKE.

Io walks towards the stairs covered with rubble. She has found a haven to rest from running across Europe.

130. INT. DERELICT PALACE HOTEL, USTI NAD LABEM, DAY

Io goes into an upstairs room and looks out of the glassless windows. On the Beneš Bridge below she sees the Statue of Prometheus passing.

131. INT. KITCHEN OF DERELICT PALACE HOTEL, USTI NAD LABEM, DUSK

Io lights a fire against the white tiles of the kitchen. she sleeps with firelight dancing on her face.

A sign forbidding all forms of fire, with icons of the pipe and the candle, with the red slash of the forbidden through them, is above her head. It reads: ZAKAZ KOUŘENI A MANIPULACE S OHNEM (*Smoking forbidden and all use of fire*).

> VOICE OF HERMES
> Let the poor cow have her forty winks
> though we're much closer than she thinks.

> IO
> (*dreaming*)

Nein.

> VOICE OF HERMES
> I'll wave my wand and make her dream
> of what's deemed Europe's worst regime –

> IO
> (*dreaming*)

Nein.

> VOICE OF HERMES
> – though Zeus approved it and endorsed
> the Führer's flames of . . . Holocaust.

Mix through the sign saying ZAKAZ KOUŘENI A MANIPULACE S OHNEM, *with candle and pipe ringed in red, to many Jewish memorial candles in tin holders with Star of David and* YOHRZEIT (*remembrance*) *inscribed on them.*

132. INT. CREMATORIUM OVENS, AUSCHWITZ, DAY

A Jewish Pilgrim places a candle in the dark mouth of a crematorium oven in Auschwitz. He gazes at the candle intently for some time.

The candle flame and oven are reflected in his glasses.

*He leaves the crematorium, and we find him at the end
of the railtrack that leads through the gateway of
Birkenau.*

133. EXT. RAILTRACK, BIRKENAU, DUSK

*The Jewish Pilgrim places another candle on the rail
track.*

*Crane up and reveal the camp and the huts, and the
lonely figure walking down the railtrack, and pick up the
Jewish Pilgrim leaving through the entrance of Birkenau.*

134. EXT. BIRKENAU, DUSK

*The Jewish Pilgrim leaves through the gateway of
Birkenau.*

135. EXT. NEAR AUSCHWITZ, POLAND, NIGHT

*The Statue of Prometheus is still, and in its body are
reflected thousands of candles of the sort lit by the
Jewish Pilgrim.*

*Crane down body with hundreds of reflections to close-
ups of candles themselves.*

*The truck that carries the Statue of Prometheus has its
trailer filled with the little Jewish nightlights we saw in
the crematoria and along the railway lines of Birkenau,
and other candles of various kinds. They burn over the
whole surface of the trailer and glow in the golden body
of Prometheus.*

HERMES

Flames when they are used for light
most undermine Lord Zeus's might.
Zeus particularly dislikes
such stolen fire in little spikes

like these, fire that renews
the eagle-ravaged hearts of Jews.
Why? Why is it fire that they choose?
These candles that can help them cope
with history and lack of hope
are anathema to Führer Zeus
who hates fire's sacramental use,
Jews flaunting in Lord Zeus's face
the fire he'd meant to end their race.

Zeus and his henchmen have a fit
whenever they see candles lit.
The only time they don't is when
they're in the hands of Zeus's men,
who happily apply their heat
to the soles of prisoners' feet.
Every 'human rights abuse'
had its proud origin in Zeus,
who deemed that Man was only fit
for dumping dead in a mass pit.

Hermes sweeps away a huge pile of burning Jewish candles.

Kratos! Bia!
Come and help me over here.

Kratos and Bia come over and jump on the trailer. They stamp out the nightlights and kick them, some still burning, off the truck.

136. EXT. NOWA HUTA, POLAND, DAY

Factory chimney in Nowa Huta. The caduceus conducts the camera's movement down from the smoke and down the chimney to the Christ and crucifix outside the steelworks.

Outside the Bar Meksyk looking at the statue of Jesus on the cross, with a smoking chimney seemingly coming from the crucifix.

137. INT. BAR MERSYK, NOWA HUTA, POLAND, DAY

Hermes sitting with a drink in the Bar Meksyk facing a smoking chimney from the industrial complex of Nowa Huta.

HERMES

When forms of fire get men destroyed
Zeus is more than overjoyed.
Zeus won't feel properly reimbursed
until Mankind endures the worst.
You'd think that he'd be satisfied
with Europe's toll of genocide.
But when he hears the children wheeze,
those brought up near plants like these,
Zeus now thinks if he bides his time
that though Prometheus and his crime
get flaunted here, that restitution
could take the form of air pollution,
children coughing, little tots
with nebulisers in their cots,
cancer and asthma, if we wait,
might, thinks Zeus, part compensate
and save him from doing something rash
like end Earth with one lightning flash.
He prefers men die from their own use
of what Prometheus stole from Zeus.
It's long been Zeus's fervent hope
by giving men sufficient rope
and simply allowing a free hand
with stolen fire, the contraband,
that fire will blow up in the face

of the whole detested human race.
The big blow up! Or bit by bit
sink Man slowly in the shit,
the slower but secure solution,
poisoned by his own pollution.
Let such factories do their work
and swathe Mankind in acrid murk.
And if not Armageddon dream a
universal emphesyma!

138. INT. PALACE CINEMA, DAY

*Old Man wheezing. Hermes delighted at the sound of
coughing and rattling phlegm.*

139. INT. BAR MEKSYK, POLAND, DAY

HERMES

So such Promethean shrines,
chemical and steel works, mines,
still anger Zeus because they stand
for the Promethean contraband,
nonetheless make him content
by blighting Man's environment.

> *Hermes looks at the two remaining vodkas on the
> table.*

I'll drink Kratos's and Bia's!
Not nectar, but who cares. Cheers!

> *Hermes knocks back one of the glasses. He is about to
> do the same with the second when he hears, then sees,
> the Statue of Prometheus being overtaken by two
> fire-engines, their lights flashing and the Boy's distant
> voice as its wailing siren.*

> *Hermes rises and leaves the Bar Meksyk.*

140. EXT. STEELWORKS, NOWA HUTA, DAY

HERMES

And now I intend to introduce
the workers to this foe of Zeus,
and hope their fierce opprobrium falls
on falsely glittering Goldenballs!

Hermes enters the steelworks.

141. INT. STEELWORKS, NOWA HUTA, DAY

Steelworkers tending vats of molten metal. Smoke and orange light.

The Statue of Prometheus enters the furnace room, with shafts of sunlight slanting through the smoke and glowing cauldrons and showers of sparks.

The scene becomes black and white, like a propaganda film for heroes of Soviet labour.

142. INT. PALACE CINEMA, KNOTTINGLEY, DAY

The picture is revealed as being on the tattered screen of the Palace Cinema, Knottingley. The Old Man shouts out to the Polish Steelworkers.

OLD MAN

Raise your clenched fists to show you praise
t'founder of your foundry's blaze!

Gradually the Steelworkers surround the Statue and, as one man, raise their fists in the Promethean pose.

Their image changes from black and white to colour.

This is not what Hermes intended. He is furious. He runs round the ring of Steelworkers shouting 'Ognia zlodzeju!' ('thief of fire'), but the Steelworkers are merely further stimulated into chanting the name of Prometheus, and making the Promethean fist.

WORKERS

Prometeusz! Prometeusz! Prometeusz!

*The Old Man is overjoyed at their response. He feels
the old 'solidarity'.*

143. EXT. STEELWORKS, NOWA HUTA, POLAND, DAY

HERMES

I should have known these stubborn Poles
still had Prometheus in their souls.
It angers Zeus. It riles. It galls
such grovelling to Goldenballs.

To Kratos and Bia:

Kratos! Bia! Get Prometheus out of here!

144. EXT. NOWA HUTA, STEELWORKS, DAY

*The golden Statue of Prometheus passes the broken
windows of the steelworks, and is reflected in grimy
pools with green hydrants.*

VOICE OF HERMES

We'll find another place and time
to bespatter Goldenballs with grime.
Leave these Poles their smog and smoke,
and may their little children choke
and croak inside a plastic bubble
and save man-hating Zeus the trouble!

145. EXT. STATUE OF HEROIC WORKER, POLAND, DAY

*The Statue of Prometheus passes by the statue of a
heroic worker with a red flag on the wall of a building
near the steelworks.*

146. EXT. BACKYARD NEAR ROADSIDE, POLAND, DAY

Io runs in and snatches a shirt from a washing line. She runs through long grass. She reaches the roadside and runs past trucks and a haycart drawn by horses.

147. EXT. BAROQUE STREETS, BRATISLAVA, NIGHT

Io rummages in dustbins and gobbles down the fish-heads she finds there. She washes them down by sucking the dregs of a discarded packet of 'Zeus juice'.

148. EXT. BRATISLAVA BRIDGE, SLOVAK REPUBLIC, DAWN

The Statue of Prometheus passes over the bridge. The Daughters of Ocean pass under the bridge, singing.

149. EXT. GIANT EAGLE MONUMENT, TATABANYA, HUNGARY, DAY

Hermes beside the eagle of Tatabanya (the 'Turul' monument). Hermes' point of view of the Statue of Prometheus being overtaken on the road below by a Tatabanya fire engine with its lights flashing and its sirens wailing (Boy in wreckers' yard making fire-engine noises).

HERMES
This is the eagle always sent
to deal out Zeus's punishment,
the one whose darkening wingspan soars
over Europe's past and recent wars,
whose shadow bulks large in the sky
when nations are about to die.
This is Zeus's favourite pet
and he hasn't finished eating yet!
He exists to make Man's spirit quake

and in the end to make it break.
The eagle's only got to fly
above a town to terrify,
and has flown more than one mission
after the Yugoslav partition,
urging Serb and Croat side
into committing genocide.
He didn't care which side killed which,
the Serbs of Slobodan Milosevic
or Muslims, it didn't matter who
so long as the death-tolls grew and grew.

Fire engine overtakes the Statue of Prometheus.

And soon the eagle's cruel beak
'll make Prometheus scream in Greek,
and shriek αιαι αιαι αιαι
to the Elefsina sky,
where burn-off flame and petrol fume
will witness the fire-thief's cruel doom.

On the road below we see the Statue of Prometheus
about to pass beneath the eagle. It is suddenly overtaken
by a Tatabanya fire engine with its lights flashing and
the distant voice of the Boy as its wailing siren.

150. EXT. WRECKING YARD, DAY

The sound of the Boy mixes through fire-engine sirens.
We see him still driving his wrecked fire engine in the
wreckers' yard.

151. EXT. BALLE HERCULANE, ROMANIA, DAY

The Statue of Prometheus passes the statue of Hercules
in the square of Baile Herculane.

152. EXT. RAILWAY STATION, BAILE HERCULANE, ROMANIA, DAY

Io looks at the train timetable, desperately weary. She rests her head against the glass door leading to the platform. The glass door is engraved with the figure of Hercules. She drops off into sleep, then suddenly runs to jump onto the departing train.

153. INT. ROMANIAN RAILWAY TRAIN, DAY

Io finds a seat on the train. The other passengers stare at her.

Io sees the Statue of Prometheus from the train.

The Ticket Collector begins inspecting tickets. He shouts at Io, then throws her off the train, shouting obscenities after her.

154. EXT. GYPSY VILLAGE, ROMANIA, DAY

Io walks towards the gypsy village, hoping to be taken in. The villagers look at her suspiciously, then begin to chase her and throw stones at her. Io flees.

155. EXT. MONASTERY, ROMANIA, DAY

A monk in black robes beats a tuaca (*a long plank carried over the shoulder and beaten with a wooden mallet*).

Outside a small building there are metal receptacles for votive candles for the living and the dead. To the sound of the tuaca *Io enters the building and steals a candle from the many burning there.*

Io runs away with the candle.

The monk now beats a much bigger tuaca, *suspended from chains.*

156. EXT. FIRE STATION, ROMANIA, DAY

The Statue of Prometheus passes an old fire engine with flat tyres. We hear the Boy's siren sound running down, then a cough.

157. EXT. FOREST, ROMANIA, DAY

The Statue of Prometheus passes a sign warning of the dangers of fire. The caduceus of Hermes points to the word FOC *(fire).*

158. EXT. VAST DAM, ROMANIA, DAY

The Statue of Prometheus crosses a vast dam.

159. EXT. DERELICT CARBON FACTORY, COPŞA MICĂ, ROMANIA, DAY

Hermes on a high vantage point of the derelict carbon works.

HERMES

This dereliction, and these hills,
I'll blizzard now with dollar bills.
Each dollar buys a missile hurled
at the champion of the human world
by these jobless carbon-worker sods
who take his side against us gods.
Or *did* with due devotion till
they deified the dollar bill.
Zeus entrusts these jobs to me,
free-trade Hermes/Mercury!
When jobs collapse they know their pal
is *D-mark*-toting Capital!
One they worshipped not far back
they now bombard with carbon black.
How were they converted to bombard
one they'd worshipped? It's not hard!

357

Hard currency is all I need,
some greenbacks and their human greed.
Lire or a bit of sterling
'll soon get these guys missile hurling.

Do your former worshippers frighten
the rebel-fisted golden Titan?
Isn't it frightening a few notes
can make Prometheans turn their coats?
For a few dollars they'll shout abuse
that gladdens the god's ears of Zeus.
And that's especially because
here, if anywhere, Prometheus *was*
patron saint of Copşa Mică,
industrial Utopia seeker.
The power-to-the-people fist
made him the gilded socialist.
Now look at all these 'socialists'
with dollar bills in their clenched fists.

> *Hermes drops dollar bills from the tower. The Copşa
> Mică Carbon Workers scrabble for them and brandish
> their dollars.*

> *The Carbon Workers throw carbon at the Statue of
> Prometheus.*

> *The scenes changes from colour to black and white.
> The scene is projected on the tattered screen of the
> Palace Cinema.*

160. INT. PALACE CINEMA, DAY

*The Old Man is on his feet pleading with the Romanian
Carbon Workers.*

OLD MAN
Don't chuck it! Don't! Don't chuck muck
at Prometheus. It'll bring bad luck.

You're desecrating the ideal
of industry, coal, iron, steel
and whatever muck that you produce
or used to till bought off by Zeus.

HERMES
(*from screen*)
Do behave! There's a good chap!
Applaud these deeds or have a nap
Or watch, in Socialism's heart,
how free-trade makes them fall apart.
I'm winning here. So either clap
these carbon-chuckers or 'shut thi trap'.

OLD MAN
Don't, brothers! Stop! All t'old bosses
'll cash in quick on t'workers' losses.
The 'free' market'll just leave you broke.
All our livings have gone up in smoke
or demolition dust-clouds.

HERMES
Just like you.
Your own demolition's almost due!

*The clouds of carbon thrown by the Carbon Workers
make the Old Man cough and sit down. He stares in
despair at the scene, and closes his eyes with horror.*

OLD MAN
(*to himself*)
Spatter Prometheus now wi' shit
but you're t'real targets getting hit.
He's tricking you, the bastard. Look
how you're muckied by t'stuff you chuck.
You cake Prometheus with chucked crud
and end, as Hermes knew you would,
with just as thick a coat of black

as t'god he bribed you to attack.
You think it's Prometheus you defile
by smearing him, and all the while
Hermes knows (that's why he's smiling!)
it's you yersens that you're defiling.
That's why that silver sod there's sneering,
it's your own souls this carbon's smearing.
He's killing two birds with one stone,
the spirit of Prometheus, and your own.

The Old Man bursts into a fit of coughing as a cloud of carbon envelops him.

The Carbon Workers bombard the Statue of Prometheus with carbon black. The image turns back to colour.

The Statue of Prometheus is black with carbon.

Io comes to the statue and tries to wash it clean. She wipes the feet clean with her hair. She rips off her ragged skirt and uses it to clean off the carbon. She begins to kiss the statue's calf and foot.

Rain begins washing off the carbon. Thunder rolls through the derelict plant.

Close-ups of carbon streaming off the gold in rivulets of rain.

161. EXT. DERELICT CARBON FACTORY, DAY

The truck carrying the Statue of Prometheus leaves the derelict factory with rain lashing down. Close-up of rain on water.

162. EXT. IRON GATES, ROMANIA, DAY

The Statue of Prometheus comes down the road parallel to the Danube, flowing into the locks of Portile de Fier

(Iron Gates). The Daughters of Ocean pass through the lock, singing.

VOICE OF HERMES
Kratos (Force) and (Violence) Bia,
who miss their old SS career,
had recent sport in two regimes
on either side these Danube's streams.
Where our sugary chorus glide
through killing fields on either side,
Bia (Violence) and Kratos (Force)
found two dictators to endorse,
the best they'd had since World War Two,
Milosevic and Ceausescu,
who made the Danube red not blue.
And poor mortals think that song redeems
the ravages of such regimes.

163. EXT. SUNFLOWER FIELDS AND BEEHIVES, ROMANIA, DAY

The Statue of Prometheus passes vast fields of sunflowers, where two Beekeepers watch it go by. Hives are loaded onto a truck and driven into the fields.

164. EXT. STEELWORKS, BULGARIA, DAY

A rainbow arcs above a run-down steelworks.

VOICE OF HERMES
Look how the free-trade rainbow arcs
in the hues of dollars, sterling, Marks,
but what they'll find at the end of it
's not gold, but a crock of shit.

The Silver Statue of Hermes points towards the hoarding surrounding Kremikovits Steelworks.

HERMES
(*pointing his caduceus*)
Though this is a Promethean shrine
the image painted there is mine.
The image of Hermes painted on a
Bulgarian steelworks. What an honour!
And with a *dogofor* (contract!) in my hand,
doing deals from land to land.
I do hope you don't mind if I gloss
such foreign words we come across,
I hate to flaunt my language skill,
and wouldn't have to, if yours weren't nil!

The god of free trade to be hailed,
now that Socialism's failed.
As god of free trade I endorse
the factory's new free-trade course.
Once they aimed at work for all,
now the weak go to the wall.

> As Hermes speaks, his image with the steelworks
> chimneys behind turns black and white, and then
> appears tattered on the fragmentary screen at the
> Palace Cinema, Knottingley, where the Old Man is
> listening and smoking. The transition is worked
> through the smoking chimneys to the smoky cinema
> and smoking cigarette.

165. INT. PALACE CINEMA, DAY

OLD MAN
But I know that it'll come,
the new Socialist millennium.

HERMES
You must be joking!
Your brain's been addled by your smoking.
You yourself are one of the weak

362

gone to the wall whereof I speak.
Your suicide by cigarettes
is not a fate that Zeus regrets.
And the free trade I promote
's to help Mankind cut its own throat.

OLD MAN

It's just as well I'll pop mi clogs
when Socialism's gone to t'dogs.
It'd be a struggle to exist
in t'world and *not* be socialist.
How could I go on existing
wi' t'war still on wi'out enlisting?
When men see all they knew collapse
t'old gods start to bait their traps.
Why else is Hermes on the loose
touting for that tyrant Zeus?
When men's great dreams are unemployed
divinities'll fill t'dark void,
distributing a specious dole
for every desperate, hungry soul.
I don't need gods, but what I need
's (one) mi Socialism, (two) mi weed.

Though it's med me think I'm allus right
and see t'whole world in black and white,
when life's so infinitely fuller
watched end to end in technicolour.
Wanting t'world all cut and dried
's a form of mental suicide.
And if you asked me now I'd say
that t'world were mostly shades of grey
coloured by a few bright flecks,
like fleeting confetti, love and sex,
and, though I know I'm bloody croaking,
the lifelong joy I've had from smoking.

Old Man exhales a savoured stream of smoke.

166. INT. BAKERY, JAMBOL, BULGARIA, DAY

A burst of fire from a large paraffin blowtorch into an oven: a Woman heats a small oven with a blowtorch.

The metal of the trays of bread waiting to be baked reflects the fire.

When the oven is heated enough the Woman withdraws the torch, puts in the trays of bread and closes the iron shutter to the oven.

167. EXT. BAKERY, JAMBOL, BULGARIA, DAY

Io, drawn by the smell of baking bread, approaches the doorway of the bakery where the Woman and her son are baking the morning's bread.

168. INT. BAKERY, JAMBOL, BULGARIA, DAY

The Woman takes bread out of oven and notices Io looking into the bakery. The Woman takes pity on her, speaks kindly to her and gives her a warm loaf, which Io clutches to her heart. Io walks away.

169. EXT. TENEMENTS, SANDANSKI, BULGARIA, DAY

Io walks, clutching the still uneaten loaf of bread given her by the kind baker woman. Two pairs of rubber-gloved hands seize her arms, and the bread falls to the ground. Io struggles free and runs through the blocks of flats, under a concrete arch and into a chemical works.

Close-up of boot trampling the fallen bread as Kratos and Bia pursue Io.

170. EXT. CHEMICAL WORKS, BULGARIA, DAY

Io runs along a railway track that runs beside a loading bay for sacks of chemicals. White heaps of chemicals lie

*on the platform of the loading bay. As she runs Kratos
kicks a cloud of white chemicals into her face. She gags
and chokes and falls to the ground. She is seized by
Kratos and Bia and dragged towards the parked
cattle-truck. She is thrown inside and driven off past
Bulgarian chemical signs and the arch of the factory
saying* NEOCHIM.

*She is now half-black from carbon and half-white from
chemicals, so that she has the brindled appearance of a
Friesian cow.*

171. INT. CATTLE-TRUCK, BULGARIA, DUSK

*Io is captured solo inside the cattle-truck, heading for an
abattoir.*

*She flings herself against the slats of the truck. She
howls. She almost moos like a cow.*

*Her left hand with the wedding ring bashes rhythmically
on the truck slats.*

VOICE OF HERMES
Now I think the time is right,
daubed as she is in black and white,
caked with chemicals and carbon. Now
stoke the furnace for our Friesian cow.

172. EXT. ABATTOIR, BULGARIA, DAY

*The truck pulls up at an abattoir. Io is goaded out of her
truck.*

*Kratos and Bia goad Io with their own version of the
caduceus of Hermes, which they employ like an electric
cattle-prod.*

173. INT. ABATTOIR, BULGARIA, DAY

One by one the cattle go into the run towards the stun gun. We see them from behind.

Two Friesian cows are stunned in turn and their carcasses fall out of the chamber onto a metal grid. They are hooked and hoisted up into the air on a chain. Their hooves rattle across the metal grid as they are dragged. More cattle move towards the stunning chamber.

The 'guillotine' doors go up and down, with echoing sonorous clangs. The colours of rust and metal and brick are close to those of Auschwitz.

Then Io is stunned and falls from the chamber onto the metal grid.

Her head bangs across the bars of the metal grid as she is dragged by the chain and is hoisted up into the air.

The pitched hum of the hoist is almost like that of a cello. Io's cello.

Close-up of head dragging across metal grid. Her face is black and white. On her white cheek there are three drops of blood like a Pierrot's tears.

The yellow plastic starter-button for the carcass hoist swings to and fro across a white immaculate tiled wall. A blue Insect-o-cutor bar is reflected in the white tiles.

174. INT. CATTLE BURNING PLACE, BULGARIA, DAY

Close-up of blue Insect-o-cutor bars with flies being electrocuted, making the sound now revealed as that of the caduceus of Hermes.

Pan up from Insect-o-cutor to Hermes: he is watching the killing from an observation window, and smiles.

175. EXT. CATTLE-BURNING PLACE, DAY

Carcasses are scooped up and incinerated in an oven not unlike that of Auschwitz. The carcasses burn and disintegrate.

Then the scoop picks up Io's carcass and feeds it into the oven. The door is sealed.

The caduceus of Hermes stirs the ashes of cremated cows and discovers the ring of Io.

176. EXT. BULGARIAN ROAD THROUGH FIR FOREST, DAY

Hermes stands before a sign in Bulgarian warning of the dangers of fire in the forest. The caduceus points to the Bulgarian word for fire: POZHAR.

HERMES

Kaputted in the abattoir,
the cow's cremated in *pozhar.*
Pozhar, the fire that in a flash
turns fine fir forests into ash.

177. INT. PALACE CINEMA, DAY

HERMES
(*on screen*)
And you, you old chain-smoking shit
can get such conflagrations lit.

The Old Man makes a defiant gesture at the screen with his cigarette. The voice of the Boy imitating a fire-engine siren.

178. EXT. GREEK FIRE HAZARD SIGN, ROADSIDE, DAY

The caduceus of Hermes sweeps down from the depicted flames to the cigarette at the bottom of the roadside sign.

HERMES

They leave their foul fire-blackened trails,
old codgers with their coffin nails.

179. EXT. STATUE OF AESCHYLUS, ELEFSINA, DAY

Hermes stands beside the Statue of Aeschylus in Elefsina.
He watches the disappearing Statue of Prometheus.

HERMES

There's one bastard passing by
to end up being chained on high,
so that the world can come to mock
Goldenballs chained to the rock,
helpless, hopeless, heaped with scorn,
here, where Aeschylus was born,
the other bastard (maybe worse!)
who hymned Prometheus in his verse.

180. EXT. MUSEUM TERRACE, ANCIENT SITE, ELEUSIS

Hermes walks from the Statue of Aeschylus to the
ancient site of Eleusis.

HERMES

But if Aeschylus had lived today
he'd have to write a different play.
He'd change his verses once he'd seen a
burn-off flame at Elefsina,
the chimneys pouring smoke above
the ancient site he used to love,
the chimneys painted red and white
that loom above this sacred site,
and how the sacred torch became
a very different form of flame,
from the initiate's pure torch
to factory fires that scar and scorch,
the corrosive, caustic clouds that eat
the marble of Demeter's wheat,

The caduceus points to a fragment of sculpture showing ears of wheat.

those clouds of chemicals that gnaw
the ancient words we stand before.

Hermes sweeps his caduceus over the inscription
ΑΓΑΘΗ ΤΥΧΗ.

HERMES

ΑΓΑΘΗ ΤΥΧΗ!
                    I'll translate –
Good luck! Not the fire-thief's fate!
And the end that Man'll come to's sticky
and shortish on ΑΓΑΘΗ ΤΥΧΗ!
Not the sort of words you'd find
wished by Zeus on poor mankind.
Zeus won't shed a single tear
to see Man's good luck disappear.
It would have long since disappeared
if Prometheus hadn't interfered.

181. EXT. ELEUSIS (ELEFSINA), DAY

Hermes points out the Statue of Prometheus chained to the rock.

HERMES

And there Man's benefactor hangs,
racked by regrets and conscience pangs.
We need no eagle now to gnaw
when conscience can consume him more.
More rending than the eagle's beak are
Dresden, Auschwitz, Copşa Mică.
He'll have to brood there on his rock
on fire and *Feuer, Pozhar, Foc,*
fire that poisons and pollutes

*Hermes looks down at his feet and sees that he is
standing in a pool of petrol.*

and smears petrol on one's silver boots!
I'll need the spring of Hippocrene
to cleanse my boots of gasoline,
I'll quit this globe Man's made so cruddy
and leave you with my understudy.

Hermes turns into his statue.

182. EXT. ELEFSINA MOUNTAINS, NIGHT

The sun begins to set.

183. INT. PALACE CINEMA, DAY

*The Old Man coughs with the eagle of Zeus on the
screen before him. The sun is setting in black and white.*

184. EXT. TATABANYA EAGLE, NIGHT

The sun sets behind the eagle of Zeus.

185. EXT. ELEUSIS (ELEFSINA), NIGHT

OLD MAN
You just get t'first drag down your throat 'n
some bugger's barking it's *verboten.*

*Figures of Miners emerge from the rocky
surroundings. They have pit helmets with their lights
switched on and also more ancient torches of flame.*

Dictators, deities, they're all t'same
forbidding men fags, fruit or flame.
First Zeus wi' fire then t'God of t'chapel's
obsession wi' forbidding apples.
One crunch into that contraband

gave men t'knowledge God had banned.
We've got t'knowledge, we've got t'fire,
we've raised ussens up out of t'mire.
Diso-bloody-bedience got us over
t'barbed wire fences of Jehovah.
But men thesens bring back t'barbed wire
round t'Bramleys and round t'bakehouse fire.
There's not one joy but what some berk'll
want it ringed wi a red circle.
Gods or men who're summat similar,
'ermes or some Town Hall 'immler,
those in power'd like t'red ring
round almost bloody everything.

186. EXT. ELEUSIS (ELEFSINA), NIGHT

The audience of Miners listens to the speech of the Old Man, who has become Prometheus. Their faces are lit by the torches they carry.

OLD MAN

Fire, that's brought Man close to t'brink
were t'first to help him dream and think.
Imagine men first freed from t'night
first sitting round t'warm firelight,
safe from t'beasts they allus feared
until Prometheus first appeared.
Watching logs burn, watching coal,
created what's been called Man's soul,
that like a – (*He coughs.*) – lung or liver gnawed
at t'orders of t'great overlord,
reasserts, gets rent, and reasserts,
for all its rending and raw hurts,
its fiery nature and its light,
its first defiance of dark night.

*Old Man lights a cigarette to the strains of an heroic
fanfare. He exhales after a deep drag. As he blows out
the smoke we cut to the face of the golden Statue of
Prometheus, who appears to be blowing out the last
puff of the Old Man's inhaled smoke.*

Fire and poetry, two great powers
that mek the so-called gods' world OURS!

*The audience of Miners roar approval and rise to their
feet and come forward to the spot beneath which the
golden Statue of Prometheus is chained to the rock.*

MINERS
(*shouting*)

Prometheas! Prometheas!

*The chant of the Miners fades back into the rock of
Eleusis and dies away slowly.*

VOICE OF HERMES
(*from statue reflected in pool of gasoline*)

Beware out there this gasoline
doesn't seep out through the screen.
Or else your audience participation
might consist of your cremation.

187. INT. PALACE CINEMA, DAY

The Old Man sees his opportunity.

OLD MAN
(*holding up smoking cigarette*)

Mi soggy-ended cigarette'll
mek bloody Hermes molten metal.
This half-smoked ciggy that I'll chuck'll
soon mek bastard's buttocks buckle.
He's stood in t'petrol and my hand
's holding t'lit Promethean brand

372

and if them boundaries don't exist
one flick of this arthritic wrist
'll mek that servile silver wet
sizzle with this cigarette!
I commit you, Hermes, in the name
of Prometheus to the power of flame.

*Old Man flicks his lighted cigarette stub into the pool
of petrol on the screen in the Palace Cinema. The
petrol ignites with a great roar and consumes the
Statue of Hermes, which screams like a man on fire.*

*Old Man rises in revolutionary triumph over the
burning Hermes.*

*He puts another cigarette in his mouth then his
triumphant expression fades from his face as he sees
the fire spread to the Daughters of Ocean, who go on
singing higher and higher until their song turns into
hideous screaming.*

*The fire spreads to the mountain and the chained
Prometheus, and again we hear the Miners screaming
in the fire of the furnace that melted them down.*

*The Old Man's cigarette drops from his mouth as he
slumps back into his seat.*

*The conflagration continues until the statues
representing both the Daughters of Ocean and
Prometheus are totally consumed, except for the right
fist of Prometheus still chained to the rock.*

As the cinema screen itself burns, the Old Man dies.

188. EXT. ELEUSIS (ELEFSINA), NIGHT

*In the pool of the melted Hermes we hear the voice of
the god. All that remains is the right hand grasping the
caduceus, the god still grimly holding on to power.*

VOICE OF HERMES
(from puddle: an icy chuckle)
Yes, they were genuinely mine,
those screams I do hope chilled your spine.
I think you mortals must agree
my screams worked well (if OTT!).
Fittingly frightening but all fake,
gods feel no wound, no pain, no ache.
It's only you ephemeral squirts
who get to feel base human hurts.
He fell for it! It wasn't hard
to pretend that I was off my guard,
to let him think he had me beat
and engineer his own defeat.
And such deceptions dug the pit
of that clapped out Promethean shit.

> *The cinema is on fire. The Old Man is dead. The whole place is going up in flames. A charred mask of one remaining Daughter of Ocean utters a note and a last expiring sigh, which becomes the sound of the Boy making his fire-engine siren noise.*

189. EXT. PALACE CINEMA, DAY

Outside the smoking Palace Cinema is parked a derelict fire engine, the one in which the Boy travelled in his imagination through Europe. The Boy is frantically pulling on the useless bell of the fire engine to raise the alarm.

The Boy jumps out of the fire engine and runs towards the cooling towers, shouting 'Mam! Mam!'

The residents of nearby houses come out to see what the commotion is.

190. INT. COOLING TOWER, DAY

The Boy runs through the derelict cooling tower shouting 'Mam! Mam!'

His voice echoes in the chamber of the cooling tower.

VOICE OF HERMES
And at his back he'll always hear
the boots of Kratos and of Bia!

The voice of Hermes echoes in the cooling towers.

The cooling towers collapse around the Boy. He runs through giant dust clouds.

The End.

METAMORPHEUS
(2000)

Metamorpheus was first transmitted on BBC2 on
17 December 2000, with the following cast:

The Poet Tony Harrison
The Professor Oliver Taplin

Music Richard Blackford with the Bournemouth
   Symphony Chorus, *Soloist* Omar Ebrahim,
   Chorus Master Neville Creed

Fixers Andrey Borissov (Bulgaria), Dee Murphy (Greece)
Dubbing Mixer Peter Davies
Dubbing Editor Jenny Silverman
VT Editor Steve Olive
Modelmakers Vicki Hallam, Codsteaks
Graphic Design Alisa Robbins
Production Assistants Marie Coyne, Valerie Mitchell
Photography Alistair Cameron
Film Editor Peter Simpson
Director Peter Symes

*Note: the dialogue for the Professor was written by
Oliver Taplin*

1. Close-up of finger of the Professor pressing a doorbell which reads ORPHEUS. *It morphs first to Bulgarian Cyrillic, then to Greek.*

THE PROFESSOR

Bugger!

2. The Professor is walking up a hill in a Bulgarian village, Bartak.

THE POET
(*voice-over*)

Bugger! says the Oxford don
frustrated by the trek he's on!
I was the one who sent him off ,
this unwary Classics prof,
my friend Taplin, off to trace
the myth of Orpheus all through Thrace
(Bulgaria as it is today
where Orpheus is now called *Orfei*,
the sign we see on this café.)

I told him 'Scholarship like yours
could open those locked Orphic doors.'

3. The Professor walks to the door and tries it. It's locked.

THE PROFESSOR

Bugger!

The Poet laughs.

*4. A restaurant in Bristol. The Poet is sitting at a table
with his Orpheus notebook. There is a photograph stuck
into it of a statue of Orpheus in Sofia, Bulgaria.*

THE POET
(*sync*)

In '98 the year before
I'd done my own Bulgarian tour
starting with this Orpheus here . . .

*The Poet points to the picture of the statue of Orpheus
in Sofia. Mix to the Poet laying flowers on the statue.*

THE POET
(*voice-over*)

. . . not much noticed in Sofia.
Orpheus torn apart, dismembered,
sings again when he's remembered
or finds some modern devotee
of the powerless power of poetry.

Gerbera, yellow, orange, red
I place behind Orpheus's head.
Call his name, or bring his flowers,
sun-coloured, to restore his powers.

VOICE

Orfei!

THE POET

Honour Orfei and you'll hear
his voice in traffic-choked Sofia.

Though over two millennia dead,
it still sings, the dismembered head,
the head of Orpheus, that head hacked
when Orpheus/Orfei was attacked
by Thracian women . . .

THRACIAN WOMEN
Orfei!

THE POET

because he was the world's first gay.
And 'Bugger, bugger!' they yelled at him
when they tore him limb from limb.

Scream.

*5. Restaurant in Bristol. The Poet and the Professor sit
at a table in a Greek restaurant.*

THE POET
(with Orpheus notebook)

I honoured Orpheus – look, this snap
shows my flowers in the poet's lap,
gerbera to seal the line
running from his muse to mine.

Oliver, you ought to trace
the myth of Orpheus all through Thrace,
Bulgaria as it is today,
follow his hacked head all the way
down the Hebrus to the sea
then to Lesbos spouting poetry.

You've got the leisure and long vacs
to follow in Orpheus's tracks.
Go on the journey I went on.
It's a great trip for a Classics don.

Food's good – wine – you can have a trip
half-scoffing and half-scholarship.

You know my notebooks, how I glue
every image, each small clue,
doodle lines in case one day
I make a film about Orfei.
Look at all this stuff I've stuck
into my new Orpheus book.

Every Orphic twist and turn
's been collected, as you know, by Kern:

THE PROFESSOR
Orphicorum Fragmenta!

THE POET
Read
those Greek texts. It's all you'll need
and broken icons of the bard
scattered on cracked pot and shard.

THE PROFESSOR
The coins!

THE POET
Those excavated clues
the Classicist knows how to use.
Scholarship like Kern's and yours
could open those locked Orphic doors.

Points to a picture in his notebook.

That's Odilon Redon that head,
still making music though it's dead.
In the Rhodopes you could even trace
ancient Orpheus in a modern face.

*Close-up of a Bulgarian boy's head, then a detail of an
Orpheus vase supered over.*

THE POET
These are some Orpheuses from my book
but he's every-bloody-where you look.
He's there in constant metamorphosis.

Look at this . . . and this . . . and this . . .
Look, even gooey Orpheus chocs
with Cyrillic *Orfei* on the box.

6. The Professor walks out of the restaurant.

THE PROFESSOR
Well, at least on this trip, I'm not going to have that
bloody bard looking over my shoulder the whole time.
And holding forth in sodding rhyme!

7. The Poet still at the restaurant table with notebook.

THE POET
Typical scholar! Scoffs his fill
then leaves the poet to pay the bill.
I bet of all my Orphic clues
the chocs 'll be the first he'll choose.

And off with the Magdalen mortar board
and after some Bulgarian broad.

*8. A nightclub in the basement of a hotel in Plovdiv,
Bulgaria, with the Offenbach 'Can-Can' music playing,
and dancers.*

THE POET
(*voice-over*)
Leaves his poor wife in the lurch
and drools at 'Can-Can' for 'research'!

THE PROFESSOR
Mmm . . . Tony didn't tell me about this underworld in
the hotel – I wouldn't be at all surprised if he came down
here looking for Eurydice.

I'm intrigued by that version of the myth that says that
Orpheus was the world's first gay – but by far the best
known story is how he went down and charmed the
Hades powers into letting him take his wife Eurydice
back from the dead. He looked round at her, of course,
and had to return to our world without her.

385

But in my researches I've been looking into the *early* myth, and I've found that the ancient Greeks themselves were far more concerned with what happened *after* that – with his violent death.

(*Voice-over.*) It's all very well that bloody bard telling me to do this and that – but following the Orpheus myth on the ground is going to mean a long climb high into the Rhodope mountains south of Sofia. After the women up there had hacked him to pieces, they threw his head and his lyre into the river Maritsa. I'm going right back to its source.

9. *The River Maritsa.*

THE PROFESSOR
(*voice-over*)

The reason why the Greek myths are so potent, why they underlie so many of our basic stories, must surely be that they have this potential for metamorphosis, to be endlessly remade, recycled in new forms . . .

But I have a new approach which may reveal something about the strength of these mythical roots. The more I think about them, the more I become fascinated by the way that although they are stories of the imagination, they are not set in some imaginary world, but in the distant past of real places. And I always want to ask: why this particular landscape for this particular myth?

With Orpheus, one starting point is that he lived in the remote mountains of Thrace (that's more or less present-day Bulgaria). Another: he was not a warrior, like nearly all the other Greek heroes. He was a poet and musician. And linking these: the power of his performance was so strong that it could cross conventional boundaries. It could even reach beyond the human world to the natural world.

10. The lyre of Orpheus floats down the river, captivating birds and wild animals, eagle, blackbird, wildcat, woodpecker, wild boar . . .

11. Gravel-diggers are working on the banks of the river Maritsa. The Professor is sitting by the river reading a book.

THE PROFESSOR
(*voice-over*)

There is no definitive version of how or why the women ripped the poet to pieces. The texts about Orpheus are all – rather like him – dismembered fragments. But I've excavated one especially intriguing version, not by a famous authority, but by an obscure poet from the third century BC called Phanocles. Phanocles was fed up with the traditional tales of gods and heroes falling for mortal women, and told stories instead of their love for beautiful young men – a gay reformulation of the Greek myths, I suppose. Only one fragment of this poem survives; and it so happens that it tells the Orpheus story, and how the women hacked him to pieces because, instead of fancying them, he was in love with a beautiful boy, Kalais.

The Professor translates from the Phanocles text.

'. . . Often he would sit in the shady groves singing of his desire, and his spirit was never at rest, but always his unsleeping passion ate away at his spirit . . . soul . . . ate away at his soul when he looked at the youthful Kalais, but the malicious Thracian women surrounded and killed him, whetting their sharp blades because . . .'

THE VOICE OF THE HEAD OF ORPHEUS

Ah! Ah!
Cease from your labour there and say
who sings in the stream.

GRAVEL-DIGGERS
ORFEI!

THE VOICE OF THE HEAD OF ORPHEUS
Your voice gives power back to me,
the powerless power of poetry.

To Fisherman midstream:

Fisherman. I float your way,
tell me who I am.

FISHERMAN
ORFEI!

THE VOICE OF THE HEAD OF ORPHEUS
Your voice gives power back to me,
the powerless power of poetry.

GRAVEL-DIGGERS
Orfei! Orfei! Orfei!

12. Hotel at Tzigov Chark. It has an Orfei with lyre on the wall outside. The Professor is outside the hotel with a notebook.

THE PROFESSOR
(*sync*)
'They cut off his head with their blades, and threw it into the water, along with his Thracian tortoiseshell lyre . . .'
Thracian women, Thracian lyre . . . This myth is different from most in the way that it's not set in the heartlands of the Greek world, but in the wild fringes. Maybe that fits with his not being conventional in his sexuality. It's as though Orpheus was trying to bring unfamiliar poetry to the wild margins.

388

13. Water park. The Professor sits near the pool reading Otto Kern's Orphicorum Fragmenta.

THE PROFESSOR

I have a guidebook through the twists and turns of my obsession. It's *Orphicorum Fragmenta*, the work of Otto Kern, a German scholar of the beginning of this century, who devoted years of his life to collecting every single fragment of ancient Greek that has anything to do with Orpheus. I wonder whether anyone before me has brought these dry pages into Orpheus' own territory?

A child splashes into the pool and sprays drops of water on the pages of the Otto Kern book.

14. Station and train, Velingrad.

THE PROFESSOR
(*voice-over*)

My friend, the pontificating poet, tries to put Orpheus back together by assembling bits and pieces in his notebooks. And in his different way Kern, the scholar, was trying to reassemble him out of fragments of texts. Now I, in my turn, try to find a shape to my journey, have to pick out a piece here and a piece there from Kern's pages. In Kern I find Orpheus the lover, and Orpheus the leader of a cult – there are many religious texts collected here from the later Orphic religion – but, first and running through all, Orpheus the poet, whose singing even survived his death.

The train goes into a tunnel. Total darkness. Scream.

15. The train journey continues. The lyre floats down the Maritsa, passing birds and cows wading in the river.

*16. A legless accordion player plays music influenced by
the lyre as cows and people go past him.*

ACCORDIONIST
(*to camera*)

ORFEI!

*17. Plovdiv. Archaeological Museum. Coin with Orpheus
stamped on it.*

THE PROFESSOR
(*voice-over*)

The central city of the Plain of Thrace, far older and more
interesting than the capital Sofia, is Plovdiv. When Philip,
the father of Alexander the Great, eventually conquered
the ancient Thracians, he named this city after himself:
Philipopolis.

The modern Bulgarians, even though they arrived long
after the era of ancient Greece, have claimed Orpheus
as their own – you see his name and image all over the
place. Yet I've ransacked the libraries for pictorial
fragments, for images of Orpheus, that go back to the
days of Phllipopolis, and I've been able to track down
only one in the whole of Bulgaria – a picture as small as
my wristwatch.

18. Roman theatre of Plovdiv.

(*Voice-over.*) Where are these inscriptions?

The Professor finds the inscription.

THE PROFESSOR
(*voice-over*)

So the city was divided into administrative divisions,
which would sit together in the theatre. One of those

was named after Orpheus, another after the Rhodope mountains and another after the river his head floated down.

19. The Professor on a bridge over the Maritsa river.

THE PROFESSOR

The river of the Orpheus story is the Maritsa. The Maritsa it is in Bulgaria. When it reaches Greece it's the Evros or Hebros in Ancient Greek.

From here the river sweeps on through the agricultural plain and industrialised cities of central Bulgaria.

20. River sequence with the lyre carried on its waters into Svilengrad.

21. The Professor in Svilengrad with a bridge in the background.

THE PROFESSOR

I've followed Orpheus eastwards about two hundred miles and to here, Svilengrad, where Mustapha Pasha, the Turkish ruler, built this fantastic thirteen-arch bridge in the early sixteenth century. Around here the river turns to the south, towards the sea, and within a couple of miles from here, on the left bank, is the Turkish border where the Maritsa becomes the Merich . . . and on the right-hand bank, the Greek border, where the Maritsa becomes the Evros or Hebros . . . and from this bridge . . . from this bridge . . .

The Professor looks up startled as he hears the Voice of the Head of Orpheus.

THE VOICE OF THE HEAD OF ORPHEUS
Ah! Ah! My name . . . my name . . .
and the name I hear them cry
from the bridge as I pass by –

PEOPLE ON BRIDGE
ORFEI!

THE VOICE OF THE HEAD OF ORPHEUS
Bulgarians, I float your way
tell me who I am –

PEOPLE ON BRIDGE
ORFEI!

THE VOICE OF THE HEAD OF ORPHEUS
Your voices give back power to me,
the powerless power of poetry

and the name I hear them cry
from the bridge as I pass by –

PEOPLE ON BRIDGE
ORFEI!

*Sequence of field of sunflowers. Sunflowers resolve
into a yellow disk with* ORPHEUS *on it which is then
revealed as the station sign at Pythion.*

22. *Station at Pythion.*

THE PROFESSOR
(*voice-over*)
Well, bugger me, that's Orpheus; and it's the image from
the painted cup in Berlin, but without the outlandish
Thracian audience. I suppose a Greek sign might not
want to advertise the foreign audience of adoring male
admirers of their myth. And this buffet must have been
through many changes, because within the last hundred

years this railway station has been Turkish and Bulgarian before it became Greek.

This whole area has been bedevilled by nationalist claims and wars and ethnic cleansings. I can tell the Greeks are very sensitive about it – after all, Turkey is just over there.

Train journey from Phythion to Didymotichon.

23. Didymotichon.

THE PROFESSOR
(*voice-over*)

The Turks conquered Didymotichon, a key fortress in the Evros valley, in 1361, and immediately Sultan Murad I set about building a mighty mosque here, to mark the conquest, and the Turks ruled this part of the world for five hundred and fifty years. It wasn't until 1923 after all the turmoil of the Balkan Wars and the First World War that finally the Evros river was made the frontier between Greece and Turkey. And it is still the frontier and, in fact, it's a military zone, and no civilians are allowed to go there and no one is allowed to photograph there.

PHOTOGRAPHY FORBIDDEN *sign.*

24. *A motor boat on the river Evros delta.*

THE PROFESSOR
(*voice-over*)

As the Evros reaches the sea, its main branch flows past the Turkish town of Enez, on the site of the ancient Greek Ainos. But now it's split into innumerable streams to form a great delta some seven miles across.

I've located some fragments of poetry in my trusty
guidebook, Otto Kern, which must, I think, have been
inspired by this landscape. One, from Simonides, tells
how the flocks of birds flew above Orpheus' head, and
the fish jumped out of the water at the beauty of his
song. There is another which is actually addressed to the
river Hebros . . .

(*Sync.*) It was dug up on a scrap of papyrus from Egypt,
and we've only got the first two stanzas, and even those
have got bits missing. It's by the poet Alcaeus or Alkaios,
who came from the island of Lesbos . . .

> *The Professor stands up in the boat the better to read*
> *the poem. He loses his hat in the river. It drifts away*
> *towards the sea.*

25. The Head of Orpheus drifts down the Evros delta.

THE VOICE OF THE HEAD OF ORPHEUS
My song was torn into shrill screams
then reborn in the Hebros streams

and in time's tide once more made strong
but only when you hear my song.

> *The Head of Orpheus passes a Greek man on a jetty.*

THE VOICE OF THE HEAD OF ORPHEUS
I was Orfei but now I'll pass
a Greek who'll call me –

GREEK ON JETTY
ORFEAS!

THE VOICE OF THE HEAD OF ORPHEUS
Orfeas! Orfeas! Orfeas! . . .

26. Quayside at Alexandropoli for ferry to Lesbos.

THE PROFESSOR
(*voice-over*)

From the mouth of the river the head drifts out across the sea, and the story has it floating to the island of Lesbos. Why there? It's a long way from here. Why should the hero who never fought in wars, who explored sexuality, the poet, why should he have ended up on Lesbos?

27. On board the ferry to Lesbos.

THE PROFESSOR
(*voice-over*)

Well, Harrison told me to search and that's what I'm going to do, even if it means ten hours on the ferry.

(*Reading sync.*) 'The head and the lyre were borne out to sea together, soaked by the grey surge. The sound of his song and the plangent lyre filled the sea and the salt-soaked shores . . . filled the sea and the briny shores . . . '

That's how the poem by Phanocles goes on, the poem in which Orpheus is torn to pieces by the Thracian women because he's turned to the love of boys. So his head is borne over the seas, past the islands, and the main island between Thrace and Lesbos is the island of Samothrace which is, in fact, the highest island in the whole of the Aegean.

28. The Professor sleeps on a bench on the ferry. The lyre of Orpheus finally washes ashore on the beach at Lesbos.

THE PROFESSOR
(*voice-over*)

There's a nice passage I have found in Kern which says
that, as the head sang its way across the seas, the wind
blew on the strings of the lyre to play accompaniment.
And so it was carried to Lesbos with music.

29. The shoreline of Antissa on Lesbos.

THE PROFESSOR
(*voice-over*)

The tradition was that the place on the northern shore of
Lesbos where the head was washed up was Antissa, once
a flourishing city, now a remote headland.

(*Sync.*) Back in the seventh or sixth century BC
Lesbos produced more than its fair share of great poets.
There was Terpandros from Antissa. He made important
musical innovations. There was Arion from Methymna.
He charmed the dolphins into saving him from drowning.
Alcaeus from Mytilini – important and powerful poetry
of politics and love. And Sappho from Eressos, Sappho,
the tenth muse, whose love poetry to her girlfriends gave
the name of Lesbos to love between women . . .

Nude sunbathers on Lesbian beach.

THE PROFESSOR
(*voice-over*)

'Some say a squadron of cavalry
and some of infantry, and some a fleet of ships
is the most glorious sight on this dark earth.
But I say: it is the woman you desire.'

A fragment of a poem by Sappho. Her poetry only exists
in fragments, because later authorities, teachers and
priests, wouldn't allow her poems of Lesbian love to be

copied or studied. We have them mainly from tattered
scraps of papyrus excavated from the sands of Egypt.
She has, in her way, like Orpheus, been torn to pieces for
not conforming and yet has survived.

This is how the Phanocles poem ends the journey . . .

'And the grey sea brought them ashore on Lesbos.
There the men gave funeral rites
to the mellifluous head of Orpheus.
And they set his melodious lyre in his tomb –
the lyre which used to charm the rocks and the cruel sea.
And his songs and lovely music filled the isle.
And so Lesbos became the most poetic of all islands.'

30. The head of Orpheus in the sea. People see the head.
The head lands on the beach. Sunset.

THE POET
(*voice-over*)
Sun and sea in gerbera hues
salute this servant of the Muse.
Gerbera, orange, yellow, red
flow in the sunset round his head.
Though his head is dead and cold
the voice still turns shed blood to gold.
The voice, that heals and seeks to mend
men's broken souls that men's deeds rend.
When men are maimed and torn apart
they call on Orpheus and his art.

31. Titles. A head in the sea.

THE POET
(*voice-over*)
I think it needs that ancient scream
to pierce the skulls of Academe

to remind them that all our poems start
in the scream of Orpheus torn apart.

32. The Professor and Cameraman in a boat on the sea

THE PROFESSOR
'. . . and his songs and lovely music filled the sea, and so
Lesbos became . . . and so Lesbos is . . . the most poetic
of all islands.'

The head in the sea turns out to be that of the Poet.

THE POET
Oliver Taplin! What the fuck are you doing on Lesbos?

THE PROFESSOR
Sssshh! We're filming.

THE POET
Sorry, love!

The Poet dives under the water.

THE PROFESSOR
Bugger! That bloody bard Harrison . . .!

*The head of the Poet shoots out of the water, dripping
blood from its severed neck.*

*The Professor stands up in the boat and screams and
lets his notebook fall into the sea. The book floats
away.*

CROSSINGS
(2002)

Crossings was first broadcast on *The South Bank Show*, ITV, edited and presented by Melvyn Bragg, on 10 March 2002.

Angus Richard Tench
Yorkshire Farmer David Bradley
Woman at Crossing Sian Thomas

Voices Yvonne Harris, Amerjit Deu, Danielle Lydon, Bill Paterson

Written by Tony Harrison
Directed by David Thomas and Tony Harrison
Music by Richard Blackford
Camera Alastair Cameron
Sound John Avery
Edited by Tony Webb
Produced by David Thomas

TONY HARRISON
(*voice-over*)
In come the letters sack after sack
for the Lady in Red to speed up the track.

ONE: CONVEYOR

WOMAN POSTAL WORKER
(*voice-over*)
In come the letters heap after heap
me a empty mail bags all night in mi sleep.

TONY HARRISON
(*voice-over*)
In come the letters load after load
panic . . . pain . . . pleasure for every postcode:

a letter for someone homeless, alone,
sent back to his mother 'addressee unknown'.
Final demands that prove the last straw
for desperate men who can't take any more,
great news for a pupil with good exam grades,
the result of a blood test for HIV AIDS.
For all the electronic and mobile phone boom
sealed letters are still the top heralds of doom.
Perhaps some of these letters are that sort of post
that might make you choke on your coffee and toast.
Brown doom from the taxman, and those sort of letters
written in red and dreaded by debtors,
pressure for payments 'long overdue',

letters with borders red, white and blue,
lingerie catalogues to revamp a lover
sent with discretion 'under plain cover',
pictures of crotchless silk panties to pose in,
pamphlets with pompous political prose in,
the, longed for by millions, lottery win
or the junk mail you chuck straight into the bin.

TWO: SALMON LEAP

In come the letters heap after heap
and all pulled into the 'salmon leap'.
Like leaping wild salmon off to spawning grounds
where postmen tomorrow do their dawn rounds,
like wild salmon leaping, and they'll be spawning
on millions of mats tomorrow morning.

Panic . . . pain . . . pleasure will go through the doors
of millions of houses. Which'll be yours?

THREE: CULLER

The sorting machine gets fuller and fuller
unless it gets clogged and they press the red CULLER.
The button's the shade of the shiny new livery
of the Lady in Red who awaits their delivery,
but, since the thirties of Auden and Britten,
when the verse and music for *Nightmail* were written,
the modern Nightmail goes North for the border
through a rail network in total disorder.
The Lady in Red with her bounty of post 's
bound north through green fields grazed only by ghosts.
The modern Nightmail threads through the map
of mining communities thrown on the scrap,
collieries culled like Shilbottle, Shotton,

winding gear felled, and workforce forgotten.
Along with culled cattle, culled kingdoms of coal,
one dumped on the bonfire, one on the dole.
The only pits now that you'll find on this route
are mass graves for cattle that MAFF came to shoot.

FOUR: ASIAN BAG-TAGGER

(voice-over)
Culling's in fashion. There are jobs on the line.
Thousands and thousands and one . . . might be mine!

TONY HARRISON
(voice-over)
But what'll really stick in their throats
when those thousands get their redundancy notes,
the insult that'll really nark them the most,
is they'll get their redundancies sent through the post.

FIVE: THE LADY IN RED

TONY HARRISON
(voice-over)
Panic . . . pain . . . pleasure will go through the doors
of millions of houses. Which'll be yours?

A thin little letter sealed with a lick
to make you elated, or make you feel sick,
mail to delight you, or letters to dread,
all kinds are carried by . . . the Lady in Red.

The Lady in Red with a quickening heart
waits for the race through the long night to start.
The Lady in Red bound north for the border 's
a thoroughbred panting under starter's orders

405

The Lady in Red in sleek royal regalia
races, when the track's not in terminal failure.

SIX: ANGUS

*Young Scottish man in cardboard box that once housed
a fridge. He has drawn in red a rectangle on which is
written* LETTERS. *It is like a letterbox flap. His name*
ANGUS *above it.*

Sleeper is woken by Lady in Red.

The Lady in Red now crossing this bridge
wakes a boy whose 'abode' 's a box for a fridge.
The Nightmail wakes him and puts him in mind
of the border he once crossed and left far behind.
He lived near Loch Rannoch, a jewel of lochs,
and he quit it for crack and a cold cardboard box.

He lays here in London longing each night
for that one bloody letter his mother won't write.
But that very letter's right over his head,
begging for news so she'll know he's not dead,
imploring in capitals ANGUS PLEASE PHONE
but it's off back to Scotland 'addressee unknown'.

BOY
(sync)

All those millions of letters and not one mine.
Fuck you, sodding Nightmail! Mam, drop us a line.

Pan down to LETTERS *on cardboard box.*

SEVEN: GREAT NORTHERN INN

TONY HARRISON
(*voice-over*)
The Lady in Red in full throttle career
gives *delirium tremens* to glasses of beer.
and passing this pub with post for the nation
ruins crucial concentration.

POOL PLAYER
(*sync*)
Jesus! I always miscue
when that bloody Nightmail comes thundering through.

TONY HARRISON
(*voice-over*)
And *he* was on top. He was winning the game

DARTS PLAYER
(*sync*)
till that bloody mail train pissed up my aim!

EIGHT: SUICIDAL YORKSHIRE FARMER

*Farmer stops his car at railway crossing as barrier
descends, red lights flash, and pulsing siren sounds.
The Nightmail appears.*

There goes t'bloody Nightmail up from t'south
through pastures made empty by Foot and Mouth.
Cows filled this county, and hundreds of mine
grazed these green fields each side of this line.
Them fields were all full. Not now they're not!
The cullers turned up and murdered the lot.

Looks at Nightmail passing.

It's that bloody Nightmail that I've got to thank
for more and more last demands from my bank.
The mail that train carries has put me so deep
in t'dungheap of debt I can't get to sleep,
and if I try counting sheep all I see in mi bed
are t'poor beasts queuing up to be shot in the head.
It goes on and on, and if it doesn't get better
and t'post goes on making me more of a debtor,
If there's one more demand in t'postman's next sack
I'll be putting mi head right here on this track.
It's t'only way left to me, laying my head
under the wheels of the Lady in Red.

> *Crossing Barrier goes up. Farmer still sits staring. The*
> *vehicle behind sounds its horn. It is a red Royal Mail*
> *van.*

I'll be back late with a skinful of drink
but I'll go to my bed and I won't sleep a wink.
I'll lay awake anxious, till t'letterbox flap
bangs afore dawn like the spring of a trap.

> *Cut to Pelaw Grange Greyhound Stadium.*

NINE: PELAW GRANGE GREYHOUND STADIUM

TONY HARRISON
(*voice-over*)

Just before the last race of the night
the Lady in Red always comes into sight.

While the Lady in Red heads off for the Tyne
this lady in red 's the first past the line.

SAD GAMBLER
(*voice-over*)

I'll leave here a pauper. I could have left rich
if I'd wagered the lot on that red-coated bitch.

408

CROSSINGS

I blued all I had from the DHSS
but not on that bitch in her new purple dress.
The dog I had quids on and seemed a dead cert
was thrown by that Nightmail and lost me my shirt.

That Lady in Red she'll be crossing the Tyne,
pools wins aboard her, but not one, I bet, 's mine.

TEN: NEWCASTLE-UPON-TYNE

TONY HARRISON
(*voice-over*)

The post train goes by with Scotland's next mail
as the Geordies are hitting the pub and club trail.

GEORDIE GIRL
(*voice-over*)

While the Nightmail goes rumbling by up above
us Geordies go clubbing and looking for love.
While the mail rumbles over the Tyne viaduct
we're out on the pull to get worsels fucked.
It's the middle of winter but we all dress as though
it were eighty degrees and not two below.
Our fantasies warm us. And this is mine –
we're in. . . . California and not on the Tyne.

TONY HARRISON
(*voice-over*)

And that was just the start of the fight,
he'll never get into her knickers tonight.
And despite the text message and mobile phone
many young Geordies 'll go home alone.
They'll end up puking then sleeping till late
unless they've got snail-mail that wakes them at eight,
or like head-jolting thunder the letterbox flap
bangs with junk mail and that catalogue crap.

ELEVEN: TEETH IN GLASS

TONY HARRISON
(*voice-over*)

He's snored since the Nightmail stopped being steam
the life that death wrecked redeemed in his dream.
Double bed. Pint glass, plenty of room
for the teeth of the bride and the teeth of the groom.
He dreams of fine bubbles from a full flute of Mumm
bursting through dentures and prickling his gum,
the toast 'Bride and Groom' on their wedding day,
the dark honeymoon bedroom at chill Whitley Bay,
the steam train that chuffed them off to the coast
with the rhythm they heard in this bed from the Post
till steam Nightmail was scrapped and the line outside
went all electric once he'd buried his bride.
Still her love letters in slow motion stream
through his door in the morning but only in dream.
That sort of ghost post and ethereal mail 's
stopped at life's crossing by the klaxon's shrill wails.

TWELVE: AIDS TEST WOMAN

Her car is stopped at the crossing. The Nightmail passes.
On mobile phone to woman friend at crossing.

Hi, it's me. No. I'm not. I'm very upset
I haven't told you the half of it yet.

I'm sorry, I know that it's too late to phone
but I'm terribly frightened. I feel so alone.

I'm stuck at the crossing. The Lady in Red,
probably carrying the post that I dread,
's streaking past me right now as we chat.

It's a red Nightmail train, that's why it's called that!

It's so bloody ironic! Having to wait
for the train with a letter that might seal my fate.

I've just had a blood test for HIV
I think that the bugger's passed it to me.
Neither did I! I'd no bloody idea
when I married the bastard he'd turn out to be queer.
I mean he's from Yorkshire, macholand, tough –
it was almost unheard of a Pontefract puff.
He soon showed his colours and was out on the trail
of, well, almost anything teenage and male.
I tried understanding how he'd got double-doored
and, stupidly, still gave him full bed and board.

I emptied a pocket with sick *billets doux* in
he'd post every day to a boy he met cruising.
Full-frontal language, pure porn, obscene
and all despatched with the head of the Queen.

My result's in the post. I've been out for the night
and forgot all about it till this train came in sight.

It's gone past. With my fate. In one of those sacks
there's a thin little letter with the weight of an axe
that falls with a thud on your neck from on high.

The barrier's lifting. I'm petrified! Bye!

The barrier pole vibrates at its maximum height.

Cut to vibrating bell above bar in Berwick pub.

THIRTEEN: BERWICK-UPON-TWEED

TONY HARRISON
(*voice-over*)
This is the Nightmail picking up speed
bound for the border past Berwick-on-Tweed.

Time for last orders. The regulars know
when the Nightmail above rocks the bell here below.

The noise of the Nightmail crossing the border's
the cue for the landlord to call for . . .

LANDLORD
(*sync*)

LAST ORDERS!

*Cut to crossing, flashing lights, siren, Sound of train
passing. Rails with early morning sun. Dawn in the
Highlands.*

FOURTEEN: POST BUS

DRIVER OF POST BUS
(*voice-over*)

The first thing I do on my run by the loch's
to empty Loch Rannoch station post box.

Then I sit in the bus and wait for the train
this time of year in snow, hail, or rain.

Though this landscape's been called the 'treacherous mires',
boulder-strewn bogland with telegraph wires,
and though it goes months and never sees sun
in spite of it all it's a soul-stirring run.
I pick up post and deliver, passengers too,
but not till the spring sun starts showing through.
In winter the bus goes past shut B & Bs 'n'
holiday cottages closed for the season.
The mail I drop there 'll probably stay
and get damp on the mat till April or May.

It's fine with just sheep. They missed Foot and Mouth
that drove men to self-slaughter, they say, in the south.
I quite like the place empty. Sunshine or no
the soul's stirred by the snow-capped pap of Glencoe.

The young kids now though, they don't want to stay.
Young Angus, Mrs Muir's son, he ran away.
His poor mother's nerves have got really bad
since she's never had news of the silly wee lad.
She still writes to the hostel, poor worried hen,
and I've had to deliver them all back again.
She's been wasting away, all skin and bone
since I brought back the first 'addressee unknown'.
This is her box. Every day there's another
cry from the heart from a desperate mother.
Often I hear between the door and the gate
her cry as each letter seems to seal her son's fate.
I'm tempted to knock when I hear the hen sob
at the post I've delivered, but that's not my job.
She's on her own, and not coping, it's very hard
when I can't even bring her a son's Christmas card.

She comes in the post-bus to Pitlochry to shop.
God knows what she'll do if they give me the chop.

Och, kids with no gratitude! She'll end up a ghost
waiting in her nightie for the bus with the post.

Who'd run off to London when he has this:
peaty burns, bogs, boulders, to me it's pure bliss!
Down in London they never see in the dawn,
the wild salmon leaping upriver to spawn.
I do, and it makes my Highland flesh creep
they call a sorting machine a 'salmon leap'.

FIFTEEN: ANGUS

Vauxhall Viaduct again, this time morning. Mail vans
pass by. Angus wakes up in his box. Close-up of Angus's
'letterbox' drawn on his fridge carton, then into:

SIXTEEN: LETTERBOX SEQUENCE

Letters fly through letterboxes

TONY HARRISON
(*voice-over*)
Millions of letters through Great Britain's doors
Panic . . . pain . . . pleasure . . . Which'll be yours?

Mail that you'll loathe, or mail that you'll like
or no mail at all because they're on strike!

The End.